Museums, Monuments, and National Parks

A VOLUME IN THE SERIES

Public History in Historical Perspective

Edited by Marla R. Miller

Museums, Monuments, and National Parks

Toward a New Genealogy of Public History

——— ✠ ———

Denise D. Meringolo

University of Massachusetts Press

Amherst and Boston

LC 2012016865
ISBN 978-1-55849-940-9 (paper); 939-3 (library cloth)

Designed by Sally Nichols
Set in Adobe Caslon Pro
Printed and bound by Thomson-Shore, Inc.

Library of Congress Cataloging-in-Publication Data

Meringolo, Denise D., 1968-
Museums, monuments, and national parks : toward a new genealogy of public
history / Denise D. Meringolo.
p. cm.
Includes bibliographical references and index.
ISBN 978-1-55849-940-9 (pbk. : alk. paper) — ISBN 978-1-55849-939-3 (library cloth : alk. paper)
1. Public history—United States—History. 2. Historic preservation—United States—History.
3. Historic sites—Conservation and restoration—United States—History. 4. Historical museums—
United States—History. 5. National parks and reserves—United States—History. 6. Nature
conservation—United States—History. 7. United States. National Park Service—History. I. Title.
E175.9.M48 2012
973—dc23
2012016865

British Library Cataloguing in Publication data are available.

Publication of this book and other titles in the series
Public History in Historical Perspective is supported by the
Office of the Dean, College of Humanities and Fine Arts,
University of Massachusetts Amherst.

For Kevin and Shane
and
In Memory of Stacy

Contents

Acknowledgments

Over the long course of this project, I have accumulated many debts, and despite my best efforts to acknowledge all of them here, I am sure to have neglected mentioning many of the kindnesses shown me. I am nonetheless deeply grateful for all the help, encouragement, and friendship I have received from many quarters.

At the University of Massachusetts Press, Clark Dougan, senior editor, and Marla Miller, editor of the Public History in Historical Perspective series, were unflagging in their commitment to this project and unstinting in their patience and guidance as I developed it. I am deeply grateful to them both. Managing editor Carol Betsch, her colleague Mary Bellino, and copy editor Susan Silver were warm and encouraging throughout the final process of preparing the manuscript for publication. I appreciated their good humor as much as their attention to detail.

I am indebted to the historians and archivists who assisted me throughout my research. At the National Park Service, former chief historian Dwight Pitcaithley directed me to important resources and pushed me to consider interesting questions. Barry Mackintosh and Janet McDonnell patiently guided me through in-house collections at the headquarters of the Park Service history offices in Washington, D.C. Barry was a particularly gracious colleague, sharing with me the research he had painstakingly assembled over his long tenure. At the Smithsonian Institution, archivists Pamela Henson of the institutional archives and Robert Leopold of the National Anthropological Archives helped me discover obscure sources and identify interesting and rarely recognized historical connections between the Park Service and the Smithsonian. Roger White, curator at the National Museum of American History, shared his research on automobile tourism, providing me with considerable food for thought regarding the early construction of "the public" by the National Park Service.

The archivists and technicians at the National Archives and Records Administration helped me navigate the confusing waters of Park Service materials held there. Because of my interest in the Washington offices of the NPS, records held at Harpers Ferry Center in West Virginia were particularly valuable. Archivists there gave me access to meeting minutes and a wealth of secondary sources. Andrea Mauck sent a remarkable response to my inquiry about the center's oral history collections: more than a thousand pages of photocopies containing the transcripts of numerous oral histories conducted with key figures in the history of the Park Service. Similarly, Marisa Bourgoin, chief of reference services at the Archives of American Art, answered dozens of questions by e-mail, directed me to a wealth of oral histories held by that institution, and helped me secure necessary permissions to use them.

I have been thinking about the ideas at the heart of this book for at least two decades. Along the way I have been encouraged and inspired by a number of teachers and colleagues. While I can't thank them all, I wish to acknowledge particularly some of my early and most important mentors. Edith P. Mayo and Charles McGovern, former curators at the Smithsonian's National Museum of American History, convinced me of both the public value and scholarly significance of public history. Stephanie Batiste, Paul Gardullo, Michele Gates-Moresi, Laura Schiavo, and Elizabeth Otterson Wiley, cherished colleagues from the George Washington University Department of American Studies, shared with me both the joy and the frustration of intellectual inquiry. I thank them for gentle critique, strong encouragement, and frequent laughter. Dr. James O. Horton has been my most steadfast supporter. He is a gifted teacher, tireless mentor, and kind friend. All of my colleagues in the Department of History at UMBC have supported my public-centered scholarship, and I am especially grateful to Kriste Lindenmeyer, Anne Sarah Rubin, R. Terry Bouton, and Joe Tatarewicz, who enthusiastically mentored me during my transition from experienced public historian to junior faculty.

I have been buoyed by loving support in my personal life as well. My parents, Nicole and George Meringolo, encouraged me to follow my passions and to find a way to make a career of them. Dear friends from childhood—Dana Silverman-Briskman, Mary Behr, and Sharon Miller Chan—have helped me keep my wits about me. My husband's parents, Minh-Triet and Greg Tucker and Ellen and Jorge Fernandez, and his great-uncle Gerry Battle have also been unfailingly supportive of my work in deeply felt ways. Neighbors Marie and Bill Randall have been virtual co-parents to our son, and our family runs smoothly because of them. Local ties have, indeed, proven essential to the completion of this work. Thanks to the Internet this book has been written in various locations around the greater Washington metropolitan region. I owe a special debt to St. Elmo's Coffee Shop in the Del Ray neighborhood of Alexandria, where I nursed many a single cup of coffee while working in the back corner.

Several institutions have provided me with support in both time and financial resources. The Department of American Studies at George Washington University granted research fellowships and gave me teaching opportunities. The Gilder-Lehrman Institute in New York funded two years of my graduate work, which included development of GWU's Center for the Study of Public History and Public Culture and the creation of a high school history program at the School without Walls in Washington, D.C. The Columbian College of Arts and Sciences awarded me two dissertation fellowships and supported my travel to conferences, and the Smithsonian Institution awarded me a dissertation research fellowship in 2000–2001. More recently, I have been the beneficiary of tremendous support from the University of Maryland, Baltimore County, in the form of two faculty fellowships from the College of Arts, Humanities, and Social Sciences, a summer faculty research fellowship in 2006, and a semester-long research fellowship in the spring of 2010. I am particularly grateful for the generosity of my colleagues in the Department of History who covered my teaching load that semester, with good will and humor.

This book is dedicated to three people who have helped me shape the better parts of who I am:

Stacy Jill Tishman, my stalwart best friend, gave me love and laughter and, as she battled cancer, insight into what truly matters in this world. Her death changed me profoundly.

Kevin Gregory Tucker has known me since I was nineteen years old. He has taught me that life and marriage and parenthood are more improvisation than science and that change and transformation are always possible.

Our son, Shane Battle Tucker, reminds me daily that life is joyful and that the small discoveries are the most profound. I look forward to introducing him to many national parks and historic sites. I expect these visits will either foster his own passion for history or send him off on a career in mathematics.

A New Kind of Technician

In Search of the Culture of Public History

———— ✠ ————

My primary problem was to take a man trained in history and make a real Park Service man out of him. Some men trained in history never fit that bill.... Some were good in the books, but they couldn't deal with the public; they couldn't deal with the physical conditions on the ground. I had to create a new kind of technician.

—VERNE CHATELAIN—

Public History and the Problem of Definition

When Verne Chatelain, the first chief historian of the National Park Service, recounted his efforts to create a "new kind of technician" during the 1930s, he implicitly understood that the historians he brought into his division were the inheritors of a distinct professional genealogy.[1] Before 1930 not a single historian had worked for the National Park Service. By the end of the decade, however, a small but growing number would be employed in the bureau's Washington, D.C., administrative offices, in each of the regional offices, and at many of its historic sites.[2] New Deal programs and initiatives expanded Park Service holdings and encouraged the development of historical programming. These initiatives enabled the Park Service to hire university-trained historians.

At the same time, it was evident to Chatelain that an advanced degree in history did not necessarily prepare historians for work in the federal government. Although trained to conduct research, many were unable to recognize material artifacts as historical documents, and few had the personality needed to deal with either government bureaucracy or tourist demands. The men hired by Chatelain and by his successor, Ronald Lee, had to adopt work habits and values as much created by the marriage of government and science as nurtured by professors and university-based colleagues in the discipline of history. It was the strange alchemy created by the mix of science, government, history, and—to a lesser extent—the public itself that forged these new government workers, forcing them to become as good on the ground as they were in the books.

Examining both the long tangle of events that eventually called historians into government service and the first decisions they made as members of the Park Service History Division offers us a window into the formation of a unique field of expertise. Chatelain's new technicians were among the first public historians, and they had a profound impact on the evolution of the field. The programs they devised in the middle of the 1930s guided interpretive development, site selection, designation, and interpretive programming by the National Park Service through most of the twentieth century. The impact of their work remains tangible, evident in the number and kind of historic sites recognized and protected by the federal government.

Public history as a specialty field, a profession, and a course of study has earned broader recognition in recent years. In the United States, the practice of history for public consumption can be traced back at least 150 years and tracked through several stages of development—beginning with preservation work undertaken by women's voluntary associations in the mid-nineteenth century, maturing with the creation of state and regional historical societies in the late nineteenth century, and gaining legitimacy in the federal government during the middle part of the twentieth century.[3] Nonetheless, public history did not achieve recognition as a formal profession until the late twentieth century.

Beginning in the 1970s a group of university historians, concerned about the scarcity of jobs for history PhDs, created an often uneasy alliance with colleagues working in government agencies and historical societies. Their conversations about the usefulness of historical study for practical job training helped implement several significant milestones in the viability of public history: the founding of the first graduate program at the University of California, Santa Barbara (1976); the minting of a professional journal, *The Public Historian* (1978); and the creation of the National Council on Public History (NCPH) (incorporated on May 2, 1980). These relatively recent events are frequently recounted in textbooks, monographs, and articles seeking to analyze or historicize some aspect of public history practice.[4] As a result, many students and instructors of public history, when asked to define the profession, point to the 1970s as the starting point.

Emphasizing the late twentieth-century ascendance of public history as a recognized field of intellectual inquiry has reinforced its stature as an academic specialty. The number of public history programs in colleges and universities grew from 60 in the 1990s to more than 110 in 2008. There is little doubt that the expanding number of public history tracks and programs in departments of history has had a measurable impact on the broader discipline. Public historians have been in the forefront of a movement to reform university promotion and tenure guidelines. Their work has helped to expand accepted definitions of scholarship so that exhibits, preservation reports, and other forms of historical analysis and interpretation may be recognized as the equivalent of books and articles for professors seeking tenure and promotion.[5] Professional associations have become increasingly welcoming to public historians not only as members but also as leaders.[6] Scholarly journals of history—most notably the *Journal of American History* published by the Organization of American Historians—include reviews of exhibits, documentary films, and websites alongside reviews of scholarly monographs. Furthermore, the ascendance of the field has had an impact on public perception. During the 1990s a significant survey of American attitudes found that a majority of those surveyed placed museums and historical societies among the most trustworthy sources for exploring the past.[7]

These milestones are worthy of celebration. Yet such intense focus on the legitimacy of public history has obscured a different set of questions—not about the profession's trajectory but about its habits of work and multidisciplinary culture. Ethnographers and anthropologists have led the charge in this direction. An important body of literature examines public history as a cultural field composed by differential power relationships among workers and between workers and visitors in specific institutions. Although this work has provided practitioners with a window into the dynamics that shape public interpretations of the past, their response to studies of this nature has often been defensive.[8]

Among public historians, the effort to define "public history" in the years following the establishment of its professional scaffolding has been ongoing and occasionally frustrating. Debates tend to circle around two general trends of thought. Some scholars emphasize the term "public," arguing that the environment in which historians apply their craft impacts the questions, methodology, and content of interpretation. Others underscore the term "history," insisting that credentialed historians perform their work in accordance to the same disciplinary standards regardless of location or audience. During the 1970s all participants in this discussion had an equal stake in achieving professional authority and stability. But defining "public" as a place or an orientation and "history" as a strict discipline has stalled public history's maturation. Most casual observers can list the kinds of jobs that public historians do: They create exhibits. They conduct research that justifies preservation of particular buildings or landscapes. They collect artifacts and analyze their significance. Yet few people can articulate the qualities that mark public history as distinct from the larger discipline. Is any historian who writes text for a website accurately described as a public historian? Is every staff member in a government history office practicing public history? What about a historian who appears as a pithy talking head on PBS? Are scholars who study the role of museums, historical societies, and monuments in the creation of public memory necessarily practitioners of public history?

That it may be difficult to distinguish public historians from public intellectuals—a better term for scholars whose work resonates beyond the academy—is compelling evidence that the field has achieved legitimacy. Given that, it seems an appropriate time to move toward a more proactive effort to historicize and theorize the attitudes and habits of mind that make public history distinctive.

A History of the Public History Idea

The professionalization of public history was, indeed, fostered by specific historical events and conditions of the mid-1970s. The United States had entered into a period of severe economic recession, worsened by energy shortages, climbing inflation, and high unemployment rates. Academic institutions were not immune to these conditions. A shortage of tenure-track jobs in history departments across the United States led many doctoral programs to shrink the number of students they accepted into their programs, and a special committee of the American Historical Association advised department chairs to send letters of warning about poor job prospects along with letters of acceptance to those admitted into the program.[9] Concerned about the future of the profession and the usefulness of higher education, historians across the country began developing new curricula and new programs of study designed to identify practical applications for intellectual work. Public history gained a firm foothold in the academy as a result of these trends.

Leaders in this academic public history movement were not primarily practitioners who had carved careers in the public sector. Rather, they were university-based historians such as Robert Kelley, who had supplemented his work as a university professor at the University of California, Santa Barbara, by serving as a consultant and expert witness for the state on matters related to water rights. Looking for ways to improve job prospects for their graduate students, academics like Kelley began to emphasize the broad marketability of a history degree, arguing that skill in research, analysis, and interpretation could be applied to a variety of jobs. Kelley's particular experience had piqued his interest in the intersection between public policy and history. Convinced that policymakers had, at best, misused history and, at worst, completely disregarded it, Kelley successfully applied for a grant from the Rockefeller Foundation to design a program that would foster better interplay between history and policy. He brought fellow historian and public policy expert G. Wesley Johnson into the project, hoping to draw on his experience in both developing specialized programs of study and managing grants from the Rockefeller Foundation. Together, they established the UCSB Public History Program as an experiment in practical job training for doctoral students in history.[10]

Seeking funding and promoting their program required Kelley and Johnson to develop a precise definition of public history. For them, the term captured their practical intentions. They sought to train students to export their historical skills to jobs outside university departments of history. At its most basic, Kelley explained, "Public History refers to the employment of historians and historical method outside of academia." Johnson recalled that the term "meant to us that historians had skills that could be used for public benefit, whether in business, government, foundations, historical societies, or wherever." They imagined sending their graduates "out, one by one, to demonstrate their value by their work."[11] Kelley saw that value as largely political. He advocated for the expansion and creation of government history offices as a way to both ease the job crisis and improve the effectiveness of public policy. Policymakers should, he believed, think like historians and recognize civic issues as taking shape in both time and place.

Kelley and Johnson were not alone in their efforts. The Organization of American Historians and the American Historical Association, concerned about the long-term ramifications of the university job crisis, organized meetings and conferences to foster creative solutions to the problem. Frequent speakers at these meetings, Johnson and Kelley touted their public history program and identified a network of like-minded colleagues from universities across the country. Scholars at the University of South Carolina, for example, were reinvigorating their program in historic preservation. Historians at Carnegie Mellon University were creating a program in applied history. Together, this expanding group of scholars developed programs of study they believed would provide history graduate students a well-imagined set of marketable skills. Their ideas gained traction in 1978 when Johnson—then a visiting professor at Arizona State University— received a grant from the Arizona Humanities Council to organize the first of several conferences focused specifically on public history, laying the groundwork for the creation of a professional infrastructure.[12]

The great bulk of this initial work took place in academic circles, reflecting and reinforcing rifts among historians that had divided the discipline since its establishment in the late nineteenth century. Federal historians participated in meetings and conferences leading up to the creation of the NCPH, and they held positions on the board of directors from the organization's first days. Yet they were wary of their academic peers' interest in public sector work. Indeed, as Johnson later admitted with a bit of self-deprecating humor, "it was increasingly apparent that there were a number of practitioners of public history out there that we were not aware of."[13] But this lack of visibility was not humorous to historians working in the federal government. Jack M. Holl, a historian in the Department of Energy, admitted he had "briefly and ineffectually tried to stem the rising tide of Kelley's public history movement in the federal government."[14]

Federal historians such as Holl and David Trask, the chief historian for the U.S. Department of State, felt a profound disconnect between their work and the goals of public history and believed that the public history movement further marginalized them. Their disenchantment was exacerbated when the Organization of American Historians and the American Historical Association circulated a questionnaire, designed to collect detailed information about the history job market, that described jobs for historians outside of academia as "alternative careers." Holl wrote, "I did not believe that the professional concerns of federal historians could ever be satisfied by an organization overwhelmingly dominated by academic historians who regarded our employment as 'alternative careers' and lumped us into a professional category of 'public history,' their short-hand term for 'non-academic history.'" The questionnaire confirmed federal historians' sense that the public history movement was strictly an academic venture, designed to legitimize graduate degrees in history, not to integrate federal historians into a more broadly defined discipline of history.[15]

In addition, far from being a viable career option for history graduates, government history divisions and archives were threatened by a job crisis of their own. The economic recession was fueling efforts to eliminate government waste and streamline the number and size of federal agencies. Several history divisions were shut down and history advisory boards disbanded. Without advisory boards to serve as a conduit to their university colleagues, the remaining government historians found themselves cut off from the profession and concerned about protecting not only their own jobs but also crucial government documents. For Holl this need seemed particularly pressing because public discourse during the Carter administration was dominated by worry over the energy crisis and the environmental impact of nuclear waste. As a result, access to energy policy documents was increasingly politicized. Unable to add permanent employees to his history staff, Holl scrambled to contract out requests for information and analysis to graduate students and junior historians. He turned to the fledgling public history movement for assistance but found little relief. Academic public historians were eager to train marketable, history-literate public policymakers, not necessarily policy-savvy historians. Holl wrote, "That was fine, but of little immediate concern to me as a practicing professional historian in the federal government."[16] To better address those concerns, federal historians organized meetings and conferences that paralleled efforts by academic public historians, and in February 1980 they formally organized a separate professional entity, the Society for Historians in the Federal Government.[17]

There is evidence to suggest Holl was correct in his assessment. At the university level, historians won financial support for courses and programs designed to broaden the appeal of history classes for majors and nonmajors alike. They encouraged students to apply the skills they learned in history to careers beyond those with "history" in the job description. For example, shortly after the creation of the society, Otis Graham, a historian of modern America, taught a public history course at the University of North Carolina Business School, titled "History for Decision Makers." Funded by a grant from the National Endowment for the Humanities, the course sought to provide future economic policymakers with tools for thinking about pressing issues in terms of time and context. While enthusiastically reporting on the success of his particular public history model, Graham also expressed concern about the impact of public history on the larger discipline. Many university-based historians were wary of public history, he explained, because public historians often went beyond historicizing political questions to formulating policy directly and making questionable predictions based on the direct comparison of past and present issues. Graham worried, "The threat to the scholar's objectivity mounts, most of us would concede, with the distance we move from Widener Library or a graduate seminar at Stanford toward the executive offices of governments or corporations."[18]

Despite federal historians' unwillingness to be lumped in with self-described public historians, they were cast in the same light when university-focused colleagues raised questions about the "objectivity" of any historian who produced scholarship on behalf of a paying client. Both public historians and federal historians invested a great deal of intellectual capital into efforts to defend their professionalism in terms defined by the larger disciplinary structure. For federal historians, this was a particularly knotty problem. Buffeted by uncertainty about the future of their programs, suspicion about the usefulness of the public history movement, and dismay about the lack of respect from the larger discipline, federal historians were often the more dogged in insisting that public sector work was no different than work by historians in university settings. David Trask argued, "This has been an issue—whether public historians are different than academics. I say 'No.' I say they just have a different constituency, they work in a different context, but that the fundamental training and purpose and functions of historians are the same everywhere." Jack Holl viewed the issue similarly: "Because I made my living practicing my craft, why wasn't I simply a paid, professional historian?"[19]

Members of the academic public history movement often reflected a similarly defensive posture in their efforts to define the field. But efforts to establish an organizational mission for the NCPH and win administrative support for new academic programs required them to define and justify their creation of a new specialization. Philip Scarpino, an environmental historian and founder of the public history program at Indiana University–Purdue University, Indianapolis, famously argued that academic and public historians shared "common ground." He wrote, "All historians conduct research; all historians analyze and interpret what they find; and all historians communicate their findings to others." Specialized training in public history would not alter historical methods or damage the discipline; rather, it would strengthen the discipline by broadening its appeal. He explained, "The differences between public history and the rest of the profession are found in the area of communication, in the audiences with whom we communicate, and in the methods that we use to communicate our scholarship to those audiences."[20]

Several scholars echoed the idea that public historians' communication with diverse audiences would help the discipline reaffirm its core values and larger usefulness. Robert Kelley argued that historical knowledge is more than simply the foundation of a "cultivated mind" or the basis of sophisticated foreign policy. Rather, historical methods are "essential in every kind of immediate, practical situation."[21] Although the focus on practicality and attention to contemporary problems often made public historians vulnerable to accusations of bias, the field's defenders insisted that a present-day perspective could generate high-quality scholarship. Theodore Karamanski, professor of public history at Loyola University in Chicago, argued that developing historical questions based on current events did not absolve public historians from adhering to standards of intellectual rigor: "All of our products, unlike many an academic monograph, contribute directly to society's daily activities, not just the life of the mind." Scholars such as Karamanski identified roots for public history in a specific disciplinary lineage. He noted the field's intellectual indebtedness to progressive historians such as Charles Beard and Frederick Jackson Turner, who sought to address through scholarship the profound social and political change they observed in the Gilded Age and Progressive Era. Following the lead of these forebears, public historians could reinvigorate the discipline's historical commitment to public service.[22]

Interestingly, most of the pioneering leaders in the public history movement stopped short of exploring the intersection of history and service, discipline and mission. For most, "public" remained a synonym for a generalized and somewhat passive "audience" and, as a result, public history programs initially focused on the products of public history work, not the process. They focused on the ways in which public history provided scholars with new avenues and methods for communicating their ideas, rather than raising questions about the relationships and motivations that drove such communication. Philip Scarpino clearly expressed the movement's reluctance to stray too far into these more challenging questions: "Public history and the entire profession would be much better served by focusing on the research, analysis and interpretation, and communication that draws us all together. I like this approach because it emphasizes those things that all professional historians have in common; it argues for the legitimacy and importance of reaching a variety of audiences; and it assigns value to the different ways historians can communicate their scholarship to these audiences."[23] Such an approach retained the expertise and authority of public historians, but it left them unprepared for the extent to which audiences, employers, and others might resist and challenge such authority.

This observation should not call into question the tremendous importance of early efforts by public historians to define their specialty. Their dialogue on this subject had many fruitful, indeed crucial, outcomes, such as fostering important debates about the definition of historical scholarship.[24] It also raised questions about the necessity of credentialing public historians and encouraged more historians to prepare for work outside of university history departments.[25] The discussion led to better cooperation among academics, museum professionals, and federal historians from a variety of bureaus, which, in turn, improved reviews of exhibits, preservation reports, archival study guides, and other history products.[26]

Unintentionally, however, the early focus on legitimacy tended to harden disciplinary boundaries, forestalling a critical examination of the important impact that specialists from other fields have had on shaping public history. It is significant, for example, that simultaneous to the rise of public history in the mid-1970s, oral history was establishing its own professional identity. Oral historians, as part of this process, actively engaged in a conversation about methodology and work culture. J. Ronald Grele, groundbreaking oral historian and author of *Envelopes of Sound: The Art of Oral History*, made one of the first attempts to articulate his field's methodology and to make connections to the public history movement.[27] Grele praised scholars such as Kelley for raising important questions about the limited and limiting perception of historians as primarily researchers or university educators. At the same time, he observed that debates about public history had failed to articulate a clear sense of mission. He broadened the public history cohort, placing oral historians inside the movement and arguing, "Those of us who currently work in the field have not clearly defined what it is we do, why we do it, and why it is an alternative to other forms of historical effort." He observed that the focus on job placement, the emphasis on policy-making, and the conceptualization of the "public" as simply the "audience" had failed to adequately conceptualize the function and value of historical research practiced outside the academy.[28]

Placing himself in the company of Karl Marx and the populist historian Carl Becker, Grele touted the belief that "every man can become his own historian." In this vein, "the task of the public historian, broadly defined, should be to help members of the public do their own history and to aid them in understanding their role in shaping and interpreting events." By imagining public historians as facilitators rather than communicators of history, Grele pioneered efforts to redefine the field, not as a product or an environment but as a collaborative practice. Grele saw public history as promising "a society in which a broad public participates in the construction of its own history. . . . If the public history movement lives up to its name, those of us who work in the field will recognize allies in the struggle to make historical consciousness a reality in American life."[29]

By the late twentieth century, public historians had finally begun to heed Grele's call. Scholars who bridged oral history and public history had introduced a better language for describing their relationship with audiences. Michael H. Frisch, for example, argued that oral historians' recognition of the ways in which interviewers and interview subjects share authority for shaping a narrative is a process that conveys to the practice of public history more generally.[30] As outgoing president of the NCPH in 2003, Rebecca Conard, professor of public history at Middle Tennessee State University, challenged public historians to identify the intellectual core of public history, tossing aside old fears about professional standing in favor of establishing a new foundation on which to build a set of best practices. Focusing on practice, she argued, provides students with a window for understanding what sets public history apart from the rest of the discipline and, specifically, allows students to recognize that "public history can be defined as the reflective practice of history."[31] In reflective practice, public historians engage in active collaboration, constantly reframing questions and improving interpretations in conversation with themselves and with their stakeholders—employers, audiences, and so on. In this way, public history requires both "shared authority" and "shared inquiry," a dynamic collaboration that ensures far more complex outcomes than simply engagement with matters of policy.[32]

Spurred on by this attention to the intellectual core—or, seen another way, the cultural value system, motivations, and beliefs that compose public history as practice—the NCPH board of directors began in 2007 to revisit its working definition of public history. Officers proposed a formal definition that described public history as "a movement, methodology, and approach that promotes the collaborative study and practice of history" and described public historians as embracing "a mission to make their special insights accessible and useful to the public." Far from finding consensus, however, their efforts reopened debate about the field's origins, content, and purpose. Members of the council questioned the notion that public history constitutes a movement and debated whether or not public historians have a methodology distinct from other historians. They resisted the idea that the insights of public historians are more or less "special" than those brought to the fore by audience members, community groups, and others engaged in sharing and preserving stories about the past.[33]

This apparently endless and often exhausting debate illuminates several important aspects of public history practice. First, public history is, at its core, collaborative. Whether they work as consultants or in museums or federal agencies, public historians conduct research and develop interpretations in concert with a variety of audiences and stakeholders. Although public historians share a commitment to the best practices of historical scholarship, they are more likely than university-focused scholars to value collaborative inquiry over independent scholarship; they facilitate conversations that allow the interests and needs of diverse partners to shape the questions that will guide their historical research.[34] Although popular histories are often false or misleading, they do speak to communal values and beliefs, and public historians tend to engage these beliefs respectfully rather than dismissing them out of hand.[35]

The collaborative aspect of public history illuminates a second important point. Public historians share authority not only with their audiences and employers but also with colleagues from a variety of disciplines. This most recent effort to define public history revealed that a large percentage of public historians views disciplinary boundaries as permeable. Contradicting the notion that public history has a specific methodology, some argue that public historians take a multidisciplinary or interdisciplinary approach to historical subject matter, integrating perspectives from a variety of partners and fields.[36] Public historians working in national parks, for example, participate in cultural resource management with archaeologists and anthropologists. Museum historians' facility with material culture requires them to adapt and adopt interpretive models from linguistics, art history, sociology, and elsewhere.[37] Historians working in the field of preservation must remain mindful of the boundaries of law and public policy, interpreting the value of a particular building or battlefield pragmatically. Far from undermining the scholarly integrity of their work, disciplinary fluidity enables public historians to advance original interpretations about the meaning and relevance of the past.

These first two interrelated points focus attention on process, raising questions about *how* public historians practice history as a collaborative and multidisciplinary endeavor. But the ongoing debate has revealed a third fundamental point. Public historians remain divided in the relative emphasis they place on the term "public" and the term "history." Examining this division more closely than they had in the past, public historians began a debate about the function and value of history. What are the implications of practicing history not simply *in* public but rather *for* the public? How is history practiced as a public service? It is clear that the fissures that opened up during the founders' effort to define public history remain perceptible thirty years later.

Some public historians continue to emphasize scholarly authority, arguing that public historians must produce responsible narratives that challenge prevalent myths about the past.[38] Others question this particular definition of responsibility. They argue that even the most troubling beliefs about the past contain evidence about the fears and values of audiences, stakeholders, and partners. By acknowledging these emotional attachments, public historians can open up dialogue and foster a mutually educational experience, allowing public historians not only to educate their audiences but also to learn something about the ways in which average people understand, use, and value the past.[39] This troubles some who view public historians as ill-equipped to identify and engage a given community's emotions. Those who emphasize the "public" side of public history, however, argue that public historians exert authority most effectively by approaching their work reflexively, constantly asking how new narratives, new questions, and new interpretations challenge their partners' deeply held and often very personal notions of identity.[40] For this group, public historians' responsibility is best understood as a question: "In whose service do we work?"[41]

Toward a New Understanding of Public History

The unfinished debate over the definition of public history is more than simply intellectual; it is historical and contemporary, practical and philosophical. To work with confidence, professionals of any stripe must stand on a firm foundation in the history, values, and purpose of their chosen field. The form and content of the ongoing debate suggests that any definition must include four crucial components: historical precedent, practitioner skills, collaborative practice, and intellectual value. This book is most fully engaged with the question of precedent. As this review of recent scholarship demonstrates, tracking the evolution of public history as part of the emergence of history as a discipline leaves us with an incomplete understanding of the conflicts and challenges historians in the public sector have faced for generations. Federal historians' initial unease in the creation of public history programs, professional associations, and standards raises important questions about the culture in which they work. We must step outside history's disciplinary box to accurately trace the emergence of history as a specialty in the federal government. This book seeks to challenge received wisdom regarding the professionalization of public history and argues that the effort to define pubic history will be improved by examining its emergence as a multidisciplinary government job.

With its focus on the federal government, this book rests on a more expansive notion of the public at the center of public history. For federal workers, the public is civic space, government funding, political constituents, and, more broadly, the citizens for whom government works. Examining the evolution of this public as a by-product of government expansion creates a road map for retracing the historical development of the field, the process by which particular preoccupations, conflicts, and understandings became institutionalized and invisible in the everyday work of public history. It is precisely these ideas that occasionally bubble up to the surface in the apparently neverending debate over definitions. Public history did not spring, fully formed, as a response to the academic job crisis of the 1970s. Rather, it evolved, consciously and unconsciously, through trial and error as government workers began to put history to work for the public. (It is only in the relatively recent past that government historians and other practitioners began to conduct history *with* the public.) This book traces the first part of that journey, drawing attention to the ways in which the slow emergence of history as a job in the federal government tended to institutionalize specific trends and beliefs in the culture of public history. Although historians eventually came to work in a variety of federal agencies and offices, this book is focused on the two government institutions most directly dedicated to the identification, protection, and interpretation of history: the Smithsonian Institution and the National Park Service. The first professionals hired to collect, interpret, and study history joined these institutions well after the turn of the twentieth century, and this book argues that the National Park Service History Division was, initially, the more important of the two for establishing history as a public service. To understand the challenges these prototypical public historians faced and the decisions they made, however, it is necessary to begin before the beginning—to examine the ways in which the evolution of government-sponsored research and education enabled the creation of both these agencies in the first place.

I am indebted both to scholars who have traced the professionalization of history as a discipline and to those who have raised important questions about the role of public history in national identity formation. But this book departs from these lines of scholarly inquiry in two important ways. First, it does not primarily focus on the relationship of public history to the evolution of historical scholarship. Too often, such a focus devolves into debates over relative stature and disciplinary achievement that do not advance our understanding of public history's unique work culture. Rather, they only return us to unproductive defensiveness about the legitimacy of historical inquiry practiced in a public setting. Second, while this book does examine the attitudes of Park Service public historians toward park visitors, it does not address the relationship between public history and popular patriotism. This subject is well covered in the growing body of literature on commemoration, memory, and identity.[42] That scholarship is tremendously important in helping us understand how publics use the past, and the critique it stimulates about the position of public historians in patriotic discourse is crucial in our commitment to enabling meaningful civic discourse.

At the same time, the critique has sometimes preceded the history. Focusing sharply on public history's complicity in reinforcing an exclusive form of patriotism has sometimes obscured the important events leading to the integration of history and government in the early years of the twentieth century. This process created an altogether new sensibility about the value of working in and with history. The contents of internal memoranda, conference proceedings, meeting minutes, and interagency debates that surrounded the formation of history collections and divisions in both the Park Service and the Smithsonian give form to the foundations of public history and, in many ways, prefigure current debates about the role of historical interpretation in public service.[43]

Perhaps most important, this book recognizes that the original public historians were only eventually historians by training. The first efforts to identify and protect historically significant artifacts and landscapes on behalf of the federal government were made by former businesspeople, college professors, self-trained archaeologists, and other practitioners of natural science. In the 1930s a handful of graduate students in history entered into this work, following in their footsteps. Together, they helped expand both the physical holdings and the educational purpose of the National Park Service in the two decades following its establishment in 1916. A few of them are highlighted in the following pages. Some, such as Jesse L. Nusbaum, were particularly good on the ground. Nusbaum had been apprenticed in the building trades as a teenager. By the age of twenty, he was a college professor, training students for work in what was called the "manual arts." He spent his summers working alongside pioneering American archaeologists, stabilizing Native American ruins in western parks and monument grounds.

Others, such as Horace Albright, were remarkably efficient and diplomatic bureaucrats. Albright came to Washington, D.C., shortly after his 1912 graduation from the University of California, Berkeley. He toured public lands as the private assistant to secretary of the interior Franklin Lane. His civil service career advanced quickly—from clerk, to solicitor, to assistant director of the National Park Service. After serving a ten-year stint as the superintendent of Yellowstone National Park, he was named director of the National Park Service in 1929. During his four-year tenure in that position, he expanded Park Service holdings into the eastern part of the United States, stretching the definition of a national park to include historic as well as natural places. Albright's work required him to bring new experts into the Park Service workforce: men such as Verne Chatelain who were "good in the books." A historian and educator, Chatelain had worked in local history, but he had little experience with national parks before Albright hired him. Only after accepting the position did Chatelain familiarize himself with the parks, taking a lengthy tour and spending time with Nusbaum and other hands-on park interpreters in the West. Chatelain finally arrived in Washington with plans to implement a new interpretive program designed to illuminate and quantify the nation's history.

Despite their differences, men such as Nusbaum, Albright, and Chatelain viewed their work through a common cultural lens. They carried with them to their Park Service jobs a distinct sense that what they were doing was something altogether new. They all struggled to find adequate words to describe their work and its value. Albright said he was "dabbling" in history. Chatelain said he was trying to "create a new kind of technician." Nusbaum said, "I was always getting something else beside what I was doing—I was always getting another job."[44] Indeed, all three men held a variety of positions inside and outside the Park Service, and each one left a distinct footprint on the soil in which public history took root. Their work informed the cultural milieu of something we now call public history; for them, it was altogether new, a body of work for which they could find no suitable name.

An Intervention for the Definition Debate

By beginning in the middle of the nineteenth century and taking readers to the 1930s, this book examines the process by which federal workers began to conceptualize the protection of landscapes and artifacts as valuable public work. It pays particular attention to the role of scientists in selecting nationally significant places, and it sheds new light on the challenging work conducted by the National Park Service between 1916 and 1933 in its efforts to carve historical landscapes out of places long identified as "natural" and "scientific." The goal of the book is to illuminate the cultural roots of the work we now call "public history" so that we may more fairly and more accurately define and critique it.

Part 1 paints a broad historical canvas, providing necessary background to students unfamiliar with the emergence of government agencies dedicated to the collection, management, and interpretation of specimens between the middle of the nineteenth century and 1916. The establishment of the National Park Service was the pinnacle of a steep and treacherous series of cultural transformations that, over time, connected the interests of science to the interests of government. Chapter 1 describes the pre–Civil War struggle to interest the federal government in research and education. Elected officials were reluctant to exacerbate sectional tensions by imposing federal authority into areas typically left to local control. Nonetheless, a coalition of scientists gradually connected the interests of the nation to the interests of science. They convinced the federal government to gather data and assemble collections that would help foster economic development and enable military planning. Pragmatic scientists took advantage of this effort, becoming adept at explaining the usefulness of their research to local boosters, military leaders, and representatives alike.

Chapter 2 argues that the needs of the nation changed dramatically after the Civil War, allowing the federal government to expand its role in scientific research, land management, and conservation. After the war, most Americans believed that the nation was changing at an uncontrollable pace. Commentators from a variety of backgrounds found evidence of novelty in social arrangements, work, and status. While many saw cause for optimism in the swirl of change, the period was marked by a general sense of anxiety about the loss of tradition and the lack of order. The longing for order and predictability lent legitimacy to science. Scientists' emphasis on objectivity, efficiency, experimentation, and repetition provided an antidote for the emotionalism and havoc stirred by modernization.

The language of science became a useful tool for reasserting federal authority in a nation so recently divided. In this atmosphere, scientists with an established track record of research on behalf of government interests joined forces with a new generation of American-educated naturalists and others. They became the directors and key researchers for new federal expeditions, agencies, and bureaus—ultimately including the National Park Service—that advanced conservation (broadly conceived) as a science, creating an institutional framework strong enough to support the emergence of new perspectives on the value of landscapes and artifacts. This section also documents the parallel development of history as a realm of inquiry and a new profession, arguing that a rift in the discipline cut against historians' efforts to craft a viable and broad professional network. The leaders of the discipline's professional association discounted the value of local and regional history and dismissed preservation as too emotional. As a result, historians' work on behalf of the government was rather marginal to the evolution of the federal bureaucracy.

Part 2 argues that the emergence of public history was enabled by the work of nineteenth-century scientists who had, over time, established the American landscape as a resource to be studied, interpreted, and managed. Given that, each chapter examines the emergence of public history at a microscopic level, looking at the decisions made from inside the institutional framework established during the nineteenth and early twentieth centuries. Chapter 3 analyzes the emergence of park museums during the 1920s, paying particular attention to the rocky but symbiotic relationship between Park Service museums and the museums of the Smithsonian Institution. Jesse Nusbaum is a key figure in this chapter, bringing professionalism and a certain amount of stubbornness to the creation of museums in the western parks. Focusing on both disputes and collaboration that took place between Nusbaum and other Park Service interpreters on the one hand and Smithsonian curators on the other amplifies the deeper significance of questions about the disposition, organization, and display of artifacts by and for the federal government. These questions laid the philosophical foundation for defining history as an arena of public service.

Chapters 4 and 5 look at the establishment and growth of the Park Service History Division between 1928 and 1942, introducing Verne Chatelain and analyzing his effort to create a "new kind of technician." Horace Albright is a central character throughout. His understanding of the Park Service mission, his vision for expansion, and his political savvy enabled the transformation of a landscape long defined as scenic and scientific into one that might be recognized as historic. The cultural conditions of the New Deal established the tensions inherent in the practice of public history. These chapters suggest that lingering debates about the definition of public history must begin with an even more basic set of questions: "Who are public historians?" and "What purposes have they served?"

Part 3 examines the complicated relationship between public historians and their audiences during the 1930s. Recognizing that early public history practices took shape during an era of uncertain class relationships sheds new light on the defensiveness underlying public historians' sense of authority and professionalism. Chapter 6, the most theoretical of the chapters, suggests that the relationship between Park Service professionals and their audience was shaped by several historically specific cultural transformations. The rise of domestic tourism expanded the class of visitors entering the parks and raised anxieties about the extent to which tourists might change the meaning of the landscape. Park Service interpreters and administrators were idealistic, believing park education could open visitors to new experiences. But the desire of park professionals—particularly practitioners of young sciences—to define and defend their expertise limited dialogue with tourists.

Ultimately, this book exposes much deeper and more tangled historical roots for the debates that have both advanced and hindered the professionalization of public history. The conclusion argues that the decisions made by Park Service historians during the 1930s had a long and profound influence on the nation's historical landscape. Fledgling public history inherited from its late nineteenth-century origins a pragmatic approach to research and an impulse to manage change. It is the core argument of this book, then, that the events leading to the establishment of public history as a federal job created an attitude toward public service that government historians and other practitioners have only recently begun to analyze more fully. This book is designed to shift debates regarding public history away from matters of definition and toward questions regarding the larger value of history practiced as public service.

Museums, Monuments, and National Parks

PART I

Science and Government

Defining the Landscape

CHAPTER I

A Matter of National Dignity
Education and Federal Authority

———— ❈ ————

There are persons who entertain the opinion that the study of natural history is only an amusement, or the gratification of useless curiosity. If they were to examine the subject more carefully, they would perceive that natural history is the basis of domestic and public economy and that it contributes essentially to the prosperity of families and the wealth of nations, by the resources which its productions offer to agriculture, to commerce, to the arts, to manufacturers, and to all the wants of life.

—JOEL ROBERTS POINSETT—

During most of the nineteenth century both the study of nature and the study of history were perceived by many as a diversion for the leisured class. By the middle of the 1830s, however, some began to argue that research was more than a private intellectual pursuit. Men such as Joel Roberts Poinsett and John Quincy Adams became early supporters of the controversial notion that the federal government should engage in scientific investigations, gathering and examining natural resources for the benefit of agriculture, commerce, the arts, and industry.[1] They argued that exploration of the continent's rich landscape was essential to the well-being of the nation. Congress was slow to embrace the notion that intellectual inquiry served the public good. Indeed, the establishment of federal science initiatives and agencies required constant pressure. Prior to the Civil War, politicians, well-connected wealthy citizens, and politically savvy scientists exerted enough influence to win federal support for a number of scientific expeditions and the establishment of national research collections, which became the material basis for a larger intellectual project that, over time, redefined the American landscape as a public resource and aligned the interests of science, business, and government. Establishing research as crucial to national ambitions was the necessary first step for creating federal agencies dedicated to fieldwork and interpretation. Thus, the history of public history began before the first historian was hired by the federal government. Indeed, it began before history as a discipline had grown from pastime to profession.

The Problem of National Culture

The philosophical shift that opened up space for researchers to enter into the civil service took place in the decades leading up to the Civil War. After the Revolution, America's political leaders struggled to find the right balance between federal and state power. From the 1830s to the 1850s, the flash point was slavery. Increasingly heated disagreements over the relationship between America's ideal of liberty and its dependence on slave labor simmered below the surface of just about every discussion regarding the size and function of the nation's governmental structure. Most representatives and civic leaders were opposed to the establishment of any program or agency that appeared poised to dictate a national culture. That is why, when funds became available for the creation of a new national institution of research and education, many politicians were opposed. They feared that such an institution would dictate the content and values at the heart of American culture and thereby destroy regional and state distinctiveness.

In many ways, their point was moot. Commonly held beliefs and sensibilities had already informed American political thought. Well before the establishment of a historical profession, for example, cultural leaders helped shape a sense of the past that guided the actions of colonists and revolutionaries. During the seventeenth century, religious leaders interpreted the colonization of the Americas as part of a historical continuum set in motion by God. They believed that divine will drove the engines of historical change, and their rhetoric has remained a relevant, if often controversial, element in American political discourse. Prominent late twentieth-century politicians—including both John F. Kennedy and Ronald Reagan—adopted John Winthrop's 1630 reminder to fellow founders of the Massachusetts Bay Company that God was shaping their actions: "He shall make us a praise and glory that men shall say of succeeding plantations, 'may the Lord make it like that of New England.' For we must consider that we shall be as a city upon a hill. The eyes of all people are upon us."[2] Despite the persistent popularity of his words in American's sense of national purpose and identity, a second generation of historical thinkers gradually replaced the Puritan adherence to God's law with a new belief in natural law. After the Revolution, men like Thomas Jefferson emphasized human self-interest as the prime motivator of historical actions, and this emphasis shaped the nation's earliest political documents.[3]

For Jefferson and his contemporaries, the study of nature and the study of the past were nearly indistinguishable. Historians have puzzled over Jefferson's ambiguous and often convoluted philosophy in these matters. Yet it is clear that for Jefferson and others like him, collecting natural, historical, and archaeological materials was part of a larger effort to compose an organizing myth, a way of categorizing and making use of the large American landscape and all of its resources.[4] In the same vein, the first national cultural institutions were designed to study and organize the natural world. None of the amateur historians among the founding fathers or their successors argued that the study of history should be a function of government. By the middle of the nineteenth century, there was no movement to employ historians in the civil service, to assemble national historical collections, or to assert governmental authority in the effort to define the continent as a historical landscape. History remained on the fringes of public life, and its marginalization was tied in complicated ways to conventions of gender. In the 1840s women's voluntary associations began to identify nationally significant historic structures and advocate for their protection, and individual donors gave time and money to preserve the homes of Founding Fathers and others. Their success defined historic preservation as women's work and the nation's most important historic structures as an extension of domestic space.[5]

If historical work took place at the margins of American culture in the years leading up to and immediately following the Civil War, however, science assumed a place at the center. Beginning in the 1830s botanists, geologists, cartographers, and various naturalists worked to convince Congress that research collections were not simply markers of individual elite status. Rather, artifacts held important clues for establishing the economic and cultural wealth of the nation. By the time the Civil War erupted, men of science had acquired government support to collect, interpret, and share information. As a result, it was scientists—not historians—who established the material conditions necessary for the later emergence of public history.

The Increase and Diffusion of Knowledge

In 1839 the leading proslavery senator, South Carolina's John C. Calhoun, angrily addressed the Senate. A watchdog for the rights of slaveholders, he stood to criticize yet another effort by Congress to impose the will of the federal government on the states and undermine local laws. Calhoun had served as vice president under both John Quincy Adams and Andrew Jackson, but he had grown increasingly angry about the reach of federal laws into the South. For him, the tipping point came in 1832, when South Carolina legislature declared federal tariffs unconstitutional. President Jackson sent the U.S. Navy into Charleston Harbor to enforce federal law. Enraged, Calhoun ran for the Senate rather than remain on the ballot with Jackson. As a senator from 1832 to 1843, he consistently and vehemently opposed any proposal he believed would endanger the legitimacy of slavery and trample on states' self-governance. Such was the case when he rose to argue, "I not only regard the measure proposed as unconstitutional, but to me it appears to involve a species of meanness which I cannot describe, a want of dignity wholly unworthy of the government."[6] This time, Calhoun's ire was not enflamed by the imposition of federal tariffs or a petition by a free territory for entry into the union. The new species of meanness he railed against was a proposed bureau that would engage in public education and foster research by American scientists.

Prior to the Civil War, education and scientific discovery were largely the provinces of elites who had been assembling collections in the United States since the founding of the nation. Inspired by European cabinets of curiosities created by aristocrats, merchants, and early practitioners of then undifferentiated sciences, wealthy Americans quantified and displayed their good taste and high intellect by establishing typological collections and assembling libraries of classical works and memoir. Thomas Jefferson amassed inventions and maintained collections of books, art, and Native American artifacts at Monticello, his Virginia plantation.[7] Charles Willson Peale, a painter and a contemporary of Jefferson, opened the first museum of science and art in the United States, inviting the general public to view his private collection of natural specimens, paintings, and other materials.[8] Both Jefferson and Peale ruminated on the importance of establishing a national culture for the young democracy, and they believed that Americans needed to display their cultural taste and intellectual achievements. To that end, the nation's first state historical societies were established during this period of nation building as well. In Boston, eight influential men—five ministers, a physician, a former governor, and a gentleman described as "a zealous antiquary"—organized the Massachusetts Historical Society in 1791. The society gathered books, letters, and papers to ensure New England would hold its rightful place as the cultural and spiritual origin of the young nation.[9] The New-York Historical Society, founded in 1804, was similarly established by local elites, including "statesmen and distinguished jurists," but it differed in emphasis from its Massachusetts predecessor. The New-York Historical Society collections approximated those of Jefferson and others, bringing together a broad assemblage of artifacts and documents. Donations included not only a library's worth of historical monographs and papers but also a number of "antiquities of this continent," including "a fine collection of objects of curiosity, deriving interest from their rarity or antiquity."[10]

The role of the elite in organizing collections, dabbling in scientific research, and pioneering local museums and historical societies did not necessarily prefigure the rise of federally funded or operated institutions, nor did it prepare Americans to accept the notion of a national culture sponsored by the federal government. Indeed, when the opportunity for the federal government to play such a role first arose in earnest, it was controversial and hotly debated. One hundred thousand pounds from the estate of British scientist James Smithson arrived in the United States in 1835, setting off a debate in Congress that would last for nearly a decade.[11] Smithson, a quintessential nineteenth-century "gentleman-scientist" who had studied chemistry at Oxford, specified that the money should be used by the United States to found "an establishment for the increase and diffusion of knowledge."[12] For some it served as a lightning rod for general anxieties about the unpredictable effects of foreign influence on the evolution of America's institutions, but the loudest voices of opposition came from Calhoun's faction, all of whom were intensely sensitive to the expansion of federal authority. In his 1839 statement to Congress, Calhoun worried that the Smithson bequest put Congress in danger of "enlarge[ing] our grant of power derived from the states of this Union." He insisted on refusing the gift on the basis that it was unconstitutional for the federal government to expand its authority into areas such as education, which should be left to states' control.[13] Calhoun's objection was, of course, clear evidence of the all-consuming power of the slavery debate in the decades leading to the Civil War—even when slavery was not the topic of discussion, the slavery question influenced political debates about states' rights.

For Calhoun and his supporters, the imposition of federal authority detracted from the noble intentions of the young democracy. Those who wished to use the bequest to create a national institution dedicated to research and education calculated "national dignity" rather differently, however. Two camps of supporters pressed Congress to accept the Smithson bequest. Although they each had a different vision for the institution it might build, both recognized that the gift represented an opportunity for the United States to demonstrate the nation's wealth and accomplishment. On the one side, a modest group of supporters emphasized Smithson's interest in the "diffusion" of knowledge, arguing that the bequest should be used to improve educational opportunities in Washington. Robert Dale Owen, a reform-minded representative from Indiana, perhaps sharing some suspicion about the reach of the federal government, argued that large-scale cultural institutions designed to formulate a national culture were elitist. He wanted to see the money put to use to create a school, and a wave of educators agreed with him. Similar suggestions from this side of the conversation included calls to create a national university or establish an agricultural study center.[14]

By far the more powerful group of supporters, however, was led by John Quincy Adams, who between 1839 and 1846 chaired a series of congressional committees to explore the nature of the bequest and to examine options for acceptable use of the funds. Adams and those in his camp were interested in using the Smithson funds for a more ambitious "increase" of knowledge among American men of letters. They proposed large-scale institutions that would enable the federal government to support and showcase American intellect and inventiveness. Richard Rush, the statesman who had worked through British legal channels to secure the bequest from executors of Smithson's estate, stated that the physical strength and natural resources of the nation were well-known, but its intellectual and moral strength had not yet garnered international recognition. He argued that federal support for an organization dedicated to scientific research would enable American scholars to stand as peers with leading scientists from the "civilized nations" of the world. Joel Poinsett, a staunch unionist and opponent of slavery from Calhoun's state of South Carolina, envisioned an even more sweeping institution that would include—along with a space observatory Adams wished to create—botanical gardens, laboratories, and libraries, as well as a series of publications for communicating the institution's scientific findings.[15] Poinsett believed the government should play a role in encouraging American scientific discovery, and he regularly injected this idea into ongoing debates about the future of the Smithson bequest.[16] For him, government support for the sciences was essential to the dignity of the nation, and he challenged detractors: "Would we expose ourselves to be denied our just title of a moral, religious, intelligent and enlightened people, by refusing to inscribe the United States of America among the names of the civilized nations of the earth?"[17]

Like Smithson, and to some extent Jefferson and Peale, Joel Poinsett was a gentleman scientist who collected rocks, fossils, and plants. His personal efforts were driven by a powerful belief that scientific observation and discovery could be useful to the federal government. Born in Charleston in 1779 Poinsett moved back and forth between the United States and England throughout his youth. He was educated in private schools at home and abroad and eventually studied medicine at the University of Edinburgh in Scotland and law in the United States. His father would have preferred him to settle into life as part of the South Carolina aristocracy, but Poinsett built a public career as a statesman and a diplomat. His parents and sister died when Poinsett was still in his twenties, and he inherited the family's entire estate. His position of privilege allowed him to engage in science as a hobby while he held a variety of elected offices and presidential appointments between 1809 and his death in 1851.

Poinsett's career began when James Madison sent him to South America to investigate revolutionary forces seeking independence from Spain. Despite the United States' official declaration of neutrality, Madison expected him to help calm the situation by intervening when tempers flared, which he did with some success. Poinsett was elected to Congress in 1821, and a year later James Monroe sent him as a special envoy to Mexico to determine if the United States should recognize its government. John Quincy Adams appointed him as minister to Mexico in 1825, a position he held until he became too involved with some of the groups fomenting civil war, and he was recalled in 1830.[18]

Poinsett's scientific ventures were at least as significant as his diplomatic efforts, and he helped shape a national program to collect, catalog, and display a wide range of scientific artifacts. He had long been interested in finding new agricultural products and farming methods that might be imported to the United States to eliminate dependence on slavery. During youthful tours of Europe, beginning in 1801, he had made an extensive study of farming practices in Italy, France, and elsewhere.[19] While fulfilling his formal duties in Mexico, Poinsett also indulged his hobby as an amateur naturalist. He kept a detailed diary in which he recorded his observations about the nation's agriculture and natural resources. He paid attention to regional economic and agricultural differences, taking care to mention where American products seemed superior and where Mexican techniques might have an advantage in the U.S. market. He sent his diary accounts in letters to the cartographer Henry Schenk Tanner, and the entire collection was published—along with a map and other materials—in 1824.[20] Later, even as he was becoming embroiled in the Mexican civil war, he experimented as an arborist, introducing the American elm tree into Mexico. He also collected samples of plants, bringing the first poinsettia (named for him) to America among his specimens. As Poinsett continued to achieve even greater stature in his public life, he also worked to create more direct connections between his scientific and political interests.

Hard Science and National Defense

Men like Poinsett engaged in the study of natural science as a hobby, paying for travel and collections with money from private fortunes.[21] There were few opportunities for less privileged naturalists who wished to make work out of full-time study. In the middle of the nineteenth century, the United States lagged behind other nations in graduate education in the natural sciences, and congressional debate continued to delay the creation of a national museum or research institute that might help legitimize the study of nature. Great Britain was ahead of the United States on both counts. That nation had established its National Museum in the middle of the eighteenth century, after purchasing and displaying a private collection of plants, fossils, and bones. By the early decades of the nineteenth century, British natural scientists enjoyed a measure of legitimacy, although their theories were certainly not immune from controversy. The great naturalist Charles Darwin first became curious about the distribution of fossils and animal species in the late 1820s. He had lost interest in medical studies and had begun taking classes with botanists and other naturalists at the University of Cambridge.

While Darwin was able to feed his interest, Americans interested in the study of the natural world had few options for graduate study. A handful of programs in prestigious East Coast colleges allowed young men of privilege to study under European scholars, but many ambitious young men of more modest means entered medical school and engaged in fieldwork as a hobby. Complicating matters, an internal hierarchy among scientists of various disciplines tended to mesh with American gender conventions, shedding an unflattering light on many young disciplines in the field of natural science. Practitioners of "hard" sciences, such as physics and chemistry, valued lab work and experimentation and tended to view natural science, with its emphasis on material collections and personal observation, as frivolous and less intellectually rigorous. The fact that women were among the pioneers of fields like botany and anthropology only reinforced the dismissive perception that these fields were "soft."[22]

Historic preservation was similarly dismissed. The gender of early preservationists dovetailed with the gendering of their avocation, limiting their ability to attract much official interest in their work. Ann Pamela Cunningham was arguably the most influential person in this pioneering generation. She was a thirty-seven-year-old near invalid when she received a letter from her mother in 1853. Louisa Dalton Bird Cunningham, while traveling south by steamboat along the Potomac, had noticed the dilapidated Mount Vernon plantation, clearly visible on a rise above the river. She wrote to her daughter, "I was painfully distressed at the ruin and desolation of the home of [George] Washington, and the thought passed through my mind: Why was it the women of his country did not try to keep it in repair, if the men could not do it?"[23] The younger Cunningham, having suffered a severe spinal injury as a teenager, was unmarried and had few prospects. She was inspired by her mother's observation to take an unconventional public stand.[24] She published an anonymous appeal in the Charleston *Mercury* on December 2, 1853, urging the state of Virginia to purchase the historic structure.[25] Other newspapers picked up her letter. Unfortunately, men in positions of authority—including the governor of Virginia—were unwilling to take seriously such an assertive suggestion made by a "Southern Matron." Women, however, were drawn to the idea. Cunningham abandoned her efforts to interest policymakers in her project. Instead, she established the private Mount Vernon Ladies Association to solicit money and urge advocacy from women in every state in the nation.[26] She tied her interest in saving Mount Vernon to a larger desire to preserve the union from Civil War, recalling, "Providence had called upon the nation's women to rescue the 'sacred ashes' of Washington during the 'darkest days of the Republic' so that his sepulcher 'could be made all powerful in regenerating and healing' the Union."[27] Her efforts succeeded, and the Mount Vernon Ladies purchased the plantation in 1859.

The Mount Vernon Ladies Association's belief that protection of a common past could preserve the union can be understood as an unsuccessful effort to define historical work as broadly useful to the nation. After the association took control of the house, Cunningham put her formidable efforts to the task of restoring it. She urged all Americans to participate because the plantation was, in her estimation, the nation's "common homestead . . . procured as a common heritage for the estranged children of a common father, the spell of whose memory will yet have the power to reunite them around his hallowed sepulchre."[28] Cunningham's domestic imagery—her portrayal of Washington as a father and the house as a place for familial reunion—only reinforced the association of historic preservation with domesticity. However successful the efforts of Cunningham or the people and groups she inspired to take action to protect other historically significant structures, preservation remained in the minds of many a private and sentimental task appropriately performed by women.[29] Practitioners in some of the natural sciences fighting a similar bias were more successful in disconnecting conventions of gender from the development of expertise. Scientific research—whether "hard" or "soft"—could capitalize on a presumption of dispassionate objectivity.

In any case, geology proved to be something of an exception. Although the study of rocks had many of the characteristics of a soft science, geologists were among the first naturalists to earn legitimacy, because their research was immediately useful. Beginning in the 1830s and with greater success after the Civil War, geologists connected their field research directly to the interests of the federal government. At first, the Department of War fostered this connection, because geological and topographical surveys of the landscape were crucial for defense. After the War of 1812, Congress made appropriations for a small topographical unit to support military objectives. At first topographers were ordered to plan military routes and defensive positions, mapping roads, waterways, landscape features, and established villages along the way. They also accompanied military scouts to "make sketches of their routes, accompanied by written notices of everything worthy of observation therein; to keep a journal of every day's movement when the army is in march, noticing the variety of ground, of buildings, of culture, and distances, and state of roads between common points throughout the march of the day."[30] At first, then, the scientific work of observing, recording, and mapping the American landscapes was conducted as a means to an end, to support the construction of military forts and transport routes. An Army lieutenant oversaw topographical work, although the unit was supervised by an engineer who directed projects on behalf of the military.

As the unit's responsibilities expanded during the 1820s to include coastal surveys and infrastructure improvement projects, topographers began to lobby for separation from the engineering unit so that their research would not be eliminated in an effort to streamline the unit's productivity.[31] Early in the 1830s John James Abert, a veteran of the War of 1812, had successfully convinced the secretary of war and Congress that geological research has usefulness all its own, independent from engineering and construction. Abert had joined the topographical survey unit in 1814, and he was assigned as the lieutenant in charge of its functions in 1829. After accepting his new role, however, he was dismayed to discover that it was largely clerical, and he echoed and amplified complaints made by others in the unit. As a result, in 1831 the newly appointed secretary of war, Lewis Cass, reconstituted the unit as the independent Topographical Bureau. Abert was promoted to colonel in charge of the bureau, and he reported directly to the secretary of war. Topographers continued to play a supporting role in engineering projects on roads, harbors, bridges, and railroads, and Abert did not let up on pressuring the secretary and Congress to recognize the value that purely scientific research might have for fostering the progress of the nation. Geology, he argued, could "open so many and so important national advantages." Geologists were poised to provide evidence that could stimulate "internal commercial prosperity [through] development of these great resources of wealth and commercial intercourse, which now lie inert and buried in the bowels of the earth."[32] Convinced, in 1834 Congress authorized Abert to use $5,000 of the bureau's appropriation to create a national geological map.

The geological mapping project lasted only two years, but it marked the beginning of a shift in the government's attitude toward science. Although Congress continued to debate whether or not to fund science for science's sake, most representatives recognized that economic interests could be served by supporting well-crafted scientific expeditions.[33] Abert found an intellectual partner in Joel Poinsett. Martin Van Buren appointed Poinsett as secretary of war in 1837, putting him in a position to finally authorize a long-debated and delayed research expedition by the U.S. Navy. During the 1820s scientists had begun lobbying Congress to equip navy ships for scientific expeditions, but they had been unable to attract sustained support. Congress had authorized a naval expedition to Antarctica in 1828, but final approval of a travel route and designation of appropriate crew dragged on. The navy objected to the prospect of bringing civilians on the expedition to conduct the research, and military officials competed vehemently for the right to determine who should retain control of the project. By the end of the decade, senatorial objections had escalated. South Carolina senator Robert Young Hayne argued that geographical discovery was not worth abandoning the fundamental principle of a restrained federal government or forming unnecessary entanglements with foreign nations. The cause temporarily lost, scientists threw in their lot with private expeditions but complained loudly that their work was overshadowed by sponsors' interest in finding viable markets and salable goods. The private expeditions were considered a failure by most supporters of science.[34]

By the middle of the 1830s, however, attitudes had shifted. The success of the Topographical Bureau in connecting military defense to scientific research had cast government-sponsored research in a different light. Congressional debate about the Smithson bequest, although still some years from a final resolution, forced senators and representatives alike to articulate the relationship of science and national dignity. Riding these trends, Joel Poinsett finally implemented the United States Exploring Expedition, linking scientific research to an international display of military strength. After a few false starts, Poinsett appointed Charles Wilkes, a naval officer who had participated in topographical surveys of the coasts, to oversee the four-year expedition by six naval ships. Wilkes divided the responsibility for various kinds of scientific research between military officers and civilians. He reserved for his officers the research with which they were most experienced, explaining to Poinsett, "All the duties appertaining to Astronomy, Surveying, Hydrography, Geognosy, Geodesy, Magnetism, Meteorology, and Physics generally to be exclusively confined to the Navy Officers." He did, however, allow that less useful scientific collecting in fields such as zoology, geology, mineralogy, botany, and conchology could be completed by members of the medical corps accompanying the expedition.[35] Poinsett, himself a botanist, was not happy with this rather dismissive attitude toward the softer sciences and advocated for the inclusion of experienced natural scientists. When Wilkes polled medical officers, no one would claim any expertise in the fields he outlined. With some reluctance, he invited seven civilian scientists to accompany the expedition: naturalists Charles Pickering and Titan Peale, son of Charles Willson Peale; geologist James Dana; linguist Horatio Hale; conchologist Joseph Couthouy; and botanists William Brackenridge and William Rich. By the time the expedition had concluded in 1842, it had cost $928,000, covered eighty-seven thousand miles, and visited most of the world's continents, including Antarctica.[36] Unlike its earlier, privately funded predecessors, the United States Exploring Expedition was a tremendous success.

The navy returned to the United States with a wealth of new collections from around the world, including four thousand animal specimens; fifty thousand plants; many thousands of gems, minerals, and fossils; and more than four thousand ethnographic artifacts, including war clubs from Fiji and flax baskets from New Zealand.[37] Amassing collections from other nations has long been a tool of colonialism, nationalism, and conquest.[38] For instance, the British explorer James Cook had collected about three thousand ethnographic artifacts over the course of his three expeditions.[39] Poinsett was surely familiar with this practice. National museums in cities such as London, Paris, and Rome displayed collections of both natural specimens and cultural artifacts to reinforce the claim to international power and cultural superiority. For the United States, a former colony without apparent claim to a unique national heritage, collections of this variety surely served multiple purposes during the early part of the nineteenth century. On a practical level, Poinsett had long believed that collections could provide the young nation with important economic information and evidence. On a grander scale, his support for the creation of a national institution with the Smithson bequest suggests he understood collections' usefulness for demonstrating America's fitness to the world.

While the United States Exploring Expedition was still at sea, Poinsett established the National Institute for the Promotion of Science in 1840 for this purpose; John James Abert was one of several geologists among the founding members. The National Institute assumed responsibility for the care of all topographical surveys and specimens collected during the expedition, as well as the specimens that had arrived with the Smithson bequest and a number of miscellaneous American antiquarian artifacts, including George Washington's field kit. These materials were all displayed in the U.S. Patent Office building, alongside various patent models.[40]

Research, Discovery, and the Advancement of American Science

Poinsett hoped that the Smithson bequest might ultimately be used to expand the National Institute. Instead, the growth of the government's scientific ventures provided an additional source of pressure, bolstering John Quincy Adams's long effort to establish a new institution. Congress authorized use of the Smithson bequest for the creation of the Smithsonian Institution in 1846. The enabling legislation adopted the language of the original bequest, rather vaguely allowing for an "establishment for the increase and diffusion of knowledge among men," and it positioned the new institution just outside the reach of formal federal control. The Smithsonian was set up as an independent federal entity whose daily operation took place outside of the three formal branches of government. At the same time, because the Smithson funds were held in trust by the Department of the Treasury, the legislation required federal oversight of the Smithsonian budget.[41] In an attempt to temper the extent to which Congress might exert political control over the institution through budgetary restrictions, the legislation also established a governing Board of Regents to provide more or less balance in influence among states, the federal government, and practitioners of science. As originally constructed, it included a group of politicians—the vice president of the United States, the chief justice of the Supreme Court, the mayor of Washington, three members of the Senate, and three members of the House of Representatives—as well as a group of civilians composed of two members from Poinsett's National Institute for the Promotion of Science and four citizens from four different states.[42]

Poinsett and the other supporters of the Smithsonian plan believed that improving American scientific achievement should be the institution's primary focus, but the role of collections in pursuing this agenda was not an immediate point of agreement. The institution's founding documents called for the establishment of a museum so that collections might be put on public display, but the first secretary of the Smithsonian, Joseph Henry, was not enthusiastic about dedicating precious staff and limited resources to collections management and public education. Henry, who served from 1846 to 1878, preferred to focus on more traditional modes of professional development, and he had made no secret of his plans.[43] He had sent a proposal to the Board of Regents prior to his appointment as secretary in which he outlined his vision for an institution that would enable isolated and underserved American scientists to engage in intellectual inquiry with an international community: "The most prominent idea in my mind is that of stimulating the talent of our country to original research—in which it has been most lamentably deficient—to pour fresh material on the apex of the pyramid of science, and thus to enlarge its base."[44] To this end, Henry put a great deal of energy into publishing, creating an exclusive vehicle for American scientists to circulate their findings and engage in scholarly discussions with scientists from overseas.

Henry's assessment of the poor state of original research among American scientists was, in many ways, correct—at least in 1846. By 1848, however, the perceived value of natural science research to national interests had taken dramatic leaps forward, opening up opportunities for geologists to engage in federally sponsored research. The discovery of gold in California and the acquisition of new territories in the wake of the Mexican-American War created an immediate need for better commerce, communication, and transportation between the East and West and illuminated the usefulness of geology to both federal and state governments.[45] Congress appropriated $150,000 to the War Department in 1853, authorizing the recently reorganized United States Army Corps of Topographical Engineers to conduct four geological surveys to identify the safest and least expensive location for railroad lines between the Pacific Ocean and the Mississippi River.[46] Congress also disseminated information gathered during the surveys; by 1860 it had published sixty reports related to the exploration of the West.[47] Similarly, by this time thirty states had initiated geological surveys to identify potentially valuable mineral deposits as well as arable land and water resources to accommodate new settlers.[48]

Expeditions by the topographical corps and engineering units became vehicles of discovery. In 1848 Colonel William H. Emory reported, "We are now in the regions made famous in olden times by the fables of Friar Marcos and eagerly did we ascend every mound, expecting to see in the distance what I fear is but the fabulous 'Casa Montezuma.'"[49] The surveyors, engineers, geologists, and topographers crisscrossing the western portion of the United States between 1848 and the start of the Civil War were not the first explorers to make their way over mountains, across rivers, and through plains. They followed in the footsteps of Spanish missionaries and conquistadors who had, centuries earlier, begun to describe the astonishing natural wonders in what is now the American Southwest. During the 1530s and 1540s Spanish soldiers encountered a geyser hot enough to cook their meat.[50] In 1540 explorers traveling with Francisco Vasquez de Coronado recorded their astonishment at the immense rock formations in a chasm cut by water.[51] From the top of the steep walls leading down to the river, the rocks below appeared as large as a grown man, but when two of Coronado's men—Captain Pablo de Melgosa and Juan Galeras—climbed a third of a way down toward the water, they discovered that the rocks were, in fact, "taller than the great tower of Seville."[52] In 1769 Father Juan Crespi, official diarist of a Spanish expedition along the California coast, observed "very high trees of a red color, not known to us."[53] As the land west of the Mississippi became integrated into the United States, fantastic stories about the Old Faithful geyser, the Grand Canyon, the California Redwoods, and other natural wonders piqued the interest of investors, territorial governments, and federal policymakers alike. They represented potential sources of mineral wealth, timber, and energy, and they promised to draw settlers and prospectors into remote corners of the West.

There were also other tantalizing stories. Beginning in the sixteenth century, Spanish explorers into present-day Arizona, Colorado, New Mexico, and other regions of the American Southwest went in search of the fabled Seven Cities of Cibola, golden outposts of the Aztec Empire. In 1539 Friar Marcos de Niza had reported finding a mysterious ancient structure that he believed to be Montezuma's castle. Francisco Coronado's party of explorers recorded similar discoveries, including a four-story structure near the Gila River in Colorado with walls six feet thick. It was so ancient, Coronado insisted, that even the local Pima Indians did not know its origins.[54] The myth of the Seven Cities inspired soldiers and scientists alike, each hoping to uncover credible evidence of a mysterious ancient civilization in North America. Emory, a military topographer, was accompanying the Army of the West on a reconnaissance mission near the end of the Mexican War when he recorded the first bit of American data in 1848. After glimpsing what had appeared from a distance to be a castle, Emory concluded that the crumbling structures he found were different from those recorded by Friar Marcos. Nonetheless, they provided compelling evidence that the Southwest "was evidently once the abode of busy, hard-working people," whose advanced techniques of irrigation and agriculture suggested they came from a highly civilized race.[55] A few years later, Antoine Leroux, the guide for an 1853–54 survey by military topographers, recorded a similar discovery: "The walls of the principal building, forming a long square, are in some places twenty feet high and three feet thick, and have in many places loop-holes like those of a fortress." Despite the presence of Native American tribes across the West, observers such as Emory, Leroux, and others tended to disassociate the remains of "ancient civilized nations" from the "ruins of another Indian village." Leroux wrote, "Who were its inhabitants, and what became of them, is hard to tell."[56]

Military notations about the ruins scattered across the Southwest invigorated a still-developing field of American science: anthropology. "Anthropology" was an umbrella term used to describe work in archaeology, ethnology, linguistics, and physical anthropology. Overseas, these areas of inquiry were dominated by the study of the Greek and Roman Empires, demonstrating the evolution of Western civilization and lending a long pedigree to the dominant European nations. The United States lacked such an illustrious past on which to hang its claims to greatness. Instead, American anthropologists were marginalized by their focus on the less auspicious Native American past.[57] The earliest practitioners of American anthropology, including Thomas Jefferson, collected artifacts near burial mounds in the eastern portion of the United States and pored over Spanish accounts of the structures in the Southwest. By the 1840s and 1850s America's self-made anthropologists were beginning to integrate these bits of information into a narrative about the evolution of America that tended to naturalize the practice of slavery, policies of expansion, and the eradication of Native Americans by whites. In 1846 the regents of the Smithsonian Institution instructed Joseph Henry to focus his energies on assembling collections that documented the natural history of the nation, including anthropological materials. Henry was notoriously uninterested in collections, and the Smithsonian did not seek out anthropological collections until well after the Civil War. Nonetheless, the institution encouraged anthropological work. Henry collaborated with independent researchers such as Ephraim Squire and Edwin Davis, each of whom had a lifelong fascination with mounds and earthworks in southern Ohio and Kentucky. In 1848, Henry published their report, *Ancient Monuments of the Mississippi Valley*, in the first volume of his Smithsonian series Contributions to Knowledge.

The publication of Charles Darwin's *Origin of Species* in 1859 provided anthropologists with a scientific framework with which to classify humans on an evolutionary scale from "savage" to "civilized." Darwin's use of animal specimens to test his theory of evolution illuminated for anthropologists the importance of acquiring collections for study and training. Few engaged in their own fieldwork, however. Instead, they purchased skulls, human remains, and other collections from soldiers and relic hunters to use as the basis for their research. Their interpretation of this information rested on a presumption of white superiority, reflecting contemporary debates about manifest destiny and legitimizing both slavery and expansion. At the same time, the popular notion that anthropological and racial fissures separated the unknown ancient "civilizations" from modern "savages" was useful to the federal government, because it meant that Native Americans and Spanish colonists had no more claim to the continent than the white founders and makers of the United States.[58] As Alfred Hunter explained in his 1859 catalog of the ethnological collections assembled by the National Institute, "The disappearance of the original inhabitants of the Western continent is not the result of destruction, but a decaying atrophy, which nothing can avert, except the cataclysm of the Caucasian strain."[59]

Collections and the Emergence of Intellectual Authority

Scientific research had both intellectual and practical value to the federal government, but its expense was always a sore point. Government expenditures for publications, expeditions, and surveys were enormous, accounting for about a third of the annual federal budget.[60] Researchers were always looking for just the right argument to justify the allocation of more government funds. At the Smithsonian, that search finally brought Joseph Henry around to the benefits of collecting. Scientific research at the Smithsonian Institution hit its stride quickly under Henry's leadership. His own research in the field of meteorology grew exponentially, in part because he could demonstrate that the ability to collect and disseminate weather data had practical applications for transportation, commerce, and defense. Henry created a network of weather researchers and data collectors through use of the telegraph, facilitating better weather prediction. But Henry's project was expensive and always in danger of losing funding if the Board of Regents or Congress determined it was no longer useful to the institution's mission. Henry took no chances, and when an opportunity to connect his project to the needs of another federal bureau emerged in the 1850s, he took full advantage of it.[61] The Patent Office building was becoming overcrowded, and Poinsett's National Institute was running out of money. The commissioner of patents, frustrated by the distraction, struck a deal with Henry in 1855. He offered him a portion of the Patent Office's annual appropriations to support the Smithsonian's meteorological projects, and, in return, Henry asked the Board of Regents to transfer all of the National Institute's scientific specimens to the Smithsonian.[62]

The arrival of these materials at the Smithsonian in 1857—along with $17,000 to cover immediate expenses and a $4,000 annual appropriation— helped fuel a growing commitment among some members of the staff to transform the institution into the national repository for all government collections, thereby cementing its central location at the intersection of scientific research and federal authority. Spencer Baird figured prominently in this effort. A naturalist with a particular interest in ichthyology, Baird arrived at the Smithsonian in 1850 when he was just twenty-seven years old, bringing along his own extensive collections. As a junior staff member, Baird spent his early years at the institution supporting Joseph Henry's publication program, but Baird's own agenda more closely matched that of Joel Poinsett. He argued that it was not enough to encourage research by other scholars, and he quietly implemented a more active program of collecting. Writing an average of 3,500 letters a year, Baird made sure that naturalists from across the country were aware of the Smithsonian's efforts to collect. His efforts bore fruit, and packages of fossils, meteorite fragments, Native American artifacts, plants, and countless other materials poured in to the institution. Baird recommended naturalists and other scientists for the various government expeditions, providing them with detailed instructions about how to collect, preserve, and document items. He also arranged free shipping to send materials back to the Smithsonian by railway, boat, and mail.[63]

Baird provided an important conduit for ambitious young scientists seeking opportunities to conduct fieldwork. After the Smithsonian Institution Building (dubbed "The Castle") was completed, Baird used it as a headquarters for expanding the usefulness and visibility of the collections. Between 1857 and 1866 he recruited collectors and naturalists from across the country, inviting them to conduct research under his tutelage and on his dime, creating a kind of resident scholar program. Baird's students adopted the scientific name of a recently discovered giant sloth fossil, calling themselves the "Megatherium Society." The leader of the group— William Stimpson—was a marine biologist who had conducted fieldwork at his own expense with Louis Agassiz in the late 1840s and early 1850s. Stimpson accompanied the North Pacific Exploring Expedition for four years beginning in 1852, and he arrived at Baird's door when he returned in

1856.[64] Other members of the society, such as Stimpson's close friend Robert Kennicott, had less formal training. Kennicott was already a well-known collector by the young age of twenty-one, however, and Baird personally recruited him to join the group studying at the Smithsonian. With Baird's support, he traveled with an expedition in Canada and Alaska for three years beginning in 1859, collecting with such enthusiasm that he inspired other members of the party to join him in gathering specimens for the Smithsonian, a task they continued even after Kennicott left.[65] When not participating in a research expedition, the members of the society worked in the Smithsonian Castle, meticulously cleaning and cataloging the specimens that became the heart of the U.S. National Museum collections.[66]

State governments also provided similar opportunities for geologists seeking support for fieldwork. James A. Hall was, in some respects, the Spencer Baird of New York. He had worked on New York's geological survey since it originated in 1836. At first, the primary function of the survey in New York was to identify coal deposits, but as research progressed, it accumulated a massive collection of fossils that attracted the attention of paleontologists and generated cutting-edge scholarship. Hall completed a survey of iron deposits in the Adirondacks before being promoted to chief of the fourth district in Western, New York. Funds were initially appropriated for a four-year survey, but Hall refused to stop his work when time ran out. He lobbied the state legislature for additional aid and sold off parts of the collections to fund more research. His work earned him recognition, and he was named the state paleontologist in 1843.[67] He established a research lab in Albany, New York, in 1852 and set up an apprentice program to train students for fieldwork and collections-based research.

Men like Hall and Poinsett created a lifeline for would-be geologists who—by virtue of their modest pedigree or region of birth—were not strong candidates for entry into the few prestigious American colleges offering courses of study in the natural sciences. Amateur naturalists from across the country wrote to both men, seeking one of the few coveted research positions on a state or military survey or the chance to work with specimens in the lab. In 1853 Baird received a letter from Ferdinand Hayden, a twenty-three-year-old medical student from Cleveland: "I am extremely anxious to spend a few years in the study of natural history. I feel I could endure cheerfully any amount of toil, hardship and self-denial provided I could gratify my strong desire to labor in the field as a naturalist. . . . I am willing to go anywhere for any length of time and labor with the utmost diligence."[68] By 1853 Hayden had become committed to establishing himself as a naturalist, but he lacked the fortune and connections to study overseas. Instead, he found creative ways to insinuate himself into the network of collectors and field-workers developing their professions on the ground. Born in Westfield, Massachusetts, he was sent to live with paternal relatives in Ohio after the death of his father in 1838. His early education was inconsistent, but the move to Ohio put him in proximity to Oberlin College. Hayden enrolled in the preparatory department, throwing himself into acquiring a remedial classical education. He was successful and gained admittance to the college proper in 1846. At Oberlin Hayden developed "a decided taste for the natural sciences," studying with and renting a room from George Allen, the school's professor of music, geology, and natural history.[69]

Although Hayden's passion lay with the study of plants and minerals, he was engaged to be married and in need of a career that could convey status and stability. For a man of modest means and few connections, the natural sciences appeared less than promising. After his graduation in 1850, he briefly studied theology, pursuing a career in the ministry with plans to continue his studies of the natural world as a hobby. Religious studies did not appeal to him, however, and Allen pointed him toward medical school, introducing him to Jared Potter Kirtland, a professor at Cleveland Medical School. Once at Cleveland, Hayden identified a small community of like-minded teachers and young alumni who served as mentors. John Strong Newberry, a recent graduate, proved particularly important. Newberry had turned his attention to geology and paleontology, and he was achieving some notoriety as a researcher.

Although Hayden dutifully completed his medical courses, he was far more interested in Newberry's willingness to teach him about fossils and rocks. He became an avid collector and began what he described as an "ambitious correspondence" with fellow naturalists. His reputation spread, and Newberry introduced him to an old family friend, James Hall, who casually invited Hayden to come to Albany. Hayden leaped at the opportunity, pressing Hall for the chance to participate in fieldwork for the New York geological survey. Another prospect arose, however. The recent discovery of large fossil beds in the Dakota Badlands appealed to Hall's ambitions, and he put together a research team to collect specimens for his New York lab. Hall's assistant in New York, Fielding Bradford Meek, was in charge of excavations, and Hayden would be employed as Meek's assistant. Hall offered to pay expenses plus $150 per month, and Hayden blustered, "with all modesty, I think I should exceed even your expectations, for obstacles have no terror to me and I trust never will have."[70] As it turned out, Hayden did little collecting on the trip. Instead, he maintained detailed field notes for Meek. He developed a geologist's eye for rock strata, and his observations were incorporated into a larger published study, bringing Hayden to the attention of military topographers and providing him with the entrée he needed. He was soon accompanying the army's topographical engineers on a number of western surveys, including expeditions on the Yellowstone and Missouri Rivers and into the Black Hills. He and Meek were reunited for a survey of Kansas, and in 1859 he traveled into Montana to identify the source of the Yellowstone, Gallatin, Snake, and Madison Rivers.

Like Hayden, his contemporary and fellow midwesterner, John Wesley Powell, created his own opportunities for fieldwork. Powell was somewhat less successful than Hayden, however, in the art of self-promotion. Prior to the Civil War, he pursued a rather modest path, perhaps influenced by his parents' austere ways. Born to an itinerant Methodist preacher in New York, Powell grew up in Ohio and Illinois during the 1830s and 1840s. Slavery, a divisive issue for the nation, was also a divisive issue for the Methodist Church. Abolitionist factions petitioned church leaders to take a firm stance against slavery, but their movement failed. As a result, antislavery members broke with the formal Methodist Church, forming a new branch of Wesleyan Methodist churches. Powell's parents were among them. His family's politics made him a target for ridicule and violence and forced him to leave school at the age of twelve. He apprenticed with a neighboring farmer and became fascinated with the study of nature as it related to his preparations for an agricultural life.

Ultimately, Powell's interests lay more in research than in farming, and he began to engage in informal field studies of his own making. Likely as a result of his father's connections, Powell studied sporadically at Wesleyan colleges in Illinois and Ohio and eventually found work teaching courses in science. When he wasn't teaching, he was traveling throughout the Midwest and recording his observations of geological formations.[71] Beginning in 1856 he began to develop a particular fascination with the geology of rivers, and he undertook a solitary series of long scientific expeditions up and down the major river systems in the Midwest. In 1859 Powell launched a small boat from Ottawa, Illinois, and traveled down the Illinois River to the Mississippi, proceeding on to the Gulf of Mexico, then reversing course and coming back up the Des Moines River.[72] He was an avid collector, and by the end of the 1850s he had accumulated almost six thousand specimens of plants and shells.

Ultimately, Powell's nearly obsessive fieldwork and his expansive private collections brought him into the orbit of a small network of innovative science educators in Illinois. Frustrated by a lack of support for research at Illinois State Normal College and recognizing that science students required access to specimens, they organized the Illinois State Natural History Society, coordinating efforts by naturalists across the state to assemble information about minerals, plants, animals, and other resources. Powell joined the society as a conchologist.[73] The society attracted the attention of the state legislature, which chartered it in 1861, assigning society members responsibility to "conduct and complete a scientific survey of the State of Illinois in all the departments of natural history, and to establish a museum of natural history at the State Normal University."[74] In Illinois Powell began to connect his work as a teacher, his avocation as a collector, and the interests of state government. His work on behalf of the museum won him a professorship, and he soon was bringing students along on state survey expeditions, paying for supplies and expenses with small allocations from the legislature.

By the 1860s, then, the interests of government and the ambitions of science were more comfortable bedfellows. The federal government had expanded its reach into both education and the economy, justifying the appropriation of funds for research by emphasizing its pragmatic application. Scientists had proven themselves useful for identifying potentially valuable natural resources and supporting national defense. In turn, the Smithsonian Institution had come to occupy an important position as the nation's repository, providing an avenue for advancing America's intellectual stature and displaying the nation's grandeur. State governments were following suit and beginning to acknowledge the value of science for development. Natural scientists working on behalf of both state and federal governments had achieved a higher-level legitimacy of their "soft" interests by demonstrating the usefulness of research (despite the fears of prewar representatives) to the achievement of national dignity. That usefulness became even more evident during and after the Civil War. Between 1860 and 1916 the relationship between science and government promised to provide an antidote to the tremendous disruptions the war had wreaked on Americans' sense of social and economic order.

CHAPTER 2

Managing the Landscape
National Parks, National Monuments, and the Use of Public Land

———— ✠ ————

I earnestly recommend the establishment of a bureau of national parks. Such legislation is essential to the proper management of those wondrous manifestations of nature, so startling and so beautiful that everyone recognizes the obligations of the Government to preserve them for the edification and recreation of the people.

—PRESIDENT WILLIAM HOWARD TAFT, 1914—

The Civil War accelerated changes already taking shape in the nation's economy, politics, and social life. Nonetheless, for many Americans the dissolution of the union and the end of slavery created a sense of sudden disruption. In the remaining decades of the nineteenth century and the beginning of the new one, a cult of novelty emerged as Americans sought to move beyond sectional hostilities and the war. The era was shaped by new immigrants, the New Woman, and the "New Negro."[1] Henry W. Grady, editor of the *Atlanta Constitution*, described a "New South," and boosters touted its emergence. Grady took to the lecture circuit, speaking on behalf of southern entrepreneurs, landowners, and politicians who needed to attract outside investors to rebuild and modernize the region. Grady portrayed the New South as feminine and free. Having been emancipated from the past, she stood "upright, full-statured and equal among the people of the earth, breathing the keen air and looking out upon the expanded horizon.... She understands that her emancipation came because, through the inscrutable wisdom of God, her honest purpose was crossed, and her brave armies were beaten."[2] The region's forward-looking posture simultaneously and stubbornly turned away from the past.

This preference for the new reflected a certain optimism regarding the demographic and economic changes evident in nearly every state and territory. The population shifted to the West, and the economy shifted as well. More of the former slaves and plantation owners alike reported to work in factories rather than in fields. Many Americans saw their standard of living improve, along with their access to citizenship. Reconstruction-era policies expanded opportunities for education, entrepreneurism, and enfranchisement.[3] At the same time, the transition from agriculture to industry and slave to paid labor created a roiling, unruly economy, prone to extreme cycles of boom and bust. The extension of basic political rights to the freed slaves incited violence throughout the South. Technological innovation and the growth of cities changed the way most Americans lived and worked. Long-held traditions and habits seemed endangered. In many instances, the past was literally dismantled: old buildings and homes were demolished to make way for new businesses, new industries, new towns, and cities.[4] For many, so much change created more anxiety than optimism. One critic captured the mood of the era when she commented on the efforts of female social reformers: "If woman has, as she asserts, the power to make human society over, she has at the same time the opportunity to wreck it. A hope always implies a menace."[5] From 1860 onward, the hopeful forces pushing America into a new century were balanced by an equal and opposite fearful pull to protect America from the menace of change.

Prior to the Civil War, Congress had been slow to create any agency or bureau it perceived as dictating a national culture. The federal government had sponsored research, assembled collections, and fostered the advancement of new sciences only when such work was couched as immediately useful to defense or economic development. After the war, however, the perceived dissolution of social and cultural bulwarks lent a different kind of relevance to education and research. Over the next fifty years, Congress and the president established new federal regulations, scientific programs, and data-gathering agencies, claiming federal responsibility not simply for identifying the nation's resources but also for managing them. Furthermore, it was not simply Taft's "wondrous manifestations of nature" that required governmental oversight. The American people also seemed to require management. Anxiety about the pace of change led reformers and politicians alike to create more efficient and predictable means for channeling the restless spirit of the late nineteenth century.[6] Federally managed landscapes, Taft recognized, were more than simply beautiful; they could provide "edification and recreation" to offset the impact of rapid modernization.[7] Over the course of fifty years, the expansion of federal managerial and regulatory authority created complex legal frameworks, professional networks, institutional structures, and a philosophical inheritance for the emergence of public history.

Strengthening the Nation's Right Arm

Scientific discoveries made during pre–Civil War expeditions were partially responsible for generating a period of tremendous technological innovation and industrial expansion in postwar America. Topographical mapping identified appropriate new routes for the railway system. Geological discovery of coal and mineral deposits opened up opportunities for the growth of the steel industry and enabled the construction of new and faster machines for producing a variety of goods. Although only a few entrepreneurial individuals became extremely wealthy, new technologies changed the fortunes and habits of most Americans. On farms, in factories, and even on battlefields, work was becoming more specialized, more repetitive, and more mechanical. The number of jobs in industry seemed endless, but the pool of potential laborers was profoundly unprepared to enter a rapidly modernizing workplace. Skilled laborers were displaced by machinery, and unskilled laborers lacked the scientific and technical education that might prepare them to operate complex machinery.

Recognizing the crisis, Justin Smith Morrill, a representative from Vermont, argued that the federal government must act to expand education. Higher education remained inaccessible to most people, but the nation's future required productive and efficient workers. "Our country depends upon them as its right arm to do the handiwork of the nation," he argued in 1858. "Let us, then, furnish the means for that arm to acquire culture, skill and efficiency."[8] At first sectional hostilities and fear of extending education to the slaves and former slaves stymied his efforts, but secession created an opportunity for the federal government to move forward on Morrill's recommendation. Passed by Congress in 1862, the Morrill Act enabled the creation of state colleges and universities. Under the terms of the law, each state could acquire and sell 30,000 acres of public land for each of its senators and representatives, using the proceeds from the sale to establish new colleges—therefore called "land grant colleges."[9] Eventually,

17,430,000 acres of public land was used in this manner. By 1870 thirty-seven states had implemented programs for teaching agriculture, mechanical arts, and military science, and forty-eight colleges were established by 1890.[10]

The Morrill Act transformed higher education in two directions. With funds provided under the new law, universities created technical programs geared for improving the skills of farmers and workers. At the same time, the availability of federal funds enabled educators at older, more traditional universities to reform their course of study. Critics of the bill had feared that the emphasis on technical education would diminish the value and stature of classical, intellectual education. Morrill had loftier goals, insisting repeatedly that the program was designed to "offer an opportunity in every state for liberal and larger education to larger numbers, not merely to those destined for sedentary professions, but to those much needing higher instruction for the world's business, for the industrial pursuits and professions of life."[11] Far from watering down the quality of higher education, the Morrill Act created opportunities for an increasing number of graduate students to study in the United States rather than pursue education overseas, and it strengthened ties among science educators across institutional lines. Several existing universities seized the opportunity created by the Morrill Act to develop research-based programs and institutes, challenging the primacy of a classical educational model. Both Cornell University in New York and the Massachusetts Institute of Technology coupled land grant funds with private donations to create the first research-oriented universities.[12] In Connecticut, Yale University science professors courted the state legislature, using Morrill Act funds to expand applied science offerings at the Sheffield Scientific School.[13] Faculty at new land grant colleges and at Morrill institutions corresponded with colleagues across the country, sharing information about the best pedagogical approaches and recommending the most qualified faculty. The shift toward research-based education also brought new attention to the importance of collections. Entrepreneurial faculty members convinced philanthropists to fund libraries and museums so that students and professors alike could engage in hands-on research.

The passage of the Morrill Act helped fortify the cultural role of science in post–Civil War America. More graduates emerged from American institutions of higher learning trained in applied research methods. They accepted positions in federal collecting institutions and in federal agencies, integrating scientific methods with policymaking and setting new standards for managerial efficiency in the decades following the Civil War. Congress looked to scientists for answers to pressing postwar problems. When alarm arose about an apparent decline in the nation's edible fish supply, for example, Congress established the U.S. Fish Commission in 1871 to monitor the situation and recommend methods to conserve the nation's supply. The Office of Economic Ornithology, founded in 1885, studied the diets and migratory patterns of birds whose habits had an effect on agriculture.[14] The Department of Agriculture, created by Abraham Lincoln in 1862, was elevated to cabinet status in 1889, bringing a variety of scientific projects into the executive branch. As scientists increasingly ran government research projects and filled administrative positions in new bureaus and agencies, they brought the influence of a broad network of colleagues into the realm of policymaking.

Law and Order

While scientists established the usefulness of their expertise by providing data to manage economic and social change more efficiently, practitioners of historic preservation sought a different kind of cultural legitimacy. Women's voluntary associations worked to protect local traditions and halt social change. Prior to the war, Ann Pamela Cunningham had hoped restoring Mount Vernon as a symbol of national unity might stave off secession. After the war, women preservationists participated in the redefinition of national unity as a privilege of whiteness.[15] In the South, preservation organizations contributed to the advancement of the "Lost Cause" myth. In 1889 Cynthia Beverley Tucker Washington Coleman of Williamsburg, Virginia, and Mary Jeffrey Galt of Norfolk, Virginia, established the first state preservation entity, the Association for the Preservation of Virginia Antiquities. While southern business leaders eschewed the past in order to build a New South, Coleman, Galt, and the female members of the association used the language of domesticity and morality to preserve the memory of the Old South.[16] Galt held that poor men—black and white alike—should remain disenfranchised until they had been taught to display proper deference to authority, and she believed that the careful selection and protection of historic sites could provide that kind of civic education.[17] The association acquired historic structures and landscapes that connected the dreams of the earliest Anglo-Saxon settlers to the "honorable intentions" of the Confederacy. In 1893, for example, the association purchased a parcel of land on Jamestown Island that included both the remains of a 1639 church and Confederate earthworks.[18] African Americans in the former Confederate states—including Virginia—rebelled against the effort by white elites to interpret the meaning of the war and the southern past. They crafted a counternarrative by organizing celebrations that connected Independence Day with emancipation.[19] Galt responded angrily to these public displays, raging against "the way in which the miserable negroes behave now about everything we hold sacred."[20] For many white observers, African American commemorative activities manifested the fearful lack of social order in postwar society.

It was not only the behavior of African Americans in the South that enflamed fears about the demise of American tradition. The influence of the new immigrants on urban life and habits fueled a similar desire to conserve prewar values, emphasizing class distinctions as the mediator of patriotism. Preserving the homes of elite families and founding fathers gave women's historical associations a stage on which to promote national loyalty. In 1890 Mary Lockwood, Mary Desha, Eugenia Washington, and Ellen Hardin Walworth established the Daughters of the American Revolution (DAR) in Washington, D.C., in part, to "teach patriotism by erecting monuments and protecting historical spots."[21] The DAR, and its sister organization, the Colonial Dames of America, promoted the study of American history as an antidote to the danger posed by the new immigrants, since "many . . . are without occupation, almost without means, and of a low order of intelligence; unable to speak our language, and ignorant of and often inimical to our laws and government."[22]

At the same time that women's preservation societies were increasing in number and cultural influence, men were working to formalize historical study and establish its disciplinary boundaries. In 1884 a network of formally trained scholars and wealthy amateurs joined together to create the American Historical Association (AHA). The AHA established qualifications for membership and standards of excellence that fostered the development of historical scholarship in the United States. The founding members emphasized the scientific nature of their work, establishing emotional detachment and the objective analysis of data as the difference between the "hard" work of history and the "soft" work of preservation. Hoping to bring history closer to the realm of policymaking, members of the AHA networked with members of Congress and worked to archive the core documents in the history of the federal government. In turn, Congress bestowed official recognition on the AHA, sanctioning its role as the arbiter of historical significance. In 1893 Congress passed a resolution calling for the preservation of presidential papers. In response, the historian James Richardson compiled the first volume of *The Messages and Papers of the Presidents*. In 1899 the government published his work as a ten-volume set.[23] In this way, AHA historians participated in the creation of an officially sanctioned American past and a publicly recognized body of scholarship, one focused on official documents rather than domestic structures, vernacular landscapes, or artifacts.

The distinction between history and preservation proved to be both stubborn and complicated. As the number of formally educated male historians increased, they began to pursue employment both inside and outside of academia. Some held dual appointments as professors of history and as directors of local or regional historical societies. Despite their academic credentials, men who did so often found that the larger profession was less than supportive. The AHA refused admittance to historians whose focus was local or regional history, believing such pursuits were too limited in scope and significance to meet standards of scholarly achievement.[24] Furthermore, although men typically presided over local and regional historical societies, women were the most active members, volunteers, and board members. Historic sites that had been identified and preserved by women's associations were intellectually (if not always administratively) integrated into the creation and management of regional identities. In other words, the effort to collect, protect, and interpret the landscapes, artifacts, and documents of regional and local history—unscientific in approach and domestic in appeal—was more often gendered as feminine, advancing the belief that all local history was largely inspirational and committed to the preservation of civic virtue. Academic historians limited their focus to national events and written documents.

By the end of the nineteenth century, college-educated experts had become a new class of white-collar professionals. Historians were no exception, but their influence was somewhat limited by the discipline's internal divisions. Scientists found employment and research support in both the public and the private sectors, hired to add a layer of efficiency to the workings of government and industry.[25] As a result, it was more often practitioners of science—not scientific historians—who lent order and stability to the unruly postwar society.[26] The expansion of scientists' political legitimacy broadened their cultural authority and general popularity. Scientific research attracted the interest of state and territorial governments, business entrepreneurs, and others. Stories about their research expeditions filtered out of government reports and into the popular press, and men such as John Wesley Powell and Ferdinand Hayden capitalized on their newfound position at the center of American public life.

Adventures in Science

The sense of disorder in the post–Civil War era was not simply social and political; it was also material. The explosion of the demand for resources amplified the need for scientific data. Between 1860 and 1880 the number of American settlers west of the Mississippi more than doubled, from 619,000 to 1.8 million. As the population exploded, settlers transformed the region's topography. In addition, rapid industrialization and urbanization east of the Mississippi put new pressure on mineral, timber, and fuel resources. Industrialists made a fortune investing in western mining and logging interests. The extraction of bituminous coal alone increased from 8.8 million tons in 1861 to 50.8 million tons in 1880.[27] The completion of railroad lines made it possible to expand logging operations in previously inaccessible areas, feeding the demand for building materials. So much exploitation of western resources stressed the landscape. Unchecked logging left behind rubble and brush on newly bald mountain tops, and the mess easily sparked into uncontrollable fires and often washed downriver in violent flash floods.[28]

Meanwhile, geologists and other natural scientists offered their services to help identify valuable mineral deposits and arable land. Ferdinand Hayden wrote to Spencer Baird about "little groups of politically minded merchants, bankers and land speculators" in the Great Plains, interested in promoting their resources to attract investors and settlers. Recognizing these circumstances as an important opportunity to advance their own standing, Hayden and others "thrust their way forward in each city to volunteer a leadership that was crucial not only to the struggling new community itself but also to the much bigger region that was tributary to it."[29]

Beginning in 1867 the federal government responded to both the stress on natural resources and the interest of investors and local politicians by allocating funds for a series of new surveys of the West.[30] Not all of the surveys were funded equally. The Geological Exploration of the Fortieth Parallel received an initial allocation of $40,000. Clarence King, a twenty-five-year-old graduate of Yale's Sheffield School, led a team of researchers along the hundred-mile stretch by which the transcontinental railroad traveled from the Sierras in Nevada to the Front Range of the Rockies.[31] He described the landscape in vivid, dynamic language, arriving at new conclusions about the creation of canyons and the destruction of ancient creatures in the West. He produced a volume's worth of information on mining in the region and debunked claims that diamonds were among the minerals deposited there. The mining report demonstrated the usefulness of King's research, and Congress renewed the survey for three years without any solicitation from King himself.[32] His formal reports to Congress constituted a massive body of scholarship, eventually constituting a seven-volume research report and an atlas.[33]

Disbursement of federal money for civilian-led projects annoyed the military's remaining scientific units. Lieutenant George Wheeler argued that the practice created an inefficient, piecemeal approach to mapping the West's resources and undermined military planning. Indeed, western military operations continued in the 1860s and 1870s as conflicts between settlers and Native Americans intensified. Wheeler, an engineering officer for the Army of California, embarked on a series of expeditions in 1869, 1870, and 1871 to map uncharted desert, mountains, and plains in California, Nevada, Utah, Arizona, Idaho, and New Mexico. In 1872 he convinced Congress to support a complete geological survey of lands west of the hundredth meridian, which he expected would cost $2.5 million and require fifteen years to complete.[34] Wheeler's survey eventually produced forty-one reports including 164 topographic maps, recommendations for road and railway routes, and assessments of agricultural potential across the region. Both Wheeler and King also acknowledged that hostility between Native Americans and settlers worsened as homesteaders and prospectors encroached on tribal hunting grounds, villages, and reservations. Wheeler engaged an ethnographer to gather information that might help control the remaining tribes.

Scientists capitalized on the strategic coalitions that made survey work possible, accessing an expanding network of politicians and investors to bolster support for their research interests. Ferdinand Hayden was perhaps the most skilled of all the survey directors in connecting stakeholders' interests to his own professional goals. He had made good political connections while conducting fieldwork in the Nebraska territory during the 1850s. After Nebraska was admitted to the Union in March 1867, word quickly reached him about a proposed survey of the state's resources. Hayden produced letters of recommendation from both colleagues at the Smithsonian and friends in the new state's legislature. His efforts were successful, and the secretary of the interior named him as the chief of a geological survey of Nebraska. Hayden was granted only $5,000 for staff, equipment, and rations, but he knew well how to stretch his meager budget. "With economy and the good will of the people of Nebraska," he wrote, "much good work can be done." He had good reason to expect support; during the planning process he was bombarded by letters of inquiry, and he proposed a publicity campaign in the state to help capitalize on local enthusiasm. He explained, "I desire to write one or two letters to the people of Nebraska desiring them to make observations, collect specimens, and send me such notes as are valuable to the survey." He also asked Spencer Baird for additional support. Although he had no money to spare, Baird did pledge to provide whatever material assistance he could, because he knew Hayden would respect the Smithsonian's status as the national repository for specimens gathered with federal funds. He wrote, "I of course take it for granted that the Materials collected are to come to S.I." Indeed, by the end of the summer season, Hayden had shipped more than thirty crates of biological and geological specimens, most of which went to the Smithsonian. He also identified deposits of limestone, clay, and sand, opening up the promising possibility that the state could make an industry in the manufacture of bricks and other building stone. His findings were met with enthusiasm in both Nebraska and Washington, and his success earned him a position on a number of other small government surveys in Colorado, Idaho, Montana, Wyoming, and Utah between 1868 and 1869.[35] Hayden's surveys of Nebraska and adjacent territories produced a near-endless series of reports, published between 1867 and 1883.

John Wesley Powell also capitalized on interest in the West, but his goals were broader than Hayden's. He wanted more than to achieve success as a collector, a researcher, or a teacher; he wanted fame as an explorer. Stories about the adventures of prospectors and hunters were popular fodder for newspapers and magazines. Wild claims by men and women who had trekked through sparsely settled regions of Montana, Colorado, Nevada, Utah, and elsewhere made exciting reading. Their tales of geysers, massive canyons, wild river rapids, and hostile Indians crafted a West that was both appealing and terrifying. In 1867 a prospector named James White had washed up in a makeshift raft on the Colorado River in Callville, Nevada, claiming to be the first man to have survived a run on the river most believed too wild for travel. White's story was carried in newspapers across the country, and it captured Powell's attention too. In the summer of 1869 he initiated an expedition along the Colorado into geological formations he dubbed the "Grand Canyon." He hoped either to disprove White's claims or to emerge as the first scientist to develop a reliable map of the nine-hundred-mile-long river and the massive canyons through which it ran.[36]

In May 1869 Powell and a party of nine men set off in four small boats from Wyoming's Green River, the chief tributary of the Colorado. He had cobbled together support from various sources. Ulysses S. Grant gave him permission to draw free rations from western army posts, a decision formalized by an 1868 congressional resolution that allowed Powell to feed up to twenty-five men. Powell traded some of the meat allowance for cash, using the proceeds to hire four hunters to accompany the trip. He purchased boats by combining money from his own salary with funds from private donors as well as research grants from both Illinois Industrial University and the Illinois State Natural History Society. Powell courted publicity from the start, promising to submit regular research updates to the *Chicago Tribune*. Only a small number of well-wishers saw the men off at the start of their journey; most of the fanfare that spring was reserved for the completion of the first transcontinental railroad. Nonetheless, Powell was determined to share his findings with a curious public and win more significant congressional support for additional research.[37]

Word about Powell's adventure began filtering through newspapers and journals as the journey became more difficult and dramatic. Just two weeks in, one of Powell's boats capsized and was destroyed in the rapids, along with a third of the team's equipment and supplies. The weather and currents were unpredictable, and members of the party grew disgruntled as hunters accompanying them failed to provide enough meat. Each night's encampment brought new dangers and setbacks. Once, a sudden wind scattered the flames from the camp fire, destroying dinner and burning several members of the party. Efforts to collect rations from far-flung, understaffed, and undersupplied outposts—often located miles from their path on the river—were time consuming and hardly worth the effort. The party made this trek less frequently, limiting Powell's ability to send regular dispatches to the press. Even when he did send the promised updates, mail traveled slowly to urban publishers. Several men left the party, and worry spread about the fate of the expedition. Imposters claiming to be survivors spun tragic, false tales that Powell's men had drowned or been massacred by Indians, and the dramatic rumors ignited a media frenzy. By the time Powell emerged, he was lauded as a hero who had mastered the wild river. With Grant in the White House, federal funds appeared for further research. In 1870 Powell received a federal allocation of $10,000 and another $20,000 came the following year, allowing him to complete his survey. During his journey Powell also arrived at some important scientific theories. He observed the flow of the river and the stratification of rock along its banks and concluded that the unique geology in the canyons had not been formed by the upward thrust of rock but rather by the gradual wearing away by the strong currents of the water. His formal *Report on the Lands of the Arid Region of the United States* won him both a new level of scientific credibility and a new public visibility.[38]

Useless Landscapes

The expeditions undertaken by Powell, Hayden, King, and Wheeler contributed to the popularization of both the West and science. Excerpts from researchers' formal reports, travelogues, diaries, and letters appeared in specialty magazines such as *Scientific American* and *Popular Science Monthly*. Publications such as *Harper's*, *Scribner's*, *Atlantic Monthly*, and other journals also dedicated several pages in each issue to scientific topics, publishing travel accounts and highlighting new discoveries.[39] In addition to dramatic stories, readers also saw powerful illustrations that helped attest to the truth of the otherwise fantastic tales. Photographers and artists accompanied the surveys, often hired by the scientists themselves to document evidence and bolster scientific findings. John Wesley Powell did not invite a photographer on his 1869 expedition into the Grand Canyon, but his later surveys were documented by the noted landscape photographer E. O. Beaman.[40] Civil War photographer Timothy O'Sullivan traveled with both the King survey and the Wheeler surveys.[41] During the Wheeler surveys, O'Sullivan positioned the camera deliberately to avoid capturing images of wagons, farms, towns, and other signs of civilization. In this way, he constructed the western landscape as desolate, devoid of people, barren, rocky, and dramatic.

Entrepreneurs such as the railroad magnate Jay Cooke began to bank on the possibility that the popularity of these stories and the images that accompanied them might attract adventure-seeking tourists. Cooke had invested heavily in the Northern Pacific Railroad and planned to develop a second transcontinental line that would pass through Montana, skimming along the west side of a particularly scenic landscape known by the name of the river running through it: Yellowstone. Unfortunately, he was in danger of losing his investment. Legends and published accounts of the Yellowstone region, located at the intersection of what is now Montana, Wyoming, and Idaho, had long interested both explorers and scientists. Army engineers had organized expeditions in 1856 and 1859, hoping to identify a navigable route to the origin point of the Yellowstone River, but neither attempt had lent value to Cooke's investment. The landscape appeared useless to both investors and the government. The terrain was too rugged for mining or agriculture, and transportation in and out of the region was difficult. Both federal and state interests determined industrial exploitation and settlement in Yellowstone was impractical. As a result, Congress reserved most of the territory for the Sioux under the 1868 Treaty of Fort Laramie. The U.S. military's Department of the Dakota—which oversaw defense of the 370,000 mile area, including Montana, Dakota, and Minnesota—was skeptical that the region would ever be safe for travelers or settlers. This was a problem for Cooke, because about two-thirds of the Northern Pacific Railroad route passed through the treaty lands.[42]

Despite these significant obstacles, complicated further by labor unrest and mechanical problems that dogged the railroad industry, Cooke gambled that growing public fascination with the Wild West would add value to his investment. In 1870 he bankrolled a publicity stunt: an expedition into Yellowstone by an assortment of Montana business owners and politicians. The expedition team included Nathaniel Langford, Montana's young tax collector whose two brothers-in-law were major investors in the Northern Pacific Railroad; Henry D. Washburne, a veteran of the Union Army and surveyor general of Montana; and Cornelius Hedges, a lawyer and writer. In diary accounts and letters, members of the expedition recorded observations about western Yellowstone. Langford and others drew detailed maps as well. Cooke was certain that their reports of the waterfalls, geysers, hot springs, wildlife, and other natural attractions would bring tourists and settlers.[43]

After their return from the expedition, each member of the party began to lobby Congress and the president to set aside the "wonderland" of Yellowstone as a public park. They generated a massive publicity campaign, giving lectures and publishing stories in newspapers and magazines. Cornelius Hedges wrote a series of articles and editorials for a Helena, Montana, newspaper, galvanizing support from locals who were, at first, reluctant to give up state land. Langford hit the lecture circuit, delivering at least twenty lectures on Yellowstone in the winter of 1870s and booking more lectures for the spring. In vivid, often poetic language he described unmatched scenery and geological wonders. For example, he reported that steaming hot springs, boiling out of a hundred natural holes and more recent fractures in a desolate basin "were as diabolical in appearance as the witches' caldron in Macbeth, and needed but the presence of Hecate and her weird band to realize that horrible creation of poetic fancy."[44]

Despite their reliance on such poetic language to sway readers to their cause, the men understood their proposal to create a federal park in economic terms. Federal protections would prevent development, limiting competition and promising Cooke impressive returns on his investment. As with other rail lines, the Northern Pacific Railroad investors controlled the land adjacent to their tracks, including the strip along the western edge of the proposed park. By selling this land for the development of towns and businesses, Northern Pacific investors would make an immediate profit and continue to ensure a steady stream of riders for the railroad. Langford understood the local value of the scheme as well. He wrote, "By means of the Northern Pacific Railroad, which doubtless will be completed in the next three years, the traveler will be able to make the trip to Montana from the Atlantic seaboard in three days, and thousands of tourists will be attracted to both Montana and Wyoming in order to behold with their own eyes the wonders here described."[45]

The promise of tourism slowly convinced locals to support the creation of a public park, but powerful opponents had launched a campaign to stop Congress from imposing federal limits on grazing, mining, and logging in Yellowstone.[46] Congress balked, unsure how to explain the public benefit of limiting the use and development of such a vast tract of land. Langford and Cooke turned to Ferdinand Hayden, Spencer Baird, and other leading men of science for help in selling their idea. Hayden had read the official reports of the expedition and attended Langford's lectures. His attempts to explore the region during earlier geological surveys had achieved only limited success, and he viewed the park proposal as an opportunity to try

again. Hayden and Cooke lobbied their political friends to support a formal, scientific expedition into Yellowstone, and Congress allotted $40,000
for Hayden to design and lead a geological and topographical survey during the summer of 1871.

In both design and personnel, the Hayden survey attempted to strike a
balance between the interests of investors and the interests of science. His
team included two botanists, a meteorologist, several biologists, a mineralo-
gist, a topographer, and a large support staff, as well as a series of photographers and artists, most notably the Civil War photographer William Jackson
and the landscape artist Thomas Moran.[47] The artist was a late addition to
the team. In 1871 he had not yet achieved fame for his paintings. Instead,
he was earning a living as an illustrator, preparing engravings for *Scribner's
Monthly* and other popular publications. In May and June 1871, he had produced illustrations for Nathaniel Langford's two-part account of his travels,
"The Wonders of Yellowstone." Fascinated by Langford's descriptions, he
wanted to see the territory himself, and he offered to pay his own way if
he might be allowed to accompany the Hayden survey. Cooke, thrilled by
Moran's interest in the project, loaned him $500 for expenses and lobbied
Hayden to include him on the survey team.

With his team in place, Hayden crafted a research plan that effectively
knitted together the interests of science and the interests of industry.
Following the mail route to Virginia City and Fort Ellis, Montana, he
planned to begin by focusing efforts to map the geology and topography
along the proposed path of the Northern Pacific. Working outward from
there, the team would examine a hundred-mile-wide swath of Yellowstone
territory, and then spend the remainder of the season conducting research
along the Yellowstone, Missouri, Green, and Columbia Rivers. His decision to focus on the train route appealed to Cooke, of course, but his
approach to the survey also won approval from his professional colleagues.
Spencer Baird wrote, "You will make more capital and accomplish more for
science by concentrating effort upon some one region like the Yellow Stone
[*sic*], than by attempting to traverse an immense section of country." By the
end of August, the Hayden survey had created topographical and geological maps and produced hundreds of stereoscopic views, large photographic
prints, and artistic sketches of the landscape. Baird wrote to the secretary
of the interior, "We think no portion of the West has been more carefully
surveyed."[48]

Hayden's five-hundred-page report to Congress emphasized Yellowstone's value to science. He testified that massive tracts of land must be set aside to enable further research by government geologists and other experts. Summaries of his report and stories about the survey received enthusiastic coverage, but the press tended to minimize scientific findings and focus instead on the natural beauty of the region. Newspapers and magazines carried stories from Hayden, Moran, and other members of the team.[49] Hayden published "The Wonders of the West: More about the Yellowstone" in the February 1872 edition of *Scribner's Monthly*. Designed to provide scientific testimony to support the fantastic observations published by Langford the previous summer, the piece nonetheless emphasized the scenery: "The writer . . . gladly bears Witness that the statements of Mr. Langford were in no respect exaggerated. Indeed, it is quite impossible for anyone to do justice to the remarkable physical phenomena of this valley by any description, however vivid. It is only through the eye that the mind can form anything like an adequate conception of their beauty and grandeur."[50] As Hayden's words suggested, articles did excite the public interest, but it was the visual culture produced during the survey that really focused support on efforts to preserve the landscape.[51] Thomas Moran had repaid Cooke's $500 loan by presenting him with some of his completed landscape paintings, and Cooke exhibited the lot of them in the Capitol in late 1871, just as Congress was considering bills to set aside Yellowstone as a national park.[52]

Faced with such compelling visual evidence, representatives from the House Committee on Public Lands crafted legislation that expanded the notion of public value. In its report on the proposed bill in February 1872, the committee addressed critics who bemoaned the loss of valuable natural resources, arguing that the Yellowstone landscape was useless, too wild and inaccessible to be valuable to industry or agriculture: "The withdrawal of this tract, therefore, from sale or settlement takes nothing from the value of the public domain, and is no pecuniary loss to the Government, but will be regarded by the entire civilized world as a step of progress and an honor to Congress and the nation." Under these terms, the value of the Yellowstone valley was not in its usefulness but in its uniqueness. The dramatic natural landscape was unmatched anywhere in the world and stood as a testament to American exceptionalism. Protecting irreplaceable national treasures from destruction was rightfully the responsibility of the federal government. The committee argued, "If this bill fails to become a law this session, the vandals who are now waiting to enter this wonderland will, in a single season, despoil, beyond recovery, these remarkable curiosities which have required all the cunning skill of nature thousands of years to prepare." President Ulysses S. Grant signed the Yellowstone bill into law on March 1, 1872, announcing that two million acres were "hereby reserved and withdrawn from settlement, occupancy, or sale . . . and set apart as a public park or pleasuring ground for the benefit and enjoyment of the people."[53]

By the late 1870s the people were, indeed, enjoying the West, although not precisely in the way that Congress, Hayden, and other park supporters intended. Nathaniel Langford, assigned as the first superintendent of Yellowstone, found that "no horde of tourists clamored at the gates of Wonderland, no worthy concessionaires bid for privileges, no funds came forth with franchise fees and . . . there was no progress."[54] Instead, as homesteaders came in greater and greater numbers, the western landscape was endangered. Hunters poached wildlife in the park. Squatters set up camp. Native Americans refused to deviate from traditional migration routes. Amateur adventurers collected rocks, plants, fossils, and other "souvenirs" from park property, threatening to undermine efforts to protect them.[55]

An Ancient American Past

In addition to popularizing the stunning geology, the surveys of the West revealed entirely different kinds of sites in desperate need of protection. Between 1870 and 1916 the human past became visible as a national resource worthy of protection in an era of relentless change. During the Wheeler surveys, O'Sullivan had become the first photographer to capture images of abandoned and crumbling cave dwellings and pueblos in the Southwest. His 1873 photograph of the so-called White House Ruins in the Canyon de Chelly challenged prevailing beliefs about the history of the continent and lent legitimacy to the study of American archaeology and ethnology.

The year 1879 proved to be a watershed in this process.[56] Wheeler added Frederic Ward Putnam, a zoologist with an interest in Native cultures, to the survey team. Putnam analyzed the research data and examined the images, publishing a richly illustrated volume on Native American archaeology and ethnology in Arizona, New Mexico, and Southern California in 1879.[57] The report excited Lewis Henry Morgan, a devotee of Darwin, who had been among the first to argue that all Native American peoples came from a single ancient origin. He wrote, "if this be so, it follows that the facts of American archaeology must be studied ethnologically; i.e. from the institutions, usages and modes of life of existing Indian tribes."The images and reports from the West gave him new reason to encourage American scientists to test this hypothesis in earnest, and he urged them to develop a systematic approach to archaeological research among the ruins.[58]

The report also appealed to federal legislators who recognized the practical applications American archaeological research might have in the development of Indian policy. This pragmatic perspective led, in 1879, to the establishment by Congress of the Bureau of Ethnology, an independent unit of the Smithsonian Institution. John Wesley Powell was appointed as the bureau's first director, and he encouraged researchers under his authority to continue the work of amassing cultural information and artifacts in the Southwest after the surveys ended.[59] The Wheeler surveys also inspired Charles Eliot Norton, a Harvard art history professor, to found the Archaeological Institute of America that same year. Norton's original ambition had been to create a vehicle for the advancement of American scholars' standing as practitioners of Old World Archaeology, but Morgan and Powell pressured him to expand his efforts into American archaeology as well.

Powell's influence was particularly important. He had arrived in Washington shortly after the conclusion of his expedition along the Colorado River, and he took advantage of his newfound fame, ingratiating himself into the city's intellectual circles. Washington in the late nineteenth century was home to a rather large assortment of scientific study groups, composed of local university professors, Smithsonian curators, government researchers, and a variety of ardent amateurs, all organized around specific areas of interest. Recognizing that the members of these associations and clubs had similar needs to acquire funding and identify research opportunities, Powell sought to bring them together. He spearheaded the establishment of the Cosmos Club. The private men's club hosted meetings, lectures, and special events that attracted not only the members of scientific associations but also prominent artists and politicians. Mingling at lectures, social events, and formal debates, the members of the club shaped a unique elite class in Washington, bound by both access to political power and control of specialized knowledge.[60] The club hosted regular meetings of a variety of scientific organizations, and a number of others were chartered in its meeting halls.[61] The personal and professional ties forged at the club created an extensive network of politically savvy scientists who could rely on their personal relationships with policymakers to successfully negotiate the creation of new research projects, new agencies, and new laws that benefited their disciplines.[62]

From his simultaneous role as president of the Cosmos Club and director of the Bureau of Ethnology, Powell helped forge relationships that legitimized American archaeology and extended federal protection to archaeological sites. Charles Eliot Norton gave in to pressure from Powell, commissioning Swiss-born Adolph Bandelier to survey archaeological sites in the American West. At first, Archaeological Institute board members refused to sign off on the project, questioning the value of information about the "barbarous" Native American cultures and insisting the institute stick to the study of the more civilized ancient Romans and Greeks. Bandelier's credentials were difficult to ignore, however. He had been educated overseas, and he had accompanied Morgan on his investigation of southwestern ruins in 1878. Powell wrote a strongly worded letter of support for both Bandelier and his project, and the expedition began in 1880. Bandelier ranged widely across the Southwest, visiting 166 sites in eighteen months and conducting a particularly close study of Pecos Pueblo in New Mexico.[63] His published accounts, carefully documented with descriptions of pottery and other evidence he had seen during his travels, supported Morgan's theory that Native Americans had evolved over time.[64]

At the same time, Powell began his own ethnological studies in the same region. He selected Frank Hamilton Cushing, curator of ethnology at the Smithsonian's U.S. National Museum, to participate in field research among the Zuni people in New Mexico.[65] Cushing's methods were controversial; he fashioned himself as a "white Indian."[66] He lived among the Zuni for several years, earning their trust by sharing American folktales and traditions, as he appropriated Zuni customs for himself. Cushing's research advanced American historical archaeology and supported Morgan's hypothesis. Synthesizing his own study of language and customs with documentation by others of the Southwest ruins, Cushing argued that contemporary Native Americans were the descendants of ancient peoples: "As gradually their language dawns upon my intellect . . . the significance . . . of many other dark things are lighted up by its morning. They are the people who built the ruins of Canon Bonita in De Chelly. In their language is told the strange history of these heretofore mysterious cities, each one of which has its definite name and story in their lore."[67] Cushing also studied Zuni material culture, further advancing the idea that the tribes had evolved from earlier ancient peoples.

In addition to contributing to a growing body of scholarship, Cushing and Bandelier began to sound an alarm about the conditions of valuable research sites. Drawn to the Southwest by O'Sullivan's photographs and by colorful accounts of the adventure in the West, collectors, antiquities dealers, and souvenir hunters were destroying archaeological ruins. Bandelier graphically described the state of Pecos Pueblo in 1881, reporting, "In general, the vandalism committed in this venerable relic of antiquity defies all description." He found ornamental carvings removed from structural beams by vandals who, "having no other means to secure immortality . . . have cut out the ornaments . . . to obtain a surface suitable to carve their euphonious names." Bandelier bemoaned the loss of scrollwork and indigenous design. "Most of this was taken away, chipped into uncouth boxes and sold, to be scattered everywhere." Arguably, scientific researchers and museum collectors had similarly removed relics and artifacts, placing them in boxes and shipping them to the Smithsonian or Harvard. Bandelier differentiated that work from the "treasure hunting" perpetrated by "inconsiderate amateurs" who "recklessly and ruthlessly disturbed the abodes of the dead."[68] His sharply worded report captured the attention of Boston's New England Historic Genealogical Society. Members began to press for the creation of federal laws to protect American antiquities. They convinced Massachusetts senator George Frisbee Hoar to sponsor the first of several bills, reigniting congressional debate about the appropriate extension of federal power and the conditions that might justify seizure of land and property.[69] The creation of Yellowstone National Park in 1872 had been a watershed moment, but legislators were unwilling to pass more sweeping legislation that might justify removal of an indeterminate number of sites and landscapes from public use; Hoar's bill failed.

Undaunted, Frank Cushing continued to court public interest and private funding for a complete archaeological and ethnographic survey to document disappearing sites and cultures. Framing the significance of his research in terms his audience could understand, he argued that archaeology was "simply ethnology carried back into prehistoric times." To punctuate his point, he brought a group of Zuni tribal leaders with him on the lecture circuit, connecting their folklore and culture to the ruins dotting the Southwest. His technique attracted the attention of New England preservationist Mary Hemenway. A well-known Boston philanthropist, Hemenway had led efforts to preserve the Old South Meeting House, and she understood Cushing's cause as similar to her own, embodying "a perspective from which to cope with the rapid changes of a new urban and industrial order."[70] She invited Cushing and his party to visit her estate and committed $25,000 a year for archaeological research in the Southwest.[71] Beginning in 1886 Bandelier and Cushing led the annual Hemenway Expedition to New Mexico and Arizona. Cushing's health began to fail in 1889, and Hemenway replaced him with a young Harvard-trained zoologist named J. Walter Fewkes, who led the expedition until the project ended in 1894 with Hemenway's death. He later joined the staff of the Bureau of Ethnology.

The Hemenway Expedition was broadly influential. Throughout the late 1880s and into the 1890s, the Archaeological Institute of America published a variety of papers and research reports compiled from its data. The team had identified and cataloged a number of archaeological sites across the region. Researchers described their deteriorated condition and pled for new laws that might protect them for the purpose of further scientific research. This time, a more politically savvy group of scientists worked together to address the concerns expressed by Bandelier, Fewkes, and others. Recognizing the need to establish a legal precedent, Powell's Bureau of Ethnology joined forces with Senator Hoar to craft new legislation to extend federal protection to a single site—Casa Grande Pueblo in Arizona.[72] Backed by a strong coalition of politically well-connected scientists, the bill was successful and Congress created Casa Grande Ruin Reservation in 1889, the third conservation area protected by the federal government in the last quarter of the nineteenth century.[73]

Creating Casa Grande was a crucial step in an ongoing and rapid period of professionalization for the disciplines of American archaeology and anthropology. The two largest local anthropological clubs—Franz Boas's Anthropological Club in New York and the Anthropological Society of Washington—merged in 1902, creating the American Anthropological Association. Leading scientists in these fields organized ethnological collections and curatorial units, bringing together materials that had previously remained undifferentiated as disciplinary artifacts in the federal survey. American archaeology also began to achieve international recognition, as exhibitions prepared by the Bureau of Ethnology, the U.S. National Museum, and other natural history museums traveled to international expositions across Europe. The study of Native American cultures achieved greater legitimacy, but the appeal of these exhibits and artifacts to tourists also had unintended consequences, increasing popular interest in the Southwest ruins. Curiosity seekers continued to excavate in the ruins for their own collections, and museums lacking the budget for research expeditions often purchased items from illicit traders.

Stronger protective legislation was clearly needed, but members of the scientific community could not agree on the best approach. Some argued that narrow laws protecting carefully targeted sites were the only viable option with a proven track record of success. They proposed to expand federal protections by creating one archaeological park at a time. This piecemeal approach was frustrating to the increasingly professional and politically well-connected body of American archaeologists. By the end of the nineteenth century, the so-called Antiquities Act coalition of scientists, tied together by their association with the Bureau of Ethnology, the Archaeological Institute of America, and the American Anthropological Association, began to agitate for passage of a more sweeping bill that would ensure broad protections for scientifically valuable ruins and artifacts.

Edgar Lee Hewett, whose political identity was shaped at the intersection of these organizations, drafted the text eventually adopted by Congress. Hewett was incredibly well-attuned to political dynamics. Born in Illinois and educated in Missouri and Colorado, he had moved to New Mexico when his wife developed tuberculosis. Once in New Mexico, Hewett began to conduct fieldwork with ruins in the canyons and plateaus in the northern part of the state. His efforts brought him to the attention of the New Mexico legislature, and he was appointed as the first president of the New Mexico Normal School in 1897. Hewett's work put him in the orbit of the men conducting expeditions in the Southwest, and in 1900 he traveled to Washington, where he met Powell and acquired some museum experience at the Smithsonian. Hewett believed strongly that the western states should have autonomy in defining and protecting valuable landscapes, but he also recognized the need for a support system from the federal government and wealthy elites in the East. He ingratiated himself with administrators of the major land-management agencies, including the General Land Office, as well as the secretary of the interior.

Hewett's relationships provided him with a bird's eye view of both the political process in Washington and the changing temper of his discipline. From this position he was able to reconcile competing demands from leaders of the scientific disciplines on the one hand and concerns of legislators and bureaucrats on the other. Hewett understood legislators' unwillingness to extend federal powers to the protection of multiple archaeological sites, and he agreed in principal with efforts to limit federal intervention in the West. Debate focused on the issue of land seizure, but Hewett proposed a different perspective. He saw the problem of vandalism as an issue for law enforcement, shifting the focus of the proposed legislation. He pro-posed language for the bill that outlined criminal behavior, making it ille-gal to damage or remove materials from ruins on federal lands. Hewett also understood that the process of park creation was too slow and arduous to really benefit endangered places. The necessity of building a popular coali-tion for the creation of each individual archaeological reserve or national park required scientists to compromise the safety of each site. Instead, Hewett's bill authorized the president of the United States to protect sites by executive order, thus eliminating the lobbying process and minimizing congressional debate.[74]

The emphasis on law enforcement and the creation of a new execu-tive power appealed to the Antiquities Act coalition, and they convinced Congress to pass the Antiquities Act in 1906.[75] The law empowered the president to designate as a national monument any "historic landmarks, historic and prehistoric structures, and other objects of historic or scientific interest" contained on property already owned by the federal government. Although the monument designation carried the implication of federal seizure, the language of the new law focused on criminalizing vandalism. The monument designation established penalties for looting and unau-thorized excavations and enabled the president to impose limits on a host of potentially damaging activities—mining, homesteading, grazing, log-ging—that were permitted on other federal lands.[76] The Antiquities Act also carefully distinguished research excavations from looting by empow-ering government agencies to issue research permits, provided that "the examinations, excavations, and gatherings are undertaken for the benefit of reputable museums, universities, colleges, or other recognized scientific or educational institutions, with a view to increasing the knowledge of such objects, and that the gatherings shall be made for permanent preservation in public museums."[77]

Enforcing National Standards

The success of the Antiquities Act was an important step in solving the problem of protection, but it created new questions. As the number of fed-erally protected sites expanded, so did debate about the standards guiding site selection and concerns about the inefficient federal approach to park management. Executive orders established twenty national monuments between 1906 and 1916.[78] During the same ten-year period, Congress continued to entertain proposals for national parks, not all of which seemed to meet the standards set by Yellowstone for scientific significance or scenic splendor. Mesa Verde National Park in Colorado, established nearly simultaneously with the passage of the Antiquities Act and strongly advocated by Edgar Hewett, was chosen as much for the large number of ancient cliff and cave dwellings within its boundaries as for its spectacular mountains and forests. Others, including Sequoia (1890), Mount Rainier (1899), Crater Lake (1902), and Wind Cave (1903), however, were selected based on rather narrow scientific significance. Furthermore, by 1915 most of the large natural parks and many of the monuments were more or less controlled by the Department of the Interior, but the department did not have a bureau dedicated to park management. Instead, responsibility for the protection and development of each site was dispersed among a variety of bureaus, including the Indian Office, the General Land Office, the Bureau of Mines, and the U.S. Geological Survey, none of which were particularly well suited to the task. The failure of the Department of the Interior to coordinate park administration attracted the attention of reformers such as J. Horace McFarland. In 1908 McFarland, a business entrepreneur from Harrisburg, Pennsylvania, dedicated his organization, the American Civic Association, to lobbying for the creation of a federal bureau to manage the parks. McFarland's organization achieved fairly rapid success, convincing the secretary of the interior, Richard Ballinger, to recommend creation of "a bureau of national parks and resorts, under the supervision of a competent commissioner, with a suitable force of superintendents, supervising engineers, and landscape architects."[79] President Taft adopted the cause as well.

Efforts to establish a National Park Bureau were stymied, however, by the increasingly complex assortment of naturalists and activists interested in protecting the environment. Two distinct philosophies had taken shape over time. On the one hand, government scientists had adopted a pragmatic approach to conservation, one that combined the interests of business owners, policymakers, and leaders in a variety of still-developing disciplines. On the other hand, the popularization of work by naturalists, photographers, and landscape artists had shaped a romantic vision of the West and led to demands for the complete preservation of wild landscapes endangered by settlement and development. Reform organizations promoting the creation of a park management bureau typically combined some ideas and arguments from each school of thought. Government reform advocates, including the American Civic Association, pushed the federal government to apply principles of scientific management to the administration of national parks, but individual members of these groups had different ideas about what qualities should guide site selection. McFarland, for one, believed that only the most beautiful scenery was worthy of federal protection. Recreation organizations such as the Camp Fire Club argued that access to the outdoors was crucial to the health of citizens in an increasingly urban and industrial America, and they advocated the protection of a broad array of natural areas. The Save the Redwoods League and the Wilderness Society concurred with the Camp Fire Club that scenic areas should be protected but disagreed about their value, calling for strict limits on outdoor recreation in protected areas.[80]

Nowhere was the discord in American environmentalism more obvious than in California's Yosemite Valley. Intense population growth in Northern California strained potable water resources, creating a crisis for the city of San Francisco. In 1901 San Francisco attorney Franklin Lane filed a declaration of water rights on behalf of the mayor, proposing to dam the Tuolumne River and flood Yosemite's Hetch Hetchy Valley to create a water reserve. Activists, politicians, and scientists lined up on each side of the issue, and debate dragged on in California and in Congress for more than a decade.[81] Pragmatic conservationists tended to side with the city, and Gifford Pinchot became the public face of their cause. Romantically inclined nature preservationists vehemently opposed the dam, and John Muir was the most vocal.[82]

Muir and Pinchot were men of two distinct intellectual generations. Muir was a throwback. He had attended the University of Wisconsin in the early 1860s, taking courses in botany and geology. He left school in 1864 without completing a degree and traveled to Canada where he continued to study plants and wildlife.[83] After the Civil War, he returned to the United States, eventually arriving in Yosemite Valley in California in 1862. His excursions in Yosemite and across the High Sierras inspired him to establish the Sierra Club, an increasingly influential advocate for complete protection of natural environments. Muir used all his energy and influence to oppose the dam, saying, "It is a monumental mistake, but it is more; it is a monumental crime."[84] Pinchot, in contrast, was the quintessential progressive. The grandson of a wealthy land and lumber baron, he had pursued studies in forestry at Yale, a program endowed by his father, and postgraduate studies at the French National Forestry School. He achieved national recognition for designing a program for sustainable use of the nation's trees, and he summed up his philosophy in the Hetch Hetchy debate by arguing, "The fundamental principal of the whole conservation policy is use."[85] Pinchot's brand of progressivism appealed to President William McKinley, who named him the first chief forester for the U.S. Forest Service in 1898.[86] Muir had support from the remaining nineteenth-century naturalists, but by the turn of the twentieth century, many of these key supporters had died. In their place, progressive politicians and reformers sought to create a balanced federal conservation policy.

The debate over Hetch Hetchy essentially ended when Franklin Lane arrived in Washington. Lane had served on the Interstate Commerce Commission under both Theodore Roosevelt and William Howard Taft, and in 1913 Woodrow Wilson tapped him as secretary of the interior. Lane worked with an able young assistant, Horace Albright, a native of California and a recent college graduate who had camped in Yosemite as a child. Albright had fond memories of the Yosemite wilderness and sympathy for Muir's perspective, but Lane was a pragmatist. He had no patience for "extreme conservationists" who he believed failed to consider public needs.[87] His position angered many, and Albright had the unpleasant task of reading and responding to thousands of letters of protest. He found it difficult to have to explain Lane's position while secretly supporting those who opposed the dam. Ultimately, opponents were no match for Lane's well-heeled and well-connected San Francisco coalition. The dam proposal passed in 1913.[88]

The National Park Service

In the aftermath of Hetch Hetchy, Lane faced a serious publicity problem. Although he supported the proposal to create a National Parks Bureau in the Department of the Interior, his role in pressing for the dam had made him unpopular with many conservation advocates. Lane's office received thousands of letters of complaint and condemnation.[89] Gifford Pinchot stepped forward, declaring that the Forest Service was better suited than the Department of the Interior to accept responsibility for the national parks, but Gifford was no better than Lane in the eyes of environmentalists. Horace McFarland summed up their position, arguing that the parks should be protected as "the nation's playgrounds," not treated as the "nation's woodlots."[90] Nonetheless, the reluctance of park supporters to definitively back Lane adversely affected congressional will to create a park bureau. Legislators refused to vote on the issue before adjourning in 1914. Lane needed a salesperson. He found one in Stephen Mather, a borax entrepreneur and member of the Sierra Club. Mather's business acumen had made him a millionaire, and his enthusiastic participation in annual wilderness retreats with the Sierra Club had earned him respect among environmentalists. The combination made him a unique asset to Lane, who loaned Albright to him, and asked the two men to popularize the idea for a park bureau in the Department of the Interior.[91]

During the summer of 1915, as Congress was preparing to vote on the proposal, Albright and Mather embarked on a well-publicized tour to answer the question, "What makes a national park?" They began their trip in San Francisco, where they attended a conference of park superintendents. From there, they set out for Sequoia, Yosemite, Crater Lake, Mount Rainier, Rocky Mountain, and Yellowstone. At each stop, they cataloged information about the most attractive aspects of each park as well as the specific problems that dogged efforts to manage each site. The tour was a resounding success. Congress established the National Park Service in August 1916, reassigning all fifteen national parks and twenty-two of the national monuments to the new agency. The preamble to the Park Service enabling legislation defines its purpose: "to conserve the scenery and the natural and historic objects and the wild life [sic] and to provide for the enjoyment of the same in such manner and by such means as will leave them unimpaired for the enjoyment of future generations."[92]

At Secretary Lane's insistence, Stephen Mather agreed to serve as the first director of the National Park Service, but he was unable to assume his position at first. In the fall of 1917, shortly after Congress had authorized the Park Service budget, Mather collapsed and was diagnosed with "nervous exhaustion." Horace Albright accompanied him to the hospital, and he and Franklin Lane agreed to cover for Mather in an absence of unpredictable length. Lane formally promoted Albright to the position of assistant director of the National Park Service, and he served as acting director for more than a year.[93] The timing was less than ideal. President Woodrow Wilson, having won reelection in 1916 with the slogan, "He kept us out of war," had reluctantly asked Congress to declare war on Germany in the spring of 1917. Albright, who had received some military science training during college, fully expected to serve overseas. "Since all my friends were going in the war, naturally I wanted to go too," he wrote, but Lane and Mather needed him at home. Lane intervened with the draft board, and Albright "was detained from day to day and month to month and was not permitted to file an application for officers training camp until late in 1918," after Mather had resumed his duties.[94] By then, the war was just about over, and Albright never served. Instead, he rode out the war years in service to the national parks.

The war made Albright's work difficult. Most nonmilitary government work slowed dramatically, and it was difficult to hire staff and acquire office space. Worse, wartime shortages tested the limits of environmental policy. Albright found himself at odds with Secretary Lane, who had once enraged Stephen Mather by saying he was in favor of wilderness protection "as long as convenient"; the war now made protection inconvenient. The Department of the Interior was besieged by demands from ranchers, business owners, and the military, who wanted access to game and grass lands inside park boundaries. A popular, patriotic song called these demands "The Battle Cry of Feed 'Em," and editorial writers argued, "Soldiers need meat to eat, not wild flowers." Lane, a strong advocate for domestic preparedness and a member of the Council on National Defense, was willing to relax park protections. In 1917 he drafted a departmental order that would have allowed large herds of sheep and cattle into Yosemite and Sequoia. Albright lost his temper and, paraphrasing John Muir, exclaimed, "Mr. Secretary, how could you possibly allow fifty thousand 'hoofed locusts' in that beautiful park?" Albright threatened to resign, but Lane ordered him to make the deal. Instead, Albright stalled, passively allowing word about Lane's proposal to filter out to members of Muir's Sierra Club. Facing both internal and external opposition, Lane was forced to compromise, and Albright implemented a dramatically scaled-back grazing plan that gave a small number of cattle access to marginal areas of the two parks.[95]

The conflict highlighted a fundamental problem with the Park Service mission. As Albright understood it, the requirement that "the parks be protected on the one hand and must be made accessible on the other, creates an inconsistency, a prima-facie inconsistency that can never be gotten around." Hoping that some park superintendents had managed to find a way to balance protection against accessibility, Albright toured the parks again in the summer of 1917. He traveled through the Rocky Mountains to Yellowstone and Glacier in Montana, toured Mount Rainier in Washington, and then passed through Yosemite and Sequoia in California. At each stop, he collected information about the complex relationship between the parks and their users.[96] He discovered that the inconsistency inherent in the federal mandate (as well as in the individual acts creating each park) was obvious on the ground. Ranchers wanted grazing rights, entrepreneurs had ideas for concessions, politicians resisted federal seizure of state land, and local boosters proposed new parks to attract greater numbers of tourists as well as new settlers. Each site superintendent had implemented unique management strategies in response to specific local pressures. As a result, each park had created its own hostilities. The large natural parks such as Yosemite and Mesa Verde had seized treaty lands, antagonizing Native Americans and setting off many of the battles in the Indian Wars.[97] U.S. Cavalry troops, first dispatched to the parks in 1886, protected the appearance of wilderness, not only by violently expelling nomadic tribes but also by helping to enforce the criminalization of hunting, trapping, and homesteading inside park boundaries.[98] The last remaining troops were expelled from Yellowstone in 1918, but the Park Service was left with the problem of having to protect the parks while also allowing users to enjoy them.

This issue was even more complicated at the national monuments. Under the terms of the law, any qualified professional affiliated with a recognized research institution could apply for an Antiquities Act permit to conduct research on monument grounds. With permit in hand, archeologists, anthropologists, ethnologists, and other scientists had the right to define the parameters of their project. Some reconstructed crumbled buildings or stabilized remaining structures. All of the permitted researchers excavated and removed artifacts. Indeed, the law required excavated materials to be set aside "for permanent preservation in public museums."[99] At the same time, the Antiquities Act did not provide for any means of enforcing the permits. On the ground, this often meant that various universities and museums were wrangling over the right to excavate particular properties or that several archaeologists were engaged in overlapping research. Furthermore, the law criminalized any activity that went forward at these sites without official sanction, often including the burial of the dead and other ceremonial activities by local indigenous groups. In real terms, this meant that archaeologists could remove human remains and religious artifacts, even on recently seized tribal lands, while Native Americans members had no legal standing to protect or move the graves.[100]

Recognizing the inherent difficulties in both the Park Service mandate and in the enforcement of protective legislation, Albright made the earliest and most influential decisions about how best to translate the agency's mandate into a reasonable set of management policies. His 1917 tour forced him to acknowledge that the only way to protect National Park Service properties in a near-pristine form was to exert even more control over their use. His first acknowledged statement of policy appeared in the body of a letter sent from Franklin Lane to Stephen Mather. The text, drafted by Albright, read in part, "The educational, as well as the recreational, use of the national parks should be encouraged in every practicable way."[101] At first glance, Albright's emphasis on education appears rather benign. His choice of the word "encourage," however, implies something stronger than simply publicity or invitation. He meant that the National Park Service might use educational programs to mediate visitor contact with park resources. Education, in Albright's construction, was a safety valve, providing visitors with the appearance of intimacy while establishing clear boundaries between them and the park landscape. During his tenure as acting director, Albright lectured and wrote widely about the kinds of encouragement that might make up the work of the new agency. Between 1916 and the end of the 1920s, his recommendations gradually coalesced as the Park Service Creed, which identifies four primary functions for the agency: promotion of health and outdoor recreation, promotion of natural history education, development of patriotism, and advocacy of domestic tourism.[102]

Between the creation of the Smithsonian and the establishment of the Park Service, then, the nation's landscape was transformed. First seen as a source of raw materials for economic development and travel routes for military defense, it gradually came to embody cultural attitudes regarding nature, federal authority, intellectual expertise, and entrepreneurial innovation. The combined effort of politicians, scientists, business leaders, and activists constructed the continent as a resource worthy of protection and needing of careful management. Over time, new federal regulations and the agencies dedicated to enforcing them differentiated useful landscapes (rich in arable land or mineral resources) from unique landscapes (useless for anything but research or tourism). This effort constructed "nature," and the federal government assumed responsibility for mediating the difference between usefulness and uselessness, experts and amateurs, legitimate research and treasure hunting, and education and recreation. Federal land agencies established managerial bureaucracies and hired a growing number of experts to establish policies for protecting landscapes from destruction and misuse by the very people the sites were designed to serve. As historians entered into this bureaucratic structure, they added new layers of meaning and value to a landscape already shaped by conflict and compromise.

PART 2

Turning Nature into History
The National Park Service and the Culture of Public History

CHAPTER 3

Losing Their Identity

National Park Service Museums and Federal Collections

———— ✠ ————

Change in the administrative policy might easily cause these objects to lose their
identity or through . . . lack of understanding of their value allow their use in such
a way as to destroy them.

—ALEXANDER WETMORE—

In 1910 twenty-three-year-old Jesse Logan Nusbaum spent ten weeks
scrambling on ancient, crumbling walls carved into the sheer face of
a cliff. Barely a year into his job as Edgar Lee Hewett's field assistant,
Nusbaum was at work, repairing the cliff dwelling on behalf of the School
of American Archaeology. Working with a small team of laborers, he
anchored each wall to the back of the cliff, using irons and turn buckles. It
seemed his fate to be there. As a child growing up in Greeley, Colorado,
Nusbaum had loved working outdoors and building structures. The son of
a construction contractor, he had apprenticed as a bricklayer, earning as
much as $5.00 or $6.00 a day, a decent wage "when the best you could get
for irrigation or setting cabbage was $1.50." By the age of eight or nine, he
was a frequent caller at the home of the town physician, Dr. G. Law, where
he admired the family's library. One book in particular attracted Nusbaum's
attention: a copy of Gustaf Nordenskiold's anthropological field reports.
The book sat on the second shelf of a fancy parlor table, elevated at the
base by brass claws clinging to glass globes. The young Nusbaum couldn't
help but linger over the table and its treasures. "Mrs. Law wouldn't let me
pick it up or take it," Nusbaum said. "She would lay it out and lay it on a
blanket on the carpet on the floor and lay it open." An archaeologist born

and trained in Europe, Nordenskiold had been the first to formally survey and excavate the cliff dwellings around Mesa Verde, Colorado, the very same from which Nusbaum found himself suspended in 1910. The book was Nusbaum's entrée into the field of archaeology. "I studied that, so by the time I went to Mesa Verde," he later recalled, "I knew everything that Nordenskiold had found; the whole thing."[1]

In much the same way that John Wesley Powell and Frederick Hayden had carved their own paths as geologists in the nineteenth century, Jesse Nusbaum accumulated a track record of fieldwork among the ruins in the American Southwest as something of a hobby. Although opportunities for education in anthropology and archaeology had improved greatly by the turn of the twentieth century, Nusbaum did not originally pursue formal training in either field. Instead, he set his sights on teaching, attending the Colorado State Teacher's College in Greeley to earn a bachelor's degree in pedagogy. By the time he finished his degree in 1907, he was looking for ways to incorporate field study with vocational education. His mentors recommended him for a faculty position at New Mexico State Normal College, where he began teaching science and manual arts. Barely twenty years old, he likely did not realize he was following closely in Hewett's foot-steps. Edgar Hewett had also studied at Colorado State Teacher's College, and he had served as the first president of New Mexico State from 1898 to 1903. He developed much of the core curriculum for the college, including a course of study in anthropology with fieldwork opportunities for students on his summer expeditions.[2]

Nusbaum arrived at New Mexico at a crucial moment. The previous year, Hewett had composed the language adopted as the Antiquities Act, and he had participated in the near-simultaneous creation of Mesa Verde National Park. He returned to New Mexico, where he successfully lobbied the Archaeological Institute of America to support his establishment of a School of American Archaeology in Santa Fe. The creation of the school in 1907 gave Hewett an institutional base from which to act as a kind of field supervisor for any request to conduct archaeological research in the Southwest. He positioned himself as the prime point of contact for high-ranking government officials who had administrative authority over Native American and Spanish ruins in the West, and he cooperated with universities and museums in the East, facilitating fieldwork by anthropologists, archaeologists, ethnologists, and their students.[3] As a result, Hewett was ready and able to respond to a request in the summer of 1907 from the secretary of the interior for a formal survey of the archaeological ruins located two miles south of Mesa Verde National Park. When the park was created, the boundaries were extended to just outside of the Ute Indian Reservation, leaving several of the most significant ruins on Ute land. Hewett drafted an amendment to the park bill, extending federal protections to scientific resources within five miles of the park boundary, much to the dismay of Native Americans, whose objections to federal agents excavating tribal lands fell on deaf ears.[4] Through the Santa Fe school, Hewett sent Alfred V. Kidder from the Peabody Museum and Sylvanius Morely, a student at Harvard, to conduct the survey. Jesse Nusbaum joined the survey team as a photographer, and he spent two seasons documenting all the major cliff structures and mapping their proximity to the existing park boundaries to make a case for the formal extension of Mesa Verde Park boundaries.

Nusbaum's early affiliation with Kidder, Hewett, and the School of American Archaeology earned him a reputation as an able field laborer and put him inside the orbit of American anthropology. In 1909 Hewett hired him as his first paid staff member at Santa Fe. He spent several summers conducting archaeological field surveys and stabilizing ruins throughout the American Southwest and South America, crossing paths with American archaeologists from Harvard and Philadelphia as well as the Smithsonian. Indeed, he often worked in tandem with Smithsonian anthropologists Neil Judd and Walter Fewkes. Judd conducted fieldwork for Edgar Hewett in 1909 and 1910, before transferring to the United States National Museum in 1911.[5] Fewkes, trained at Harvard, conducted excavations at both Casa Grande and Mesa Verde for the better part of a decade or more. Nusbaum completed extensive stabilization work at Mesa Verde's Balcony House cliff structure in 1910, despite having little experience or training.[6] His work there finally led him to pursue a formal education in anthropology and archaeology. In 1911 he followed his Smithsonian colleagues to Washington, D.C. He and Judd took courses at George Washington University, and Nusbaum apprenticed with Judd at the U.S. National Museum.[7] Between 1916 and 1921 he conducted excavations and gathered collections for the George M. Heye Foundation's newly established Museum of the American Indian in New York.

An Era of Promising Development

Jesse Nusbaum might have continued his work in museums, having made a place for himself among Smithsonian archaeologists and anthropologists, but Stephen Mather needed someone with his particular set of skills. Mather had been receiving letters of complaint about the administration of Mesa Verde National Park for years. In 1915 a visitor from New York warned him that nepotism and political influence were wreaking havoc in the park. The park superintendent, Thomas Rickner, freely admitted he had acquired his position as a result of his political connections. He had been operating a butcher shop prior to his selection as superintendent.[8] The park rangers at Mesa Verde were supposed to control access to the ruins, accompanying visitors to the cliffs and providing them with information while limiting their access to the fragile structures. In practice, however, most of the rangers were employed part-time and their work at the park was a means to another end. Several were local ranchers who established a trail to move cattle into the park for grazing. Others ran private tourist businesses in direct violation of Park Service rules. Edgar Hewett complained about one park ranger in particular, Charles Kelly, who spent most of his time running a livery stable. Rickner hired another ranger, his daughter's husband, Fred Jeep.[9] She ran the camp lodge, sometimes acting as a tour guide, and he won praise from casual visitors and scientists alike for his exhaustive hiking and climbing trips into the cliff dwellings. When Horace Albright visited the park in 1917, he found that "the administration and protection of the park, as well as its operation as a tourist resort was very much a family affair."[10]

By 1920 the situation at Mesa Verde was untenable. Park visitors complained that the locals used the park as their private campground. Nusbaum himself later recalled, "there was no control whatever for the protection and preservation of ruins. Anybody that came into the park could drive their car any place they wanted to go where there was a road they could get over; they could go into the ruins, crawl through the windows, on top of the walls, take photographs. They were doing a great deal of damage."[11] Local park boosters began to complain heartily, publishing editorials in Denver newspapers that faulted the Park Service for shoddy administrative practices. Their anger provided Mather with precisely the right justification to make a change. He wrote, "I have long felt that we should have a man who is not only a good administrator, but also an archeologist. However, we want to be sure that the man we get to replace Mr. Rickner is the proper caliber."[12] Jesse Nusbaum was that man. He came highly recommended by Neil Judd and withstood a firestorm of opposition from Colorado representatives who believed selection of a park superintendent should be a local political matter. When Mather announced the appointment in his annual report of 1921, he emphasized Nusbaum's credentials and professionalism: "The Mesa Verde National Park is entering an era of promising development. On May 23, 1921, Mr. Jesse Nusbaum, of Colorado, a young archaeologist of experience and reputation for successful work in the Southwest, was appointed . . . to fill the vacancy caused by the resignation of Mr. Thomas Rickner. . . . The peculiar nature of the historical exhibits in this region and the necessity for their protection and restoration along approved scientific lines precluded consideration of anyone but a trained archaeologist."[13]

As superintendent, Nusbaum acted immediately to control not only access to the ruins but also excavated artifacts and the stories being told about the ruins. Unlike his predecessors, who had lived in a town outside the park, Nusbaum set up residence inside park boundaries. In such proximity, he saw how badly site administration had devolved. At first, Ranger Fred Jeep had been a reliable guide. A 1915 visitor called him "a very competent and enthusiastic guide." Two years later, Horace Albright recalled that "Dr. Fewkes thought he was a man we ought to develop and keep in the Service."[14] By 1921, unfortunately, Jeep had lost interest in protecting the site. Instead, he had begun trading in antiquities. He excavated ruins throughout the park, selling artifacts to collectors and undermining work by Smithsonian archaeologists. Nusbaum recalled, "Whenever he found that Dr. Fewkes was going to excavate a ruin, he took fellows on government payroll to that ruin and stripped all he could find out of that ruin before Fewkes got busy to excavate it." A group of young boys took over Jeep's role as interpreter. "When a car would come in they would run up and compete with one another to get on the running board of the car and guide the people to the ruins," Nusbaum said. "The stories they were telling them were so atrocious. There was nothing to them."[15] Nusbaum fired Jeep and expelled the dubious tour guides from the park. Learning that Jeep had been stashing his loot locked up in a small log cabin in the park, Nusbaum threatened him with prosecution under the Antiquities Act. Reluctantly, Jeep turned over the keys.

Nusbaum found that the building originally had been set up as a small museum. A series of exhibit cases contained artifacts Jeep hadn't had the time or heart to sell. Nusbaum recognized the space might serve the park more effectively: "I knew we had to have a museum to protect these things, [and] I knew the people had to have information." During Nusbaum's tenure, expansion of the park's museum became a priority, the centerpiece in a comprehensive interpretive plan designed to protect the park, manage its resources, and engage visitors. "I realized that there was only one way to create the interest in Mesa Verde and give out the information so that people would have a . . . fair understanding of the ruins and their significance, what we knew about the people. That would be by means of interpretation."[16] Nusbaum expanded educational offerings in the park. He arranged for local Navajo Indians to perform traditional dances, and he prepared campfire talks on a variety of subjects. His work caught the attention of private park boosters as well as the central Park Service Administration. Almost immediately after taking control of the park, Nusbaum began requesting appropriations to replace the log cabin with a more professional museum to be built at the base of the most significant cliff dwellings.

No federal money was forthcoming, but Mather found a way to direct funds to Nusbaum. In 1923 Stella Levinston, a park enthusiast from San Francisco, arrived in a car bearing Mather's official seal. "She came in with her chauffer. . . . She said, 'Those collections you have got in those cases in that log cabin are liable to burn up some time and I am concerned.'" She presented him with $5,000 to build a fireproof museum building. The following year John D. Rockefeller surprised Nusbaum with a visit, arriving with the Colorado Fuel and Iron public relations director. After a tour of the ruins, Rockefeller promised to fund completion of the museum and to cover the cost of new exhibit cases as well.[17] Nusbaum's success won praise from Stephen Mather, who boasted, "What will be probably the most remarkable example of museum construction in the entire park system is developing in the Mesa Verde National Park under the supervision and guidance of Supt. Jesse Nusbaum, a born organizer and doer, with excellent training as an archaeologist, he brought with him upon his appointment as superintendent in 1921 a record of achievement in museum construction and archaeological research work that might be envied by many older scientists."[18] Indeed, Jesse Nusbaum's interpretive work did attract attention from older scientists, not all of it positive. He became a central character in a crucial and often underestimated chapter in the evolution of American museums.

The Intellectual Significance of Park Museums

American museums enjoyed a relatively short period of broad cultural influence, which reached a high water mark during the last thirty years of the nineteenth century. The staff and founders of private institutions such as New York's Museum of Natural History, university-centered museums such as Berkeley's Museum of Vertebrate Zoology, and government-run establishments such as the Smithsonian's U.S. National Museum existed at the center of scientific advancement.[19] Geologists and other naturalists had built these institutions, creating seminal collections of specimens that formed the bedrock of scientific research and discovery. Fieldwork by ethnologists and anthropologists expanded museum holdings of cultural materials. Their work bolstered the nation's claims to greatness, placing the United States inside a logical narrative of the "natural history of civilization, of man and his ideas and achievements."[20]

The intellectual role of American museums had already begun to shift rather dramatically by shortly after the turn of the twentieth century, however. Franz Boas, the most influential American anthropologist of his generation, left his position at the American Museum of Natural History in 1905 and two years later published an essay in *Science* criticizing the role of museums in structuring scientific knowledge. He expressed doubt about the value of collections, arguing that deeply entrenched practices of collecting, organizing, and displaying artifacts tended to oversimplify human culture and stifle discovery. Boas and his followers, who were beginning to advance a philosophy of cultural relativism, objected to museums' portrayal of human history as the natural story of evolution and their tendency to display cultural artifacts on a continuum from "savagery" to "civilization." Boas's criticism had a profound impact on the cultural function and perceived stature of museums in the United States, generally speaking.[21] During the first quarter of the twentieth century, anthropologists retreated from museums, taking the most intellectually cutting-edge research on human cultures with them to university anthropology departments. Museums of natural history were cut off from the process of scientific advancement, and established museums—from Chicago's Field Museum to New York's American Museum of Natural History—declined as renowned scientists left their employ. Most museums shifted their focus, and public education moved from the margins to the center of many institutional missions.

The effects of this cultural shift had an important and somewhat different impact on government-run museums because the authority of federal institutions was not based on the same calculus as that of private institutions. The stature of the Smithsonian depended less on the individual renown of museum staff members and more on the strength of its unique networks and relationships. The Smithsonian Institution, already approaching sixty when Boas's comments disconnected scientific research from natural history museums, served as a conduit, linking government, commercial, and scientific interests. Private institutions almost immediately lost a measure of legitimacy when Boas and his followers began questioning the value of natural history museums for advancing scientific disciplines, but Smithsonian anthropologists and ethnologists lost little at first. Indeed, the passage of the Antiquities Act in 1906 promised to elevate rather than dilute the Smithsonian's cultural role, since the Smithsonian had, by then, a well-established track record as the repository for all specimens and artifacts excavated from public lands. It appeared that items excavated under a government-issued permit would necessarily become part of the national collections.

The creation of museums by the National Park Service gradually tested this assumption. At first, park museums appeared poised simply to serve Smithsonian interests. By most accounts, John Bigelow, a major in the Ninth U.S. Cavalry, organized the first park museum in 1904, when he was the acting superintendent of Yosemite National Park, in Horace Albright's home state of California. Bigelow had cultivated a working relationship with Joseph Grinnell, director of the Berkeley Museum of Vertebrate Zoology. Together, Bigelow and Grinnell developed a series of museum displays, providing visitors with a glimpse of Yosemite's wide variety of animals and plants.[22] Albright, having grown up camping in Yosemite, was undoubtedly familiar with the park's displays. When he took over as superintendent at Yellowstone, he adopted Bigelow's park museum model and set aside "space in one of the large Government buildings at headquarters and started his park naturalist on the collection of exhibits and the preparation of botanic, mineral and animal specimens which [had] already resulted in a very remarkable museum collection."[23] Albright, Bigelow, and others understood that exhibits and collections in the parks would provide visitors with an opportunity to see natural specimens up close without damaging the park landscape.

Park museums were, from the outset, different from Smithsonian museums, in that they were designed to help increase the number of site visitors

and to limit their interactions with the landscape, not to advance specialized knowledge or promote research. At first, then, the two federal bureaus
had little reason to interact, much less compete. The Antiquities Act began
to complicate their relationship. Smithsonian anthropologists and ethnologists acquired Antiquities Act permits from the Department of the
Interior, the U.S. Forest Service, the War Department, and the Bureau of
Indian Affairs to conduct research among Native American tribes and on
the grounds of national monuments, removing specimens for Smithsonian
collections. At first, small on-site museums lacked the standing, the staff,
and the budget to assert their value as federal collecting institutions and
therefore had no recognized right to retain and display materials excavated
during fieldwork, even if those materials were found within steps of the
park museum door.

As early as 1906 Frank Pinkley had been requesting federal funds to
open a museum at Casa Grande. Unlike most of the other monuments,
which were too isolated to attract significant numbers of visitors, Casa
Grande had a relatively high rate of visitation beginning in the 1880s. On
its way to Tucson, the Southern Pacific Railroad stopped in the town of
Casa Grande, about twenty miles from the monument. Many settlers and
prospectors exited the train there to travel farther west by wagon; the best
route took them right past Casa Grande. Drawn to the strange ruins, visitors stopped, carved their names into the adobe walls, and removed bits
of wood from ceiling beams or "fragment[s] of pottery and specimen[s]
of adobe and plaster."[24] That destruction led the General Land Office, the
agency which originally administered the monument, to hire Pinkley as a
full-time custodian in 1901.

Archaeologists supported Pinkley's effort, arguing that the creation of
monument museums would help enforce the Antiquities Act, keeping artifacts safe for inspection by trained archaeologists and out of the hands
of private collectors. Pinkley had demonstrated his deference to official
researchers, providing labor support to their excavations at Casa Grande
without interfering in efforts to collect specimens for deposit in the U.S.
National Museum. His primary goal was to protect the ruins from destruction by tourists and vandals. He planned to create a museum and library
for use by students of archaeology and anthropology, hoping that increased
field study would help control access. He told Horace Albright, "At the rate
attention has been given to our monuments, there'll be no need to remem-
ber them. Before long they will have been washed away or crumbled away

by sun and rain or hoisted away by tourists and merchants."[25] The network of government and university scientists understood Pinkley's agenda. In 1912 J. Walter Fewkes wrote, "It is to be hoped that a museum for Casa Grande antiquities may be erected later near the ruin and that in it may be placed not only all specimens gathered from the reservation and its neighborhood but also such books, maps, and other materials as pertain to the ruin in order to increase the educational value of this example of the culture of the former people of the Gila Valley."[26]

Although Frank Pinkley was generally well liked by men such as Fewkes and his colleague Neil Judd, he was neither a professional archaeologist nor an experienced fund-raiser. After the Park Service took over the site in 1918, Pinkley had some modest success, assembling a small collection of artifacts for his museum. In his annual report the following year, Stephen Mather offered mild praise for Pinkley's "collection of prehistoric implements and other relics of interest to the visitor" as well as the Casa Grande "library on archaeology and ethnology that is quite comprehensive." Mather was considering Pinkley's request for funds to build a more permanent museum to house these collections.[27] Despite apparent—if tempered—enthusiasm, however, Mather never went out of his way to find money for the project. More than once, his annual reports indicate that improvements at Casa Grande were modest because the Park Service budget was too limited. Pinkley, for his part, seems not to have pursued outside funding. Instead, he cobbled together his own resources, setting aside bits of his official budget and committing a portion of his office space to create artifact displays. Mather acknowledged that Pinkley's small display "has become one of the most interesting features of the reservation and has been thoroughly enjoyed by the traveling public. Dr. Fewkes uses it for all his talks on archaeology."[28] By 1923 Pinkley had set aside about $1,200 from funds allocated for site improvements and had made use of Native American labor to build a five-room adobe structure for dedicated use as a museum.[29] Nonetheless, the Casa Grande project never matched the scale of Nusbaum's museum at Mesa Verde.

Nusbaum's museum ushered in a new era of professionalism for Park Service anthropology and park museums.[30] At first, Neil Judd, Edgar Hewett, and Walter Fewkes expected that Nusbaum would extend access to his colleagues, supporting their efforts to excavate artifacts for the Smithsonian's national collections and to foster development of relevant scientific disciplines. As the Mesa Verde museum grew, however, Nusbaum proved to be a formidable foe, determined to keep artifacts on-site and to limit damaging excavation of fragile ruins. Almost immediately after he had succeeded in gaining control of Mesa Verde, Nusbaum entered into conflict with Walter Fewkes, who had been conducting excavations of Mesa Verde ruins on behalf of the Smithsonian's Bureau of American Ethnology almost every summer for more than a decade. Fewkes had helped build the popularity of the park, leading tours of the ruins and giving talks to visitors. His excavations, however, had left several of the cliff dwellings in terrible disrepair. Fewkes argued that site maintenance and restoration after excavations were complete was the responsibility of the Park Service. Nusbaum complained that not only had Fewkes left the ruins exposed and vulnerable to tourists and weather, he had also damaged the surrounding landscape in his efforts to reach and then clear an excavation site. Mather responded in 1923 by announcing a moratorium on further research in the park, allowing time for necessary repairs under Nusbaum's supervision. Fewkes protested and the secretary of the Smithsonian refused to intervene, leaving it to Mather and Nusbaum to keep Fewkes out of the park. Ultimately, the secretary of the interior became involved in the matter, forcing the Smithsonian to suspend its research operations temporarily.[31]

The Usefulness of Artifacts

The end of excavations did not end conflict between the Park Service and the Smithsonian. Instead, Jesse Nusbaum began to inquire about the status of artifacts Fewkes had removed from the site and deposited at the Smithsonian. Arno Cammerer—acting director of the Park Service in 1922—asked the agency's attorney, Edwin S. Booth, for an opinion on the matter. Booth's response challenged the Smithsonian's status as the only appropriate federal repository for materials collected under the Antiquities Act. Prior to the creation of park museums, Booth argued, the Antiquities Act had been interpreted in such a way that most of the artifacts excavated on public lands were deposited in the U.S. National Museum. But the creation of new federal agencies with more direct authority over the landscape and its contents surely required a new procedure. Booth wrote, "Congress certainly did not intend that objects . . . should be transferred to the Smithsonian Institution so long as they are useful to the branches of the Government by which they were collected."[32] Under the terms of the

Antiquities Act, then, these objects could most certainly be understood as useful to the Department of the Interior's National Park Service and its museums. More broadly, Booth's response opened up conversations about the myriad of ways in which government collections might be useful, lending more authority to park museums' educational endeavors.

For the Smithsonian, the value of artifacts derived from their usefulness to the federal government. The institution had collected anthropological information and materials from its earliest days, and the Bureau of Ethnology pioneered research in American anthropology. As the Smithsonian expanded and the number of museums and divisions grew, anthropology was established as a division of the U.S. National Museum in 1883, and it was enlarged to one of the museum's three departments in 1897. The paleontologist Charles Walcott, who became Smithsonian secretary in 1907, oversaw considerable institutional expansion. Born in Utica, New York, Walcott had spent two years working as James Hall's assistant in the office of the state paleontologist. He joined the U.S. Geological Survey in 1879 and rose through the ranks to become its director, a position he held until he was recruited by the Smithsonian. Under Walcott's direction, the Smithsonian opened the National Museum of Natural History in 1911.[33] Beginning in 1912, likely spurred by the creation of this new museum, curators at the U.S. National Museum began to reorganize their curatorial divisions with some frequency. Technological artifacts, donated by American manufacturers and large-scale industrialists, were removed from anthropological and ethnographic divisions and placed under the control of an independent Arts and Industries Department in 1919.[34]

Despite these bureaucratic shifts, throughout the 1920s all the Smithsonian curators continued to understand artifacts in terms of their location on an evolutionary continuum. This emphasis was embedded in the organization of collections into types: pottery, clothing, weapons, money, and so on. In turn, the typological organization of collections shaped exhibits that communicated a relentless narrative of progress. A communications exhibit, mounted at the U.S. National Museum during the late 1920s, provides a vivid example. Designed with input from Smithsonian ethnologists, anthropologists, and historians, it was composed of four cases that presented advancement in communication, both as a function of developing human culture and as evidence of technological prowess. Throughout the exhibit, anthropological models served as a touchstone against which to measure both calculations of progress. The untitled introductory case depicted various methods of transporting written messages—foot messengers, the pony express, and airmail. The leap from messengers to airmail was made obvious by the presence of the life-size model at the center, given the title "Indian Scout." Neil Judd provided advice about the groups of Indians who had the best "primitive runners" and therefore the best messengers. His handwritten notes read, "Hopi Indians best runners in North America, Zuni 2nd, Tarahumari Indians, NW of Mexico City, very (illegible) runners." The second exhibit case, "Visual Communication," included light ships, army semaphores and heliographs. Again, evidence of technological progress was juxtaposed against a "primitive" model demonstrating "Indian Smoke Signaling." Judd's handwritten notes state, "Plains Indians chief users, Arapahoes." The third case, "Aural Communication," did not include a model to represent prehistoric techniques, but it did include tom-toms. Finally, "Static Telegraphy" represented the height of technological advancement and focused on the mechanics of communication in a more modern age. No human forms appeared in this last exhibit case.[35]

Similar examples can be found throughout the annual reports and exhibit records maintained by the institution. These records suggest that the progress narrative was, at the very least, reinforced by curators' relationships with—indeed their dependence on—donors from major industries. The connection between curators and manufacturers helped advance the institution's professionalism by expanding the number of collections and professional staff. Accepting a steady stream of machines and products required both constant revision of curatorial units and the addition of new curators and assistants for these new units. At the same time, all the collections delivered to the institution allowed little opportunity for curators and administrators to consider the meaning or significance of industrial artifacts beyond their intrinsic qualities. Without such reflection, the narrative of progress became ever more entrenched, appearing not subjective and interpretive but objective and scientific.

The weight of industrial donations was particularly obvious in an example from the leather exhibit, displayed by the Division of Agriculture and Mining. Curators intended the display to demonstrate the production of finished goods from raw materials in the leather-manufacturing industry. Instead, the exhibit constantly expanded, with the collection of leather artifacts, tanning agents, and industry tools. As new shipments arrived from leather manufacturers, objects were simply added to the display. Temporary labels described methods of production, chemical composition, and design, and the addition of new artifacts served only to document the industry's progress and expansion. Annual reports repeatedly describe the need to rearrange and condense the exhibit, but it remained for decades a mish-mash of objects and chemicals with little interpretation beyond a visual progression of tools and products.[36]

During this period of expansion, history began to gain more promi-nence in the institution. Over time, the Department of Anthropology had assembled a small collection of American artifacts. They were absorbed into the Arts and Industries Department in 1919. There, artifacts originally collected by anthropologists, ethnologists, and others were subdivided and reclassified into six curatorial units dedicated to history: antiquarian, cos-tume, military, naval, numismatic, philatelic and pictorial. As these unit names suggest, the Smithsonian curators defined historical significance not in terms of an artifact's original context in time or place but rather by its observable physical qualities. Nonetheless, curators argued the history collection was "originally designed to illustrate the history of the U.S. and with that object in view, all available material relating to notable events and personages was assigned to the division."[37] The appropriate use and mean-ing of the collection became a source of internal debate.

Emphasis on famous people and events lent historical collections a broad public appeal and kept its curators busy with public inquiries and loan requests. During the 1920s historical commemorations became increasingly popular as the heightened patriotism of World War I led local governments, ethnic associations, and veterans groups to stake a claim in the construction of American patriotic identity.[38] The 1924 creation of a federal commission to mark the two-hundredth anniversary of George Washington's birth spurred local jurisdiction to plan celebrations, and by 1930 Smithsonian curators were spending a tremendous amount of time responding to requests for information. The curators reported providing "much information pertaining to colonial costumes . . . to various individu-als and organizations who have participated in pageants and other activi-ties in connection with the GW Bicentennial Celebration."[39]

History curators, including T. T. Belote and Carl Mitman, viewed this intense popular interest in Washington as a unique opportunity for expan-sion and exerted pressure on the secretary to support the creation of a "special building for historical museum purposes."[40] Ethnologists, in con-trast, found much to complain about in the popular interest and research requests. The divisional report notes, "The Washington Bicentennial

Commission and its various subsidiaries received the lion's share of attention and service. Men and women were supplied with Indian costumes, with Quaker robes, with Virginia planter's wife's dresses, with the dresses of Puritan ladies, with frontier costumes, and with such additional objects as they desired for use in Flag Day and other pageants."[41] The scientific curators complained that loaning objects for pageants and parades had severely taxed their collections and threatened their ability to maintain viable research collections.[42] By 1932 the Department of Anthropology had dramatically reduced the number of items it made available for loan, and ethnology curators sought to extend protection to historical collections as well, by arguing, "Americana, when divorced from the hallowing influences of personage, becomes ethnology for the purposes of cataloging, even though antiquarian interests are frequently far removed from scientific ethnology."[43] Herbert Krieger called such popularity "an evil that has crept into the handling of our study series," and he cautioned, "Carefully balanced planning and persistency in action are in order if Ethnology is to maintain pace with the many newly established museums throughout the country."[44] Krieger, an ethnologist, was certainly aware that Smithsonian scientists had lost some of their stature as most cutting-edge research had moved into university departments and out of museums. The natural science museums that opened during the 1920s were far more focused on educating visitors than producing scholarship.[45]

For similar reasons, park museums might very well have been on Krieger's mind as well. Over the course of the 1920s a growing number of National Parks had arranged exhibits in ranger stations, superintendent's offices, and—sometimes—dedicated museum buildings. The content of the displays had expanded as well, moving beyond botany and zoology and increasingly into ethnology, anthropology, and archaeology.[46] This expansion was part of the worry expressed by Krieger and other Smithsonian curators who feared losing access to new collections, but it also had a more profound influence. The specific introduction of archaeology as an intellectual framework for understanding artifacts in parks challenged Smithsonian curators' assumptions about the meaning of artifacts and created a framework for thinking beyond science, to consider the influence of history and culture on the landscape.

The museum at Yosemite played an important role in ushering in these changes. Ansel Hall, a botanist with a degree in forestry from the University of California, had joined the Yosemite staff in 1919 as a naturalist and information specialist. His role at Yosemite was to improve visitor education, and his immediate efforts included the establishment of interpretive programs and the production of a series of guidebooks. As part of his effort to make the park more broadly accessible to visitors, he also focused his energies on the park museum. He acquired funding from the Laura Spellman Rockefeller Foundation to move exhibits out of the administration building and into a permanent museum.[47] The new museum opened in 1922—the same year that Booth rendered his opinion—and it attracted thirty-three thousand visitors by the end of its first summer. The museum's six exhibit rooms included displays on ethnology and history as well as the usual displays on geology, natural history, and botany.[48]

Hall's success in expanding the Yosemite museum was rewarded, and he rose through the ranks of the Park Service.[49] He was appointed the first chief naturalist of the National Park Service in 1923, and from this position he became an increasingly vocal advocate for the establishment of park museums, particularly in the West. The year of his promotion, he attended an international museum conference under the auspices of the American Association of Museums (which had been established in 1906), and he redoubled his efforts to inject new standards of research and display in the parks. Although his formal education had been in forestry, Hall's employment in the western parks had led him to develop a keen interest in American archaeology. Between 1923 and 1937 he raised private funds to sponsor field research in several western parks, and he enlisted distinguished archaeologists to lead groups of scouts on educational digs.[50] Hall's emphasis on archaeology is significant. Prior to World War II, curators of ethnology and anthropology tended to wield the most influence in determining collections policies and designing displays at the Smithsonian. On the ground at national parks and monuments, however, archaeologists increasingly determined the usefulness and meaning of park collections.

On these study missions, participants—including Nusbaum, Hall, Hewett, and others—developed a unique, interdisciplinary approach to fieldwork.[51] Archaeological excavations at parks and monuments contributed to an explosion of questions that tested archaeology's disciplinary boundaries. An intellectual fissure began to form in the United States between old world archaeologists on the one hand and a younger generation of researchers on the other, who are now considered by many as pioneers of historical archaeology. Old world archaeologists tended to distinguish pre-Columbian historical artifacts from post-Columbian ones. Their insistence on an intellectual break between the "prehistoric" and the "historic" lent legitimacy to museum ethnology, providing a philosophical justification for distinguishing "ethnological" from "antiquarian" artifacts—and both "ancient people" and Native Americans from "historical figures." American (somewhat distinct from British or other European) historical archaeologists embraced their connection to anthropology, viewing their research as part of a larger scientific effort to understand human culture. They also began to question some of the assumptions made by ethnologists. Interdisciplinary fieldwork forced some archaeologists to begin to recognize historical and cultural continuity alongside patterns of settlement, warfare, and conquest.[52] The examination of both pre-Columbian and post-Columbian artifacts under the same scientific lens (whether individual scientists preferred the term "anthropology" or "archaeology") tended to undermine perceptions of difference in the interpretation of artifacts, placing Native American, European, and American material culture on the same continuum.

Even in its infancy, the practice of American historical archaeology threatened to alter the meaning of artifacts in the Smithsonian collection. Applying the same methodologies to "prehistoric" and "historic" artifacts fueled debates about the meaning and value of the three-dimensional items held in government repositories. Practitioners began to combine fieldwork with archival research to develop in-depth understandings of the cultural and historical forces that had produced particular products—whether mission churches or pueblo villages. This technique placed historical archaeologists in an ill-defined space, somewhere between and most definitely outside of two disciplines—history and archaeology. In some European nations, scientists and political figures alike recognized prehistoric cultures as part of a common past. In the United States, however, the maintenance of a sharp distinction within archaeology was part of a larger ideological project to reinforce the belief that indigenous peoples were irrelevant to the nation's historical past.[53] Traditional historians were complicit. Their insistence that written documents were the only appropriate source of historical information enabled archaeologists to claim artifacts for science. Historical archaeologists' efforts to balance textual research and fieldwork weakened their claims to disciplinary expertise, because it marked them as neither historians nor archaeologists, and it created a perpetual "crisis of identity" among practitioners.[54]

This identity crisis was compounded further by the distinct sense that

American historical archaeology lacked a broader kind of cultural usefulness. Practitioners challenged the disciplinary boundaries that had marked
pre-Columbian "savages" as the prehistoric subjects of archaeological fieldwork and European "civilizations" as the subjects of history. Without a
distinct break in the timeline, there was no apparent heroic, conquering age
that marked the birth of America. Historical archaeologists in the United
States, unable to point to a single moment of America's triumphant emergence, were routinely ridiculed for their focus on "the unrespectable."[55]
Their interdisciplinary approach delayed the maturation of their discipline
and undermined their sense of authority. Practitioners did not organize a
professional association—the Society for Historical Archaeology—until
1967, and most historians point to the decades after World War II as the
discipline's formative years. Smithsonian anthropologists—including Neil
Judd—eventually joined the supporting ranks of historical archaeology, but
not until after the war. The Holocaust made older notions of cultural hierarchy shameful and pushed government scientists to reexamine their commitment to evolutionary models of human civilization. Between the two
world wars, however, the world and its past looked different, and Smithsonian anthropologists, ethnologists, and archaeologists (of the old world
variety) clung to artifact categories that reinforced a narrative of progressive development over time.

In the National Park Service, historical archaeology provided a framework for challenging the Smithsonian's status as the only official government repository and helped bolster the agency's efforts to retain and interpret artifacts on-site. Actively combining archaeology and history enabled
Park Service technicians, superintendents, and rangers to argue that artifacts derived their meaning from their unique relationship to specific park
landscapes. Park Service attorney Booth had argued that parks must be
"made as attractive and inviting as possible in order to induce the people to
visit them and participate in the benefits that Congress intended to bestow.
. . . That the maintenance of the museum . . . adds greatly to the attractiveness of the Mesa Verde National Park can not be doubted, and that it
gives information and pleasure to the people that they could not gain in
any other way during their visits to the park is certainly true."[56] This opinion changed the meaning of the anthropological and ethnological artifacts
excavated by Fewkes with an Antiquities Act permit.

Booth had defined artifacts from the perspective of tourists, not the
perspective of scientists, and argued that their primary usefulness was in

their ability to provide pleasure and information to average visitors. Curators in the U.S. National Museum and scientists in the Bureau of American Ethnology were appalled.[57] They worried that using collections to entertain and educate the general public would threaten the integrity of scientific research. In this calculation, the status of American historical archaeologists, already weakened because they remained disconnected from a narrative of progress, would be threatened if not aided by an association with the Park Service. Recognizing this, Neil Judd wrote, "It is obvious the Interior Department intends to develop an independent system of museums, each designated a national depository, administered by the National Park Service. That decision seriously threatens future archeological exploration by the Smithsonian Institution and the gradual perfection of our division of American archaeology." Trying to distinguish his goal of "perfecting" American archaeology from the mission of the Park Service, Judd wrote, "There can be but one official depository, but specimens from that depository might be loaned to other federal departments to assist them in performing their several functions, as, in the case of the Interior Department, the entertainment of visitors to national parks."[58]

Collections, Education, and Entertainment

Neil Judd's distinction between the Smithsonian's role as an "official depository" and the role of park museums as sources of entertainment is not simply condescending. It is significant for its effort to account for diverse forms of authority represented by different government agencies. In Judd's estimation, Smithsonian collections provided a public service by supporting the missions of other government agencies. Permanently depositing collections in more than one federal museum would limit their accessibility to researchers and the government, curtailing Smithsonian expansion and limiting the usefulness of federal collections. In contrast, the Park Service mission to entertain its visitors provided a form of public service that could be accomplished without exclusive access to scientific materials. At the same time, and as Judd astutely noted, the Park Service was clearly interested in advancing its reputation beyond entertainment. Its effort to retain artifacts was reinforced by the development of increasingly better-appointed park museums. Judd expressed the mounting anxiety of his Smithsonian colleagues when he pointed out that the Department of the

Interior "administers most public lands" and that the Smithsonian's future research "must necessarily revolve about ruins on the public domain, including National Parks and monuments."[59]

An incident in 1927 added a new layer to the debate. On July 1, 1927, Jesse Nusbaum was promoted to a dual position as chief archaeologist of the National Park Service and supervisory archaeologist of the Department of the Interior. In this capacity, he advanced the argument that artifacts collected anywhere in the region of a park belonged in the appropriate park museum. Indeed, such institutions—however small—could provide a valuable public service by enforcing Antiquities Act permits. That fall, Dr. R. S. Lipscomb, a physician who had been working at the Ute Mountain Indian School at Towac, Colorado, hired a group of reservation boys to conduct illegal excavations. They uncovered a piece of pottery decorated with what Nusbaum described as a "hunchback flute player," a design now typically called kokopeli. Lipscomb brought the piece to Mesa Verde, hoping its display in the museum would attract a buyer. When no buyer materialized, he wrote to Nusbaum in late August, and asked him to forward the bowl to Fewkes at the Bureau of American Ethnology. Nusbaum refused. He claimed ownership of the artifact under section 16 of the Uniform Rules governing the Antiquities Act: since the artifact had been illegally excavated—without a permit or sponsorship from a cultural institution—it was rightfully the property of a national repository.[60]

Nusbaum took this opportunity to argue that the museum at Mesa Verde—and, by extension, all park museums—was a viable national repository. Nusbaum wrote to the Smithsonian acting secretary Alexander Wetmore and assistant secretary of the interior John H. Edwards, asking them to authorize his "permanent retention of this bowl in the Mesa Verde National Park Museum, a national depository for such material so seized." He wrote to Lipscomb that the museum, "made possible by generous friends of this park, is nevertheless a national depository for such material, just as much as the . . . National Museum and the Smithsonian Institution of Washington, and as such is maintained by Federal appropriations. Therefore, it is strictly a government museum, and as such may become the depository for the reception of such artifacts as may be excavated illegally on lands under the jurisdiction of the Department of the Interior." Unsurprisingly, Smithsonian administrators and curators were uncomfortable with the implications of Nusbaum's argument. If park museums could claim status as national repositories, placing them on par with Smithsonian museums, then the status of Smithsonian scientists would be diminished. One field ethnologist wrote to the Bureau of American Ethnology, "If all finds, ruins, etc. on government land, national parks, monuments and national forests are to be controlled by the archaeological department of the Department of the Interior, it will seriously handicap the work of the Bureau and also of the Smithsonian, and naturally I would hate to see such a thing come to pass."[61]

Nusbaum's claim to the artifact threatened to diminish the general authority of the Smithsonian by complicating the concept of artifact "usefulness." The Smithsonian continued to insist that an artifact's usefulness lay primarily in its contributions to professional scientific knowledge, not in its cultural role or its attractiveness to general audiences. Edwin Booth had suggested that such artifacts were particularly useful to park museums because they were attractive and contributed to tourists' ability to enjoy public space. In defending his desire to keep the confiscated bowl at Mesa Verde, Nusbaum added yet another calculation of "usefulness." His arguments suggested that the value of an item rested neither exclusively on questions of audience interest nor on questions of scientific expertise. Rather, as Nusbaum explained to Lipscomb, "the bowl should continue to remain in the [Mesa Verde] Museum, as a part of the Museum collections, where it will be seen and studied and of much greater value to all than in storage in the U.S. National Museum." In other words, the bowl was primarily useful for magnifying the broad educational value of park museums. On October 13 John Edwards approved Nusbaum's decision to keep the bowl at Mesa Verde.

Unfortunately, Nusbaum's stature as an archaeologist and an upper-level staff member of both the National Park Service and the Department of the Interior was ultimately insufficient. He failed to convince the Smithsonian that this was the appropriate course of action. Secretary Wetmore chimed in to the debate on October 19, constructing a defense of the Smithsonian's ownership that attempted to enforce a sharp distinction between the mission of the Smithsonian and that of the Park Service. He argued that while the Smithsonian supported the idea of park museums "for the benefit of tourists," the institution held to the belief that such museums should reinforce narratives of progress and evolution. He argued that park museum exhibits should be "composed of examples of the usual materials available at the different sites." In contrast, "unique specimens, of value for scientific study, should come to the larger museums—where the government is concerned, to the National Museum. Great rarities or unique specimens have significance to the student, but to the average tourist usually mean nothing more than another peculiar object. The story to be brought to the public eye can be exemplified fully with types of ordinary things."[62]

Distinctions between "unique" and "ordinary" or "tourist" and "student" were anathema to Nusbaum's concept of education. Wetmore's argument reinforced the idea that federal museums provided a public service by reinforcing the nation's claims to greatness, representing all scientific specimens as icons of a logical narrative of progress. Lest he offend Nusbaum's integrity, Wetmore went on to say that while Nusbaum was eminently qualified to understand and display archaeological artifacts, there was no guarantee that future park superintendents would be so qualified: "Such change in the administrative policy might easily cause these objects to lose their identity or through such lack of understanding of their value allow their use in such a way as to destroy them."[63] Nusbaum deflected this charge, insisting that future park administrators would possess the specialized knowledge necessary to ensure the proper display, preservation, and storage of archaeological artifacts. In so doing, he advanced support for an interdisciplinary model of site management, pointing out that the service had cooperated fully with universities and colleges, museums and scientists, to ensure that archaeology and public education were well served on-site.

On October 21 Edwards reversed his previous decision in favor of the Mesa Verde Museum and ordered Nusbaum to forward the Lipscomb bowl to the U.S. National Museum. The director of the Park Service immediately encouraged Nusbaum to disregard that order and to submit further information that might help overturn the decision. Nusbaum's response continued to give shape to an emergent philosophy about the legitimacy of park museums and the nature of public service. Nusbaum continued to define park museums as the institutional equal of Smithsonian museums. He pointed out that the Smithsonian and the Mesa Verde Museum both originated when "liberal and far-sighted friends or a single individual noted the need for preserving permanently materials accumulating and improperly cared for." But he insisted that the driving force behind the establishment of these institutions—the service which they provided—was less exclusive than the Smithsonian believed. He argued that materials in federal museums, when "properly housed and cared for, would be a great educational asset."[64] In defending his position, Nusbaum had harnessed the sensibilities of historical archaeology, elevating the unrespectable science to a pillar of government service. He argued that park museums like the one at Mesa Verde are national depositories dedicated to the preservation of the history and culture of the area in which they are located, a mission consistent with the terms of the Antiquities Act. While Wetmore's argument rested on the Smithsonian tendency to categorize objects in terms of scientific value, Nusbaum posed a much more dynamic relationship among objects, history, and culture.

Inherent in Nusbaum's argument was a more empathetic attitude toward the needs and interests of museum visitors. While Wetmore claimed museum visitors could comprehend only familiar and apparently seamless progressions of artifacts, Nusbaum assumed that visitors were capable of comprehending the value of artifacts in terms of both predictable progressions and cultural change: "The 'usual materials' tell a common-place story to the public and the 'unique and outstanding' specimens add the highlights and enhance the value of said exhibits, by showing diversification, change, progress, and advancement, etc. For this reason, they are usually prominently displayed." Nusbaum's interest in museum visitors was reflected in the Mesa Verde Museum's active program of interpretation and education. "There is always a 'Museum Assistant' on duty in the Mesa Verde Museum when the building is open to explain exhibits, answer questions and assist the visitors in their quest for knowledge. Every facility is extended to visitors, scientists and students at all times. . . . As far as we know, no visitor to the Mesa Verde has failed to inspect the park museum since its establishment. It is therefore serving 100% of the travel to this park, and fulfilling its purpose in the broadest possible way."[65]

Nusbaum's position was strongly supported by John Edwards; Arthur Demaray, acting director of the National Park Service in 1927; and the lawyer for the Department of the Interior, who argued that paragraph 16 of the Antiquities Act left the matter wholly to administrative discretion and certainly did not require the Park Service (which, of course, did not exist in 1906) to surrender any objects collected by or under its jurisdiction or on its lands. That paragraph reads, "Any object of antiquity taken, or collection made, on lands owned or controlled by the United States, without a permit, as prescribed by any act and these rules and regulations, or there taken or made, contrary to the terms of the permit, or contrary to the act and these rules and regulations, may be seized wherever found and at any time, by the proper field officer or by any person duly authorized by the Secretary having jurisdiction, and disposed of as the Secretary shall determine, by deposit in the proper national depository or otherwise."[66]

These arguments created a nervous reaction among the federal government's other anthropologists and ethnologists. Neil Judd argued that Congress surely had not intended for the Park Service in general and Mesa Verde in particular to duplicate the work of the Smithsonian, an agency created more than half a century earlier.[67] Walter Hough, head curator of anthropology at the Smithsonian, strongly supported Judd's opinion and noted that the Interior Department's solicitor had conveniently ignored the specification that artifacts should be deposited in national repositories "in Washington."[68] Furthermore, the arguments over the disposition of artifacts collected illegally on public lands did not end with the small bowl at Mesa Verde. In 1933 Judd wrote to Mathew Stirling regarding shields and a doll in a cradle collected in Torrey and St. George, Utah. He argued that the material should be forwarded to the U.S. National Museum rather than the Laboratory of Anthropology at Santa Fe, a Park Service entity.[69] Underlying the terms of the ongoing disagreement between the Park Service and the Smithsonian was the potential of the service to radically revise the discipline-specific meanings that had been assigned to artifacts during years of museum collecting and exhibition. While the Smithsonian's own history curators generally deferred to those in the science divisions when it came to categorizing and interpreting the institution's artifacts, a new breed of Park Service professionals in the 1920s were unwilling to show such regard. Gradually, they were developing the idea that an artifact's meaning and significance came not from its location on a continuum of progress or its contextualization in an ahistorical depiction of culture but rather from its physical and historical location among peoples on a landscape. In short, the meaning of artifacts was most often unique, not typical.

Prior to World War II, then, park museums became an intellectual hothouse in which a new branch of scientific inquiry—historical archaeology—began to take root. At first, most park and monument museums focused on biological and geological specimens. By the 1920s, however, a number of them had begun to collect and display Native American artifacts, excavated on park grounds, and to contextualize them in terms that challenged the evolutionary narrative favored by Smithsonian anthropologists and ethnologists. Competition over the right to collect and display Native American artifacts in particular threatened to undermine the Smithsonian's stature, and the institute's scientists launched a rather aggressive campaign to establish their legal right to these materials. Throughout the 1920s letters containing demands and even insults flew between curators, administrators, and scientists from the Smithsonian and superintendents, administrators, and rangers from the Park Service. These records document the formation of new philosophies regarding the usefulness and meaning of artifacts, the value of government museums, the authority of the Park Service, and, more broadly, the meaning of the past.

CHAPTER 4

Ignorant and Local-Minded Influences

Historic Sites and the Expansion of the National Park Service

———— ✠ ————

The purpose of history is to find one's place in the region of which you are a part.

—VERNE CHATELAIN—

At one point, exhausted from yet another prolonged debate over the Hetch Hetchy dam proposal, Senator James Reed of Missouri complained, "The Senate of the United States has devoted a full week of time to discussing the disposition of about two square miles of land located at a point remote from civilization in the very heart of the Sierra Mountains and possessing an intrinsic value of probably not to exceed four or five hundred dollars."[1] Reed's pointed frustration was symbolic of a larger problem for the National Park Service. By 1925, nearly a decade after its establishment and a half century after the creation of the first national park, the National Park Service remained more or less a regional land management agency. Of the forty-three parks and monuments it administered, only one—Acadia National Park in Maine—was in the eastern half of the United States.[2] While most members of the House and Senate appropriations committees generally supported the Park Service and were willing to commit federal funds to maintain existing parks, they were reluctant to continue adding parks to a system that seemed to serve so few Americans.[3] It was true that visitation had grown steadily. By the end of fiscal year 1922, more than one million visitors had enjoyed the parks and nearly 172,000 had seen the monuments.[4] Nonetheless, in the first half of the 1920s, parks and monuments in the West remained for the most part accessible only to the wealthy. Most people had neither the time nor the means to travel west for pleasure. Western politicians saw some economic benefit from the tourist trade, but legislators on the East Coast—and particularly those in the South—grew impatient and unwilling to commit additional time, energy, and federal funds for the disposition of land in areas too remote to benefit most of their constituents.

Regional Tradition, National Heritage

Stephen Mather recognized the problem. If his agency did not begin to manage a truly national landscape, it was in danger of losing property and stature to government bureaus with similar mandates. In his 1923 annual report he wrote, "I should like to see additional national parks established east of the Mississippi, but how this can be accomplished is not clear."[5] Hoping to demonstrate the benefits of national parks to southerners in particular, Mather set as a priority the creation of a national park in a "typical section of the Appalachian Range." Such a park would most certainly have a beneficial economic impact on underdeveloped southern regions, because any well-selected portion of the mountains would be within a day's drive for two-thirds of the American population. As automobile ownership and auto tourism broadened, the park could attract day trippers as well as overnight auto tourists. At Mather's urging, the secretary of the interior created a Southern Appalachian National Park Committee to scout locations. Their inquiries stirred up tremendous popular enthusiasm. Small communities in Tennessee, North Carolina, West Virginia, and Georgia sent testimonials and approving letters to the National Park Service and spearheaded fund-raising efforts for the purchase of land.[6] Mather counted on local support for his expansion effort, and he made note of it in his annual report, writing, "The tremendous popularity of the national parks has impelled progressive people of other states not fortunate in having a National Park within their boundaries to look for scenic areas . . . that might measure up to national park standards."[7]

Nonetheless, the expansion effort met with some resistance, and it exposed knotty philosophical differences about both the future of the National Park Service and "park standards." The Forest Service objected to the imposition of Park Service administration in any of the eastern forests. The secretary of agriculture, Henry C. Wallace, wrote to the chair of the Senate Committee on Agriculture and Forestry, "The region is totally different from that in which the National Park System was conceived and developed. It has been extensively lumbered and the remaining areas of virgin forest are for the most part small and scattered."[8] Ultimately, local enthusiasm trumped the objections of the Forest Service and won over southern politicians. The committee's work resulted in the so-called Three Park Bill and the establishment, in May 1926, of three eastern parks: Shenandoah National Park in Virginia, Great Smoky Mountain National Park in Tennessee and North Carolina, and Mammoth Cave National Park in Kentucky. Nonetheless, Wallace's critique rang true. Most park advocates, including Mather himself, believed that the agency should administer a system of natural areas, selected for outstanding scenery and protected in pristine form. Yet, few unspoiled areas existed east of the Mississippi. Advocacy organizations began to question Mather's standards. Every move to expand the size and number of parks came under scrutiny from private organizations such as the Camp Fire Club of America and the National Parks Association (NPA).[9]

During the nineteenth century, geologists, anthropologists, and other practitioners of natural science had attached meaning and value to scenic but otherwise useless landscapes in the American West, justifying the creation of national parks and national monuments and establishing new categories for federal land management. By the middle of the 1920s, however, it was clear that the Park Service needed a new set of experts to help justify the creation of eastern parks. Mather and Albright invited museum professionals, educators, and, finally, historians, to help them establish standards to guide park selection. Although their original goal was specific—to enable the expansion of Park Service holdings in the East—over time their efforts also redefined the existing parks by overlaying historical meaning onto the older natural and scientific landscapes. History had public value. It became a tool of development, enabling states in the South and Northeast to attract tourists. It provided a canvas on which local boosters could portray regional culture. And, as Verne E. Chatelain, the first Park Service chief historian suggested, it served the public good, encouraging Americans to find their place in the nation.[10] The Park Service history program transformed vernacular landscapes and local traditions into components of a national heritage.

Education and Expansion

Pressure from private advocacy organizations forced the National Park Service to reconsider both the qualities and the value of parks. By the late 1920s Robert Sterling Yard, executive secretary of the NPA, was among the most vocal critics of expansion. Yard's position likely surprised Mather. The two men had been friends since the 1890s, and Yard had served as the best man at Mather's 1893 wedding.[11] In the early decades of the twentieth century, Yard had been a reporter and editor at the *New York Sun* and the *New York Herald* before rising to the position of editor in chief at *Century Magazine*. He was a vocal supporter of national parks, and he and Mather shared a common commitment to "scenic parks and scenic values."[12] In 1915 Mather enticed him away from Century, paying him privately to work as director of publicity for the Park Service. When new government regulations prevented Mather from paying Yard's salary, Mather provided the funds to establish the NPA and transitioned publicity work to the organization. As executive secretary, Yard published a regular circular, promoting tourism in the parks and explaining the value of protected lands. In his 1919 Book of the National Parks, dedicated to Mather, he wrote, "The national parks of America include areas of the noblest and most diversified scenic sublimity easily accessible in the world. . . . The American people is [sic] waking rapidly to the magnitude of its scenic possession; it has yet to learn to appreciate it."[13]

Mather and Yard believed the Park Service mission was to teach people to appreciate nature. Horace Albright had emphasized education in his earliest statements of policy, and the educational value of the parks was reiterated by successive secretaries of the interior. Unlike Albright, however, Yard and Mather viewed education as an intrinsic value, a quality of nature itself, not a programmatic imperative. Mather and Yard viewed the parks as "museums of nature" and conceived NPA publicity as a tool for training Americans to appreciate them. Yard explained, "When we speak of education in connection with our national parks we mean two things. One is the education of the people to the glories and the magnificence and the uses of their national parks; the other is how the national parks can be used for the education and inspiration of the people."[14] Yard and Mather believed, simply, that exposure to nature would inspire visitors to relent in their undignified search for recreation and accept nature conservation as a more important national value. They found an articulate supporter in John

C. Merriam, a founder of the Save the Redwoods League, renowned pale-ontologist, and Park Service enthusiast. Merriam argued that only expo-sure to the "higher values" expressed by nature in national parks could enlighten visitors to appropriate park use, guaranteeing the "unbroken maintenance of primitive conditions."[15]

Park superintendents often advocated a more pragmatic approach to education, one that would connect the parks to classrooms, attract more visitors, and, as a result, promise greater appropriations. During their 1922 conference, park superintendents passed a resolution agreeing that parks should "supplement the work of schools by opening the doors of Nature's laboratory, to awaken an interest in natural science as an adjunct to the commercial and industrial work of the world." Educational development of this type floundered while Mather was focused on expanding the number and location of parks, however. Indeed, the superintendents had made their pledge as part of an acknowledgement that "the educational and economic value of the national parks to the nation is restricted by insufficient [pro-grammatic] development."[16]

Mather recognized the value of educational programming even more as he pushed to expand Park Service holdings in the East. The inspirational qualities of some landscapes were not so obvious to the untrained eye. The Park Service pursuit of less visibly stunning landscapes strained the friend-ship between Mather and Yard. In Yard's assessment, most of the eastern parks failed to meet high standards of scenic beauty. He feared their inclu-sion in the National Park system would endanger the future of the agency. While Mather worked to create a truly national collection of parks, the NPA and other conservation organizations envisioned a lean and focused service, one that protected a small number of pristine natural landscapes. Yard believed that the creation of parks in the East threatened this vision: "In magnificence of included scenery, in variety, in scientific importance and in ample spaciousness, these parks must do justice to the National Park System. None but the noblest examples, painstakingly chosen, must be admitted."[17] At first, Mather was entirely supportive of this statement of standards promoted by the NPA. He echoed Yard's language in the 1923 report, insisting, "National Parks . . . must continue to constitute areas con-taining scenery of supreme and distinctive quality or some natural feature so extraordinary or unique as to be of national interest and importance as distinguished from merely local interest. The national park system as now constituted must not be lowered in standard, dignity, [or] prestige."[18]

By 1926, however, Mather and Yard had begun to disagree about what constituted "distinctive quality" and "national importance" in the consideration of new park properties. Yard wanted to protect the Park Service "trademark": "When Zion National Park was created in 1919, the whole world knew from the simple announcement of the fact that another stupendous scenic wonderland had been discovered. But when pleasant wooded summits, limestone caves, pretty local ravines, local mountains and gaps between mountains become National Parks, the name 'Zion National Park' will mean nothing at home or abroad."[19] While he approved of Great Smoky Mountain National Park, he was less enthusiastic about the creation of Shenandoah: "Areas better fitted for national parks than Shenandoah have been turned down. It can be duplicated anywhere in the Appalachians. . . . Looking to the future, the Shenandoah Park is going to raise an avalanche of bills in Congress to produce national park areas that are really state parks—commercial propositions. A different standard for the East is going to appear."[20]

In many respects, Yard was correct. Different standards of value were already attached to the eastern landscape. In large part, that was a result of the Civil War. Military operations had shifted from West to East, leaving men of science to define the value of the landscape beyond the Mississippi River while the events of the Civil War sanctified eastern forests and fields, by turning them into battlefields and cemeteries or by constructing forts and earthworks. Since the 1890s the War Department had managed a large number of these sites east of the Mississippi. Battlefields may not have embodied the kind of visible, intrinsic, and universal values Yard preferred, but they certainly appealed to tourists and commemorative societies. Beginning in the 1890s the Civil War battlefields had been a stage for the performance of patriotic identity. Veterans associations and their sister organizations held reunions of troops from both the Union and Confederate troops. Carefully choreographed reenactments helped convey the message that the soldiers on both sides were noble, committed to the same American values and united by the common experience of battle.[21]

The popularity of these events and of the battlefields themselves created an opportunity for the Park Service, one that Horace Albright had recognized early on. During his tenure as acting director in 1917, Albright had argued that the War Department sites should come under Park Service control. Albright, noting that it was the National Park Service, not the War Department, to whom potential visitors turned for information about battlefield hours and programs, argued, "The question is whether these parks should not also be placed under this department in order that they may be administered as a part of the park system. The interesting features of each of these parks are their historic associations, although several of them possess important scenic qualities."[22] War Department officials doubted that an agency, primarily dedicated to the protection of nature, was equipped for the task of preserving historic places.[23] Albright tried to overcome this perception, arguing that the agency already managed historic properties: "Many of the monuments and at least three of the national parks were established to preserve the ruins of structures that have historic associations of absorbing interest, or to mark the scene of an important event in history."[24] The NPA fought efforts to incorporate historic properties into the National Park holdings. In Yard's estimation, these places were, at best, associated with locally significant events. They embodied an entirely different set of standards that might justify the creation of a separate system for management by a different agency, but their inclusion in the National Park Service would only dilute park standards and destroy the value of the Park Service trademark.[25]

On the ground, however, visionary superintendents and strong-willed custodians had begun to recognize that the trademark operated less as an intrinsic value and more as a programmatic policy. They had implemented campfire talks, guided tours, formal educational partnerships, and park museums to protect vulnerable landscapes and explain the value of the Park Service brand. The highly visible and successful work in museum development conducted by Jesse Nusbaum at Mesa Verde and Ansel Hall at Yosemite slowly began to translate into a broader educational initiative. Chauncey J. Hamlin, president of the American Association of Museums, had met Hall in late August 1921 during a brief visit to Yosemite. Hall made an impression on Hamlin, who asked him to accompany his son, Chan Hamlin, on an extensive tour of Europe beginning in August 1923. Hall and the young Hamlin traveled for a full year, and Hall took the opportunity to explore national museums in all the major European cities to develop a model for a system of park museums.

Impressed by Hall's intellectual approach, Hamlin established a Committee on Museums in National Parks designed to bolster Hall's ideas. The committee reviewed the educational potential of park museums and proposed establishing natural history museums in each of the larger parks.[26] The committee concluded that these museums would prepare "the visitor for a profitable sojourn within the reservation, thus enabling him the better to understand the physiography, the fauna and flora, and, in short, preparing him to use these parks and their resources as instruments of instruction."[27] The American Association of Museums presented the report to the Laura Spellman Rockefeller Memorial Foundation and secured two important grants: $5,000 for the committee to continue its work and $70,500 for the completion of the Yosemite museum. This report encouraged the National Park Service to implement a centralized museum program under Hall's charge, a significant step in the professionalization of park interpretation. The project was both celebrated and popularized in the magazine *Science,* which reported enthusiastically that the "new and modernly equipped institution ... is expected to become one of the greatest treasures of scientific and natural history exhibits."[28]

The creation of a museum program also had important consequences for enabling Park Service expansion beyond scenery and science and into history. The association's recognition that museums might serve as instruments of instruction, and the extent to which that conclusion attracted generous philanthropic giving, changed Stephen Mather's understanding of education. He began to recognize Park Service expansion as something that required more than the acquisition of real estate. At Mather's request, the secretary of the interior, Roy O. West, appointed a committee to study "educational problems" in the National Park Service. The committee, which included John C. Merriam, was composed of men who each had an impressive scientific career. Several had also distinguished themselves in government work. Harold C. Bryant, a paleontologist and naturalist, had developed guide programs for Glacier and Yosemite National Parks. Hermon Bumpus, a biologist, was the first director of the American Museum of Natural History, a founder of the American Association of Museums, and a strong advocate for park museums. Vernon Kellogg, an entomologist and founder of the National Research Council, had held several government positions. Frank R. Oastler, a medical doctor, had been among the first to explore Glacier National Park. Funded by another grant from the Laura Spellman Rockefeller Memorial Foundation, the committee undertook a massive field study of educational programs at Park Service sites.[29] Committee members became convinced that the piecemeal, park specific approach to educational programming had created uneven quality and exacerbated the unequal distribution of money in the parks.

The committee's preliminary report, issued in January 1929, compelled the National Park Service to improve both external relationships and internal professionalism and provided Mather with a stronger base from which to justify expansion. The committee recommended the creation of a permanent educational advisory board composed of outside experts as well as the establishment of a Park Service education division in Washington, "directed by a man with the best of scientific and educational qualifications," a professional, not a political, appointee.[30] The work of implementing this plan would have to fall to someone other than Stephen Mather, however. He suffered a stroke in 1928, and Horace Albright stepped in to aid his ailing friend for a second time, gradually taking over day-to-day responsibilities. Mather resigned on January 12, 1929, and Albright officially accepted the position as director of the National Park Service, just days after the Committee on Educational Problems in the National Parks had issued its preliminary report. Mather died a year later.

As director, Albright asked the committee to expand its inquiry, exploring the viability of historical education as a responsibility of the National Park Service. The committee resumed its work at the start of Herbert Hoover's administration on March 4, adding two new members: the geographer Wallace W. Atwood, president of Clark University, and the ethnologist Clark Wissler, a curator at the American Museum of Natural History and professor of anthropology at Yale. Each member of the committee selected a particular topic and group of parks to study. The research conducted by Clark Wissler would prove to be particularly crucial. He embarked on a tour of the Park Service archaeological sites, including Mesa Verde, and took responsibility for conducting a "special study of the problem of the National Parks as they may teach the greater lessons of human history." In the two decades since the passage of the Antiquities Act, the archaeological sites and national monuments had been more or less controlled by scientific interests. Wissler proposed that such sites might provide a "great opportunity for appreciation of the nature and meaning of history."[31] Wissler's words would prove to have a profound effect on the expansion of both park holdings and educational programming in the area of history.

While the committee engaged in its final study, Horace Albright sought formal approval from Congress and the president for a plan to centralize control of existing historic properties under the Park Service. Albright and Yard had rather different perspectives on where the sympathies of incoming President Herbert Hoover and key members of his cabinet might lie. The near simultaneous change in the presidential and Park Service administrations presented Albright with precisely the opportunity he needed to start fresh, arguing that the distribution of monuments and sites among various federal agencies was inefficient and expensive. The NPA understood Albright's larger agenda, however, and they believed Hoover would prove to be their ally. Reports in the NPA information circular interpreted comments Hoover had made while secretary of commerce in 1924 as evidence that he shared the group's dedication to scenic standards: "My own thought is that the national parks—the parks within the responsibility of the Federal Government should be those of outstanding scientific and spiritual appeal, those that are unique in their stimulation and inspiration."[32] The NPA was also enthusiastic about Hoover's key cabinet choices, particularly Ray Lyman Wilbur as secretary of the interior. "There is no uncertainty about his attitude," the NPA reported. "'The standard for the creation of a national park is a high one,' he has stated, 'and it must be maintained by the exclusion of scenic areas possessing merely local appeal and not having the essential element of national interest.'"[33]

Albright, however, was well acquainted with Wilbur, as well as with Hoover's new secretary of war, James W. Good. As chair of the House Appropriations Committee during the 1920s, Good had led an inspection tour of the national parks. He had spent considerable time at Yellowstone while Albright was superintendent there.[34] Wilbur had been the president of Stanford University and one of the original members of the State Park Commission in Albright's home state of California. Albright leveraged his personal connections with both men, meeting with them to advance the cause of Park Service expansion. In short order, he won their support for his plan to centralize control of the existing national monuments and the various battlefield parks under the National Park Service. During the summer and fall of 1929, Albright and Wilbur crafted a reorganization plan for the Department of the Interior, defining three areas of departmental responsibility: protection of public lands, development of natural resources, and implementation of educational initiatives. Albright wrote the Park Service portion of the reorganization plan, taking the opportunity to make a strong case for the transfer of historically significant sites.

In the meantime, Robert Sterling Yard and the NPA continued to lobby against the effort, arguing that "ignorant and local-minded" influences should be kept out of the park system.[35] Yard's assessment of historic preservation was harsh, but not entirely incorrect. Historic preservation remained largely a local venture, driven by idiosyncratic evaluations of beauty and vernacular expressions of patriotism.[36] During the years between the two world wars, nostalgia for a near-imaginary bucolic past provided a respite from postwar disappointments and an antidote to the hedonism sparked by the booming economy and youth-oriented culture. Wealthy elites began to engage in historic preservation as a hobby. John D. Rockefeller, whose tremendous wealth came from his family's monopoly of the oil industry, made the restoration of Williamsburg, Virginia, his pet project. Beginning in 1926 Rockefeller's reconstructed colonial village capitalized on the popular colonial revival movement in architecture and furniture and reflected the growing popularity of American history. The sesquicentennial of the Declaration of Independence in 1926, commemorations of the Revolutionary War, and celebrations of the bicentennial of George Washington's birth reinvigorated a movement by patriotic associations across the country—including the Daughters of the American Revolution and other women's preservation groups—to mark historic sites, claiming a special place in the nation's past for just about every small town. Henry Ford, whose automobile industry had ushered in modern America, opened Greenfield Village in 1929, a museum complex designed to celebrate the slower pace of a lost agricultural America.

The rise of popular history coincided with the growing maturity of the discipline of history. The first professors of history had joined the faculties of American colleges and universities in the 1870s, but by the end of the century a high percentage of American historians were still pursuing graduate education overseas.[37] Prior to 1882 no U.S. institution of higher learning offered a doctoral degree in history. The earliest programs to do so—Johns Hopkins University and Yale University—granted the first recognized history PhDs that year to John Franklin Jameson and Clarence Bowen respectively. Jameson proved particularly influential in setting the tone and agenda in the development of the discipline, leading efforts to establish the American Historical Association. The AHA sought to advance historical scholarship in the United States, and members established a journal, developed a mechanism for peer review, and gradually expanded the number and influence of formally trained historians. By 1929 thirty-nine history programs across the country offered doctoral degrees in history, and the number of history PhDs awarded grew annually.[38]

At the same time, by the late 1920s most professionally trained historians had begun to distance themselves from historical commemorations and from historic preservation. AHA leadership was not blind to the importance of identifying and protecting historic resources, but they were focused almost exclusively on documents. Between 1900 and 1917 the AHA undertook a massive program to survey public records held by various state institutions to ensure that the documents were accessible to scholars, and John Franklin Jameson began lobbying for the establishment of a National Archives building. Jameson and his colleagues saw the protection of public records as a necessary step for ensuring the continued advancement of the discipline. In the same way that nineteenth-century museum collections had contributed to the professionalization of various natural sciences, a national collection of documents and manuscripts, Jameson argued, would provide the material necessary to bolster the expertise of historians. The National Archives would serve as a "powerful agency in the development of American scholarship."[39]

Yet Jameson's philosophy departed in meaningful ways from that of early curators of scientific collections, particularly those in the Park Service. Those professionals had sought to balance the interests of science against the interests of the public and had put collections on display for average visitors. Jameson was insistent in his belief that the responsibility of the federal government to protect nationally significant documents was entirely distinct from the growing popularity of the past. Advising colleagues about how best to ensure Congress would fund the archives building, Jameson commented "these things are matters with which public opinion has little to do." His lack of interest in the general public was reflected in his lobbying strategy. He was confident—incorrectly as it turned out—that he would be more successful once Republicans controlled the White House and Congress, stating, "I think Republicans are a little more interested in things like good filing systems than the Democrats are, because they come more largely from urban centers and less largely from Squashville and Podunk."[40]

For Albright, however, the popular appeal and locally defined significance of historic properties did not undermine their value. They were simply problems to be solved with careful planning and professionalism. Clark Wissler's recommendations to the Committee on Educational Problems in the National Parks provided the necessary roadmap. In the committee's final report, issued on November 29, 1929, Wissler articulated the case for Park Service control of historic sites. His report to the committee laid out a framework for historic site selection as well as interpretation. He proposed that the Park Service develop a plan to identify new historic sites that might "serve as indices of periods in the historical sequence of human life in America." He envisioned educational programming for historic places that combined site-specific narratives with contextualizing background. In addition, Wissler acknowledged that sites previously identified as scientific could be reimagined as historical, and he suggested, "a selection should be made of a number of existing monuments which . . . may, as points of reference, define the general outline of man's career on this continent."[41]

Trained as an ethnologist, not a historian, Wissler recognized that "man's career" was not always reported in documents. More often, it was represented in material remains. His report served as an intellectual linchpin, connecting Jesse Nusbaum's museum work to the establishment of a service-wide history program. In much the same way that Nusbaum had caused archaeological artifacts to "lose their meaning," Wissler redefined entire archaeological landscapes, recontextualizing them as part of a broad historical narrative, and finally undoing (at least philosophically) the artificial distinction between "prehistory" and "history." Furthermore, illuminating the historical qualities of monuments in the American Southwest helped justify the establishment of historic monuments in the East by eliminating the perceived distinction between scientific and historical sites implied by the language of the Antiquities Act. While the act had presumed these qualities to be intrinsic to the monuments, the committee report, and Wissler's portion in particular, understood the problem of education as programmatic. Integrating monuments and historic sites into the Park Service collection required the creation of an explanatory narrative, one that might help visitors recognize a logical structure on otherwise isolated and unintelligible places. Most important, crafting a new narrative would require the creation of new professional categories in the upper echelons of Park Service management.

National economic changes put Albright's plans on hold, unfortunately. Hoover had accepted both the plan to reorganize the Department of the Interior and the argument to shift administrative control of most of the monuments and the War Department sites to the National Park Service, but the stock market crash in October 1929 delayed further action.[42] As the Depression took hold, President Hoover folded Albright's ideas into his proposed panacea for the economic crisis, arguing that government streamlining would cut costs and decrease spending. As his popularity sank among legislators and voters, however, Hoover found it impossible to pass any of his proposals through Congress. Transfer of the War Department's collection to the Park Service was put on hold, and Albright looked outside the federal government for support.

He found a lively historical program and important allies just next door, in the state of Virginia. William E. Carson, head of the state's Conservation Commission, took Albright on a tour of the historic markers his group had erected along Virginia highways. He also arranged for Albright to tour historic sites along the James River and to visit Colonial Williamsburg as the guest of John D. Rockefeller. Albright and Rockefeller had much in common. Rockefeller had a long history of commitment to the National Park Service, and he had dedicated a considerable amount of money to the development of park roads and museums. He had also thrown his support behind Park Service administrators in the often-contentious battles to acquire new parks or expand park boundaries. Albright shared Rockefeller's sensibilities as well as his disdain for those who opposed efforts to make the parks more accessible. Privately, they dismissed members of the NPA and others of like mind as "purists."[43] The two men joined forces. Rockefeller put together a plan to connect Colonial Williamsburg to other historically significant places in Virginia by the construction of a scenic highway. Albright lobbied Congress and the president to extend federal protections to historic sites in Virginia connected to George Washington and the Revolutionary War. As a result, in 1930 two national monuments were established in Virginia by executive order. The George Washington Birthplace National Monument, although almost immediately discredited, was established on January 23, 1930.[44] Colonial National Monument, established on July 3, 1930, preserves both Yorktown Battlefield and a portion of Jamestown Island, the original English colony.[45] The first two historians in the National Park Service— Elbert Cox and B. Floyd Flickinger—joined the staff at Colonial.[46]

With the creation of these two sites, Albright succeeded in implementing his plan for Park Service expansion. He sought to capitalize immediately on his success. He toured a variety of historic areas, trying to gauge their worthiness for inclusion in the Park Service collection, including Saint Augustine and Castillo de San Marcos in Florida and Scotts Bluff in Nebraska. Wisely, he also heaped praise on Rockefeller, working to keep his patron's loyalty attached to the development of a history program. He corresponded frequently with the donor, giving him credit for "the Colonial Historical Park . . . , the educational program of the Service with its museums, [and] the purchase of lands at George Washington's Birthplace." He described these milestones as "outstanding achievements of my administration" and he gave Rockefeller credit for his success[47] At the same time, if Albright had Rockefeller to thank for enabling physical expansion, he owed as much to Clark Wissler for fostering programmatic expansion. Convincing Congress or the president to designate additional historic monuments or parks would involve more than simply Rockefeller money or popular approval (which became more difficult to come by as the Depression worsened); it would require professional assessment. Wissler's report provided him with the outlines of a philosophical and administrative framework in which to construct a collection of historic places for the National Park Service.

Shortly after the creation of Colonial National Monument, Albright implemented the specific recommendations made by Wissler and other members of the Committee on Educational Problems. He created a Branch of Research and Education, selecting Harold Bryant to serve as the assistant director. Next, he began his search for just the right man to head the historical division under Bryant.[48] He found him in Dr. Verne Chatelain, "a professional historian with experience in research, interpretation, and report writing."[49] Born in 1895 in York, Nebraska, "right smack in the middle of Western history," Chatelain had nursed a fascination with history from the time he was a child. "That country in which I was born reeks with history—western trails, the story of Lewis and Clark and the Missouri River, and the development of the Railroads west of the Mississippi River; the Indian story, the Civil War in relationship to Kansas, the Underground Railroad into Nebraska—so my community was much interested in history." Chatelain had followed his passion to Peru State Teachers College and then to graduate school. He earned an MA in history at the University of Chicago and a PhD in the history of policy at the University of Minnesota. At the time he was hired by the Park Service, he was teaching history at Peru State.[50] He arrived in Washington on September 10, 1931, without, he claimed, "any preconceived ideas about things. I had only the most casual conversations with Mr. Albright. . . . I had to get my feet on the ground."[51]

Once on the ground, Chatelain quickly assessed the problem. The Park Service had assembled a collection of historic sites and archaeological monuments—now combined under his authority—but "no one had any clear idea of what ought to be done" with them.[52] Bryant, Chatelain concluded, was "a very great Park Service man, in my opinion, but a man who was trained in the western park point of view and who was a scenic park man." The program for scenic parks was, Chatelain thought, already quite well developed by the time he arrived, but history as a responsibility of a federal land–management agency was "a completely undeveloped field . . . and the thinking of the Park Service people was generally with reference to scenic parks and scenic values, rather than historical values."[53] Chatelain had little experience in the national parks, so Albright sent him on a tour of the Southwest in November 1931. He visited Mesa Verde National Park and spent some time with Jesse Nusbaum.[54] During the tour, Chatelain praised Nusbaum and interacted frequently with Frank Pinkley, but he still "found very little evidence of any kind of program which served as an example or precedent for what we wanted to do."[55] He was struck by the novelty of his work, recalling, "While it would parallel the scenic program of the Park Service to a certain extent, I knew that there were major points of differ-ence." The difference for Chatelain came partially from his sense of isolation as a historian in the Park Service. He was "pretty much by myself except for a couple of fellows down in Yorktown." It also came from his effort to develop a new approach to historical programming.[56]

A Completely Undeveloped Field

At first, Chatelain had understood his job would be to develop a history education program for the Park Service. As he surveyed the variety of his-toric properties, archaeological monuments, and natural parks held by the federal government, however, he recognized that the task was much big-ger. "There was a great deal to be done in the way of investigating areas, of presenting—from the standpoint of the Park Service—a rather complete picture of American history." The Park Service historical program could harness historical research and education as a tool for transforming a rather disconnected group of regionally significant places into a truly national collection. In light of this, Chatelain's task of education began with his superiors. His immediate supervisor, Harold Bryant, "didn't know a thing about the historical program." But Chatelain found tremendous support from the members of the advisory board on park service education, who counseled him to "build slowly but to strike out boldly." With some con-vincing, "Bryant and Albright both began to see that this wasn't merely an educational program; that it was a development program."[57]

Although he found enthusiasm inside the Park Service, Chatelain felt detached from his professional peers. Historians had become increasingly divided into two camps. By the second decade of the twentieth century, a significant and growing number were employed as directors, curators, and archivists in historical societies, managing collections and producing scholarship related to local history. They actively engaged local fraternal organizations and patriotic groups in the effort to identify and preserve the past. AHA leadership was dominated by traditional-minded scholars who valued published work made relevant by its focus on nationally significant events and individuals. Traditionalists were disdainful of the provincialism in state and local historical societies. They believed that special interest organizations lacked objectivity and gathered collections with sentimental rather than scientific value. The close relationship curators maintained with community-based groups ensured that historical societies were well-funded and useful, but most traditionalists were uninterested in making history more popular or accessible for the masses.[58] The pragmatism that marked historical work at the local and regional level is often associated with Carl L. Becker, who served as president of the American Historical Association in 1931. His presidential address that year famously defined history is an act of memory, applied with purpose by Mr. Everyman in the performance of everyday activities.[59]

Becker's broadly democratic notion of history shocked traditionalists, but it did not usher in a new era. Rather, he recognized and acknowledged the work conducted by local and regional historians in an effort to end lingering and mutual hostilities among scholars. This animosity had a material impact on the profession. Although museum directors and curators might be eligible for membership in the AHA, their visibility and influence was limited.[60] They were relegated to the least prestigious committee assignments and kept out of leadership positions. John Franklin Jameson, as editor of the *American Historical Review,* regularly rejected articles on local history as "antiquarian," too limited in scope to achieve broader relevance.[61] Regional historians pushed back against the lack of recognition and respect by organizing a separate professional association in 1907.[62] Seven representatives from state archives and historical societies in Nebraska, Montana, Kansas, Iowa, Missouri, and Minnesota formed the Mississippi Valley Historical Association (which later became the Organization of American Historians). Following the lead of the AHA, the MVHA set standards of professionalism and created a journal to facilitate peer review and publishing. The regional focus of the MVHA only reinforced Jameson's disciplinary chauvinism: "The American Historical Association people, and instructed persons in the West . . . have watched [the development of the MVHA] with something of the same distrust with which a sagacious pointer would examine a turtle. I doubt if it will do any harm."[63]

Ultimately, the work conducted by Verne Chatelain was more directly successful than any effort made by Carl Becker in forging a new link between the agendas of historians in the MVHA and the AHA. Regional historians harnessed the energy of local clubs and preservation associations to help identify, collect, and preserve specific pasts. More traditional-minded historians worked to identify large patterns in the development of a common past.[64] In developing a history program for the National Park Service, Chatelain would necessarily do both. As he embarked on this task, he recalled, "I got very little real help from so called historical architects, from archaeologists or from historians. I could not turn to agencies like the American Historical Association and get any good ideas."[65] Instead, he drew on his own experience. During graduate studies in Minnesota, Chatelain had worked with Solon J. Buck, a scholar of American agricultural history. Buck is perhaps best remembered as the second Archivist of the United States, but between 1914 and 1931, he juggled two positions as a professor of history and superintendent of the Minnesota Historical Society. He was active in the MVHA, and he had served as its president in 1923. As his research assistant in 1929, Chatelain acted as assistant superintendent at the society for about eighteen months.[66]

The Minnesota Historical Society's origins were not much different from those of historical societies established on the East Coast in the nineteenth century. Created in 1849, the society's mission was to collect and preserve Minnesota's official records, to document the transition toward statehood. Like antecedents in the East, the Minnesota Historical Society also occasionally gathered materials that documented the state's antiquity. For example, in the late 1860s members capitalized on growing interest in ethnology by supporting a study of the Dakota language undertaken by Smithsonian linguists. The society was run entirely by volunteers until 1869, when J. Fletcher Williams became the first paid curator. Williams focused his attention on documenting Minnesota's political history and seeking donations of money and official papers from the state's leaders. At first, collections were stored in unused rooms in the capitol. After the building burned in 1881, the society spent years searching for an appropriate, fireproof space and pressing the legislature for designation as the state's official archives. In 1914 the American Historical Association sent the agricultural historian Herbert Kellar to review the society's collections. He reported on the dire conditions in which they were stored and pressed the state to extend stronger protections to the documents. Solon Buck emerged as the champion for the Minnesota Historical Society, moving the collections to the university campus until a new museum was dedicated on the sixtieth anniversary of Minnesota's statehood in 1918.[67] A year later a state law authorized the society to act as a repository for state documents.[68] After taking over as director, Buck expanded the scope of local history work in Minnesota, and Chatelain witnessed firsthand the important role that history might play in facilitating community identity.

Solon Buck defended his so-called antiquarian interests by arguing that all American history was, in fact, regional history. American history teachers and writers were, in his estimation, simply preoccupied with "the local history of New England and Virginia," mistaking it for the national past.[69] His arguments fell on deaf ears, as historical societies and archives began to formalize the effort to collect and preserve official state documents, and the AHA returned its focus to issues of national history.[70] Regional historians defined their success in different terms, distancing themselves from the limitations imposed by the AHA. Clarence Alvord, who served as president of the MVHA in 1908 and as editor of its journal from 1914 to 1923, commented, "The whole movement in western and southwestern history grew up to manhood without much recognition from the American Historical Association."[71] Buck credited historical societies for successfully transforming local history into mainstream history, and he challenged Minnesotans to follow the lead of states like Massachusetts, home to more than three hundred local historical societies by 1922.[72]

Driven by this goal, Buck oversaw a massive expansion of the society's activities. Prior to his arrival, society meetings had focused primarily on business matters, and historical content was typically an afterthought, a keynote address during dinner. Buck made a radical departure from this formula in 1921. He used the annual meeting as a platform to launch a comprehensive plan for promoting and coordinating historical activities across the state. The meeting provided attendees with specific instructions for collecting, preserving, and managing historical records. Willoughby Babcock Jr., curator of the society's collections, urged hereditary and patriotic societies to partner with the society, allowing the professional curatorial staff to coordinate and correlate their work, while guarding against duplication and ensuring thorough coverage of state history. Because the society lacked sufficient space, R. W. G. Vail, the society's librarian, urged schools, churches, libraries, women's clubs, farmer's organizations, and other local groups to establish historical societies in their own communities. He pledged to support these local institutions,

providing guidance for the preservation of vital local records. Invited speakers contextualized the society's proposal, describing model programs in other
states. Joseph Schafer, superintendent of the State Historical Society of
Wisconsin, described the work of the local Daughters of the American
Revolution, which had created signage to mark historic sites and trails.
Shafer argued, "Most people are tremendously interested in themselves, in
their families, and in what their relatives have done, and by taking advantage
of these natural interests it would be possible to build up historical-minded-
ness among the people of our own and the next generation."[73]

Throughout the 1920s women's clubs and patriotic associations played a
central role in preserving state history. They were acknowledged frequently
in annual Minnesota Historical Society reports, particularly for their role
in keeping the society afloat financially. Members of the Minnesota DAR
and similar organizations testified before the state legislature to obtain
state funds, and they financed various preservation projects. DAR members
also focused their substantial energy on historic preservation in Minnesota.
Their work began with Sibley House, home of the first territorial governor,
Henry Hastings Sibley. The majority of the state's DAR chapters contributed to the restoration of the building, aiming to transform the house into
the "Mount Vernon of Minnesota." They gathered furniture "of the type
it contained when occupied by General Sibley."[74] Women also made an
effort to remind the Historical Society staff of the importance and validity
of their work. In June 1922 the museum hosted a special meeting of the
Ladies Shakespeare Club, which presented the Historical Society with "an
enlarged photograph, appropriately framed, of the late Professor Emeritus
Maria Sanford of the University of Minnesota."[75]

Chatelain was impressed by the society's pioneering work in bringing
historic sites under the banner of state history.[76] He conducted a formal
study to measure the impact of heritage groups on the systematic production of state history. At the Historical Society's annual meeting in 1929, he
presented the results of his study, detailing the influence of popular history
on the expansion of historical professionalism. At the turn of the twentieth
century, he found, most historical activity had been privately financed, but
public support began to grow during the Progressive Era as part of the
push for public education. The first substantial trend in this direction came
in the West, with Wisconsin serving as a model. By the end of the 1920s
a number of states across the country had implemented comprehensive
schemes of public financing for history. He concluded that the availability

of public money had a positive impact: "Public financing will stimulate and produce a more comprehensive scheme and will be better adapted to carrying the message of history to all the people."[77]

Chatelain's conclusions conveyed quite logically to the Park Service. Indeed, it was the eighteen months Chatelain had spent as assistant superintendent in Minnesota that most interested Albright. Chatelain surmised, "I think it was a case perhaps of Albright looking over the field, checking into some things perhaps that I had done in Minnesota, and maybe talking to one or two people like Sol J. Buck who knew me very well."[78] He drew on his experiences in Minnesota to develop a model he might apply to Albright's vision for expansion. In Minnesota, curators, librarians, and historians had helped patriotic societies and women's clubs recognize the larger patterns, coordinating local efforts to clarify an overarching narrative of state history. Similarly, Chatelain envisioned himself as a coordinator, helping to build the educational program in all of the parks, historic and scenic alike.[79] It was a good starting point, but it was an imperfect fit. In Minnesota, Buck had been able to start more or less from scratch, providing enthusiastic organizations with new tools for selecting and protecting historic resources. Chatelain's task in the Park Service was somewhat more complicated. Located in different states, preserved by different organizations, and associated with different, regionally specific values and meanings, the historic properties held or coveted by the National Park Service each presented unique challenges that the imposition of historical values might help overcome.

Historical Mindedness

The challenge of integrating locally significant places into a national collection became obvious almost immediately, and it required a more complex calculation of expertise than either traditional or pragmatic historians had to offer. The creation of Colonial National Monument had put the National Park Service into conflict with members of the APVA. Federal control of Yorktown Battlefield was not terribly controversial, but the park boundaries extended onto Jamestown Island. The older and most influential members of the organization considered Jamestown their "sacred charge" and a source of "inspiration." For them, it was a site that demonstrated America's place at the pinnacle of white civilization.[80] They led pilgrimages of schoolchildren to the site, organized elaborate pageants, and erected plaques and monuments to commemorate the deeds of individual Jamestown leaders and families. The seizure of Jamestown by the National Park Service stirred lingering sectional differences marked by a general distrust of the federal government, what one adviser called an "old and natural feeling in the south." At the park's creation, Albright had won the trust of many of the younger female members of the APVA members, but they did not wish to "ride roughshod over the opposition or hesitation of certain influential members."[81]

The National Park Service was no stranger to boundary disputes, but the stakeholders at Jamestown were fighting something more complicated than private property. APVA members conceded that the site of the first colonial settlement was nationally significant, and therefore appropriate for management by a federal agency. Identifying its location became a priority.[82] The APVA and Park Service disagreed, however, about the best method of discovery. The local history organization had relied on written and oral sources, including property records and family narratives, which suggested that the first fort and settlement had been located east of the lands held by APVA. Association board members repeatedly argued that this evidence should shift Park Service attention away from their property. Seeking a stronger platform for asserting its authority, the Park Service turned to the Smithsonian Institution for support. Frank Setzler, the curator of archaeology at the Smithsonian Institution, recommended a scientist—J. C. Harrington— to direct site research. Harrington implemented a systematic program of archaeological research at Colonial that required him to conduct excavations on both Park Service and APVA property. His initial report refuted long-held beliefs about the location of the original settlement: "The six months' extensive excavations at the site . . . indicate quite definitely that the first settlement was not at that location. This is indicated by the complete lack of seventeenth-century artifacts of any description, and the fact that no structural remains or soil disturbances from palisades or wooden houses were found."[83] The report convinced APVA members that their historical approach had been flawed. Ellen Smith and Ellen Bagby were sufficiently moved by the findings to recommend that the association conduct a thorough review of its "archaeological problems."[84]

Chatelain viewed the problem at Colonial somewhat differently. The site had been created before the Park Service had developed a system for historical programming. Under these conditions, his task was necessarily twofold. He had to define a program of work for historians in the existing parks, and he had to develop a set of standards to guide future site selection. He explained, "It is unsound, uneconomical and detrimental to a historical system and policy to study each individual area when presented and without reference to the entire scheme of things. The setting up of standards for national historical sites and the listing and classification of areas pertinent to the development of the Nation seems of the utmost importance." To establish standards, Chatelain first had to gather information about the number and scope of historically significant places around the country. By the spring of 1933 he and Floyd Flickinger had begun a comprehensive survey of historic sites. It was a daunting task: "Each state has literally scores of places, some of them hundreds. In its survey of strictly military sites, for example, the War Department had under its consideration approximately 7000 sites. Historic places other than military constitute another imposing aggregate." Accumulating information about these places—most of which had been preserved by the actions of some small club or local organization—was, Chatelain argued, a bit like examining a jigsaw puzzle: "Each isolated piece by itself means little. The complete picture, if we are not aware of the various pieces that make it up, is only mildly interesting. The psychological appeal of the jigsaw puzzle . . . is in the fact that many pieces, having variety in shape and color, can be fitted together. How that is to be done is the puzzle, just as how our society has come to have a particular form or pattern in America is the historical problem."[85]

Chatelain also recognized that jigsaw puzzles were misleading. Any of several patterns might reveal themselves in the pieces. In assembling a history policy it might be tempting to focus on the pieces, settling on a single pattern to guide site selection and therefore acquiring every site affiliated with a president, every home associated with a prominent American, every major battlefield, and every military monument. Chatelain advocated an entirely different approach: "The historical work of the National Park Service is dependent upon the acquisition of an historical mind by those who control its administration, or at least upon their willingness to leave the problem to the historically minded. . . . Unless there is a real philosophy of history, it will be easy enough to spend our time in academic discussions over this or that museum or antiquarian problem, and never seriously tackle the bigger task."[86] For Chatelain, the "bigger task" was to "breathe the breath of life into American history for those to whom it has heretofore been a dull recital of meaningless facts to re-create for the average citizen something of the color, the pageantry, and the dignity of our national past."[87]

Distinguishing between the "dull recital of meaningless facts" and the "color" and "pageantry" of the past put Chatelain out of step with the members of his discipline. He began to see an advanced degree in history as simultaneously necessary and insufficient for historical work in the National Park Service. The Depression-era economy created a shortage of academic jobs, and Chatelain found no lack of well-educated historians willing to work for him, but, he recalled, each one had to be "trained in the special techniques of Park Service historical work which were, in many respects, not the kind of techniques that you would at all get in a university class in history. . . . He had to know, for instance, how you develop a historical museum, how a spinning wheel works, or a water wheel powering a grist mill. He had to know the many historical artifacts that you find in historical museums—how they fitted into the life of the people. In many respects, he didn't have the slightest idea of those things." Chatelain implemented his own training programs, focused on the needs of visitors, not the demands of the discipline. He encouraged his staff to go beyond the understanding of historical details and to think about "what kind of program we would offer . . . for the general public when the man who supports all this, the taxpayer, came around to view the results."[88]

There is evidence to suggest that Chatelain sought out models for the kind of pragmatic program he had in mind and that he was more influenced by educational theorists than historians. In 1933 Glenn Frank wrote an article—several copies of which were filed among Chatelain's papers—in which he described public educators as "salesmen of knowledge." Frank was a writer, editor, and popular lecturer who had served as editor in chief of *Century Magazine* during the early 1920s. He believed that students should guide higher learning, with professors serving largely as facilitators. After Frank spoke in Madison, Wisconsin, in 1924, a regent of the University of Wisconsin successfully lobbied for his appointment as the university's president.[89] At Wisconsin, Frank established an experimental college that offered no formal classes and assigned no grades. Instead, students worked collaboratively, designing research studies that reflected their own interests and experiences. In the article Chatelain had saved, Frank argued that effective public education depended on a "trinity of social servants": the investigator, the administrator, and the interpreter. He saw no shortage of men to fill the first two roles, but good interpreters were in short supply: "The interpreter stands between the laymen, whose knowledge of all things is indefinite, and the investigator whose knowledge of one thing is authoritative. . . . The investigator advances knowledge. The interpreter advances progress."[90] Frank's philosophy echoed Chatelain's experiences in Minnesota and his sense of himself as a facilitator. Furthermore, Frank's rather radical experiments in collaborative learning shed new light on Chatelain's use of the term "historical mindedness." Chatelain understood that historians could play a powerful public role, transforming individual sites into a map of national identity that visitors might use to locate themselves inside the American past. At the same time, he understood that the discipline of history was insufficient. He had to take "a man trained in history and make a real Park Service man out of him . . . a new kind of technician."[91] Although Chatelain's tenure with the Park Service was brief, he played a crucial role in defining the sensibilities that might turn historians into "real Park Service men."

CHAPTER 5

Real Park Service Men

On the Ground and in the Books

———— ✠ ————

The New Deal was just made to order for us.

—VERNE CHATELAIN—

Horace Albright took over as director of the National Park Service in January 1929, on the eve of the Great Depression. As the economy worsened, Albright found himself in a familiar position. As acting director during World War I, he had worked on a shoestring. After he left Washington to serve as superintendent of Yellowstone, he remained Mather's close confidante, and he played an important role in preparing and defending the agency's budget. Throughout the 1920s he was often called to Washington to testify in defense of Park Service spending. By the time he took over as director, however, "Money was so scarce; they used to think many times before they would call a man in to Washington on duty."[1] As the economic crisis deepened, Albright and his core administrative staff had little time to engage in long-term planning or consider the potential effects of any policy decisions. Afterward, Chatelain and his colleagues scarcely knew how to explain the situation during those hard times. Only those who had "lived through the Depression and seen how the Government was run—day by day, crisis by crisis" could fully comprehend the challenge of trying to shape a logical history program during the 1930s.[2] Albright agreed, "We didn't have any time to think about the long range. . . . We were meeting day-to-day crises."[3]

The Depression, of course, went far beyond the offices of the National Park Service. It was unprecedented and far-reaching. By late 1932 more than eleven thousand of the nation's twenty-five thousand banks had failed. Reduced access to cash sharply limited investment in new businesses and industry, and production dropped to precipitously low levels while unemployment soared. Although estimates vary, most historians agree that 25 to 30 percent of Americans were unemployed and at least another 20 to 25 percent were underemployed, as factories cut back on hours in response to diminished demand. It is fair to say, then, half of Americans were living on a drastically reduced income. Unsurprisingly, most blamed the seated president, Herbert Hoover, for their plight. Although he made some late attempts to answer pleas for relief, his response was insufficient. Franklin D. Roosevelt, the charismatic governor of New York, defeated him handily in the election of 1932. His campaign promise of a "new deal" for Americans won him more than 57 percent of the popular vote.

Roosevelt assembled both a formal cabinet and an informal array of advisers—the so-called brain trust—the combined members of which peppered him with ideas, proposing a host of innovative responses to the crisis. After his inauguration on March 4, 1933, Roosevelt was prepared to act immediately. During his first hundred days in office, he passed legislation to reform the banking industry, provide immediate relief to farmers, and create work for thousands of unemployed laborers. Although the first measures passed without much debate, Roosevelt's program quickly became controversial, and many of the original New Deal programs were declared unconstitutional. Roosevelt worked with his trusted advisers to repackage and rename them, creating a second New Deal that strongly resembled, and in some cases expanded, the first. Making minor changes in programs' administrative structure blunted criticism, while allowing the administration to continue exerting tremendous influence over matters that had previously been left to the private sector.[4] For the National Park Service, the programs provided funding and labor to implement all of Albright's plans and more. As Verne Chatelain recalled it later, the New Deal "was made to order," providing the Park Service with labor and money to create the work program he had imagined.[5]

The National Park Service and the New Deal

Indeed, Roosevelt's programs created a New Deal for the entire Park Service. Almost immediately, he latched onto the plan, developed under

Herbert Hoover, for a reorganization of the federal government. In the process, he dramatically expanded the number of Park Service holdings in the eastern portion of the United States. Horace Albright saw to that. In April 1933 Roosevelt invited Albright along on a Sunday drive into the mountains of Virginia. The president wanted to inspect the fishing cabin Herbert Hoover had built near the Rapidan River in the Shenandoahs. He also wanted a tour of the winding highway, Skyline Drive, then being built by the National Park Service through the mountains in Shenandoah National Park. Albright made the most of his time in the president's limousine, taking the opportunity to explain his proposal to transfer the War Department parks to the National Park Service.[6] By then, Albright had already spent years negotiating with the War Department and lobbying Congress, and his efforts were stymied not only by the advent of the Depression but also by internal disagreement among War Department administrators about the usefulness of the Civil War battlefields. When one assistant secretary insisted that "they needed them for training of officers," Albright began to appreciate the fact that the military had overlooked the sites' real value. "They weren't interested in the tourists at all; they weren't interested even in telling the stories on the Battlefields."[7] At many of the battlefields, the role of telling stories had been taken over by private tour guides and commemorative organizations, fracturing the story of the war into local and regional bits.[8]

Albright felt confident that the creation of the History Division and the establishment of the first historic monuments in the Park Service had prepared the agency to make better use of the battlefields. Roosevelt agreed. He instructed Albright to draft an executive order placing all of the sites under administrative control of the National Park Service.[9] Although years of effort had been spent justifying the expansion of Park Service holdings, in the end the transfer was rather sudden. Roosevelt signed two executive orders. The first, 6166, dated June 10, 1933, justified government reorganization as part of economic recovery and reassigned to the National Park Service the responsibility for a number of ongoing commemorative activities as well as the parks and monuments in Washington, D.C. The transfer of the War Department sites—the order penned by Albright— was implemented by Executive Order 6228, signed on July 28, 1933. In late August the National Park Service acquired all fifty-seven War Department historic sites as well as seventeen monuments that had been administered by other agencies.[10] Viewing the transfer as the culmination of his career,

Horace Albright resigned on August 8, 1933.[11] His longtime associate director, Arno Cammerer, took over, ushering the Park Service through the Depression years.

In addition to increasing the number of Park Service holdings, Roosevelt's programs also dramatically expanded its budget and labor force. In less than a decade, money and workers from emergency programs transformed the Park Service landscape, making it more accessible, better protected, and more comprehensible than it had ever been. In 1933 the Park Service received less than 11 million dollars for administration, protection, and maintenance of all its holdings. By 1939 the annual appropriation was nearly 27 million dollars. A full 40 percent of its budget between 1933 and the end of the decade came from emergency funds. Before the New Deal programs ended, at least five emergency agencies provided money and labor for park projects. The Federal Emergency Relief Administration developed recreation facilities in a number of National Parks.[12] The Civil Works Administration employed more than thirteen thousand laborers on road improvement and landscaping projects.[13] The Public Works Administration provided funds and workers that enabled the National Park Service to develop recreational and educational facilities on less scenically or scientifically valuable land adjacent to several of its parks. These funds also went for the purchase and installation of museum equipment throughout the park system.[14] The Works Progress Administration focused needed attention on planning and development for regional, state, and municipal parks, and the National Park Service lent its expertise to this program, broadening its influence and building good will with state and regional preservation groups.[15] The Civilian Conservation Corps had the most significant impact on Park Service development. CCC workers lived in encampments on the park grounds and implemented projects designed by the Park Service. CCC workers built roads, campgrounds, rest areas, and visitor centers in a variety of parks, including the military parks and battlefields. At the program's high point in 1935, the Park Service oversaw 118 CCC camps in national parks and 482 in state parks, employing 120,000 laborers.[16]

The New Deal also enticed well-educated intellectual workers to consider government service. Under the terms of the CCC and other programs, work projects had to be designed and supervised by knowledgeable professionals, a dictate that compelled the Park Service to hire more staff. Prior to the New Deal, it had been difficult to attract young men with graduate degrees to work in Park Service education and interpretation.

The problem applied equally to naturalists and historians. After his arrival in Washington in 1930 as assistant director for the Branch of Research and Education, Harold C. Bryant traveled all around the country trying to convince graduate students in the natural sciences to take the civil service exam, but the test proved to be a poor indicator of success. A significant number who passed were simply ill-suited to interpretive work. Bryant had to admit that many of the men hired "weren't the right kind of people: either they didn't like people and avoided them, or they didn't know [how] to make the story interesting." Strong academic recommendations did not necessarily predict success either. Some of the most intellectually successful students were "thoroughly interested in specimens of plants instead of the real living ones out of doors. . . . They went back to teaching and we got good outdoorsmen to take their place."[17]

As the economy worsened, however, the pool of interested graduate students broadened. Chatelain embraced the opportunity, actively recruiting young historians who might not have otherwise considered government service. At first, those looking to hire professionals to oversee development on park properties preferred engineers and scientists, but, according to Chatelain, "Nobody had thought in their wildest moments about appointing historians."[18] He recognized the New Deal work projects would allow him to build up the history program quickly. He was particularly concerned about the status of the battlefields. "In places like Gettysburg, the tourist interest was naturally very high, but the opportunities to get a reasonably credible, accurate story with all the devices that would make for a clear understanding of what happened there was simply lacking. The national program simply didn't exist."[19] At some of the most popular battlefields, commercial tour guides had filled the information vacuum, providing tourists with more myth than history. At most of them, however, there was simply no program at all.

The CCC enabled Chatelain to restructure historical tourism, designing projects for one park at a time and hiring historians to supervise them. Chatelain wired the chairs of History Departments across the country, asking for the names of graduate students who might consider working for the Park Service during the summer. Soon, he found, "I was hiring PhDs a dime a dozen."[20] Thomas Pitkin had just recently completed doctoral studies at Case Western Reserve University in Cleveland, Ohio, when he answered the Park Service call for historians, an opportunity he recalled as a refreshing antidote to the dire academic job market: "The academic world in the continuing Depression was bleak. . . . A $2600 government job looked as big as a barn door."[21]

By hiring historians for temporary positions as technicians and supervisors on CCC projects, Chatelain could identify those best suited to the unusual Park Service work environment. A notable number of young men came from his alma mater, the University of Minnesota. Carlton C. Qualey had been in the graduate program with Chatelain in 1929, and he completed a master's degree in history there before beginning doctoral studies at Columbia University.[22] Charles M. Gates had begun his doctoral studies at Minnesota in 1930.[23] Thomas Pitkin worked with Gates at a regional office in Indianapolis, where the pace was hectic and unpredictable. Pitkin and Gates represented the Park Service on cooperative projects with the state parks, but they were also often asked to inspect historic properties on behalf of the service, generate reports, and conduct other work as necessary. The work did not resemble the systematic pace of scholarship to which the young men had been trained. Pitkin recalled, "There was no pattern to this. The Washington office simply responded to local pressures as they came in direct from the field historians, to make the inspections and report."[24]

Although Gates and Qualey left the Park Service after only a short period of service—each went on to lead distinguished careers in academia—University of Minnesota graduate students were generally well suited to Park Service work, and a number of them remained in government service. One particular cohort had begun studying at Minnesota around the same time. Herman Kahn, George Palmer, Edward Hummel, Ronald F. Lee, and Herbert Kahler all signed on for Park Service summer work together in 1933. Herman Kahn stayed with the Park Service from 1933 to 1936, before transferring to the National Archives and beginning a career in the Presidential Libraries system. George Palmer went on to serve as superintendent of several Park Service properties, including the Statue of Liberty and Hyde Park, before moving up to a leadership role in the regional offices. Edward Hummel served as superintendent of Colonial National Historical Park in the late 1940s and as assistant director for Policy and Program analysis in the 1960s. Ronald Lee and Herbert Kahler, both of whom began their careers as historical technicians and supervisors for New Deal work projects in the battlefield parks, followed closely in the footsteps of Verne Chatelain, serving as the second and third chief historians of the National Park Service.

Chatelain practically handpicked Lee as his successor. Lee left Minnesota for Tennessee in the summer of 1933, having accepted a position as historical technician at Shiloh National Battlefield. There, Lee demonstrated the kind of diplomacy required of Park Service technicians. He quickly befriended the staff. The site superintendent had been a War Department employee. Lee found him to be very kind and welcoming but also "unfamiliar with the programs of the Department of the Interior and all of us were without any advance knowledge of what the CCC program in a historical battlefield was going to accomplish." Recognizing that the transfer of War Department sites had made the staff nervous about job security, Lee worked to put everyone at ease and back to work. He expanded the historical staff, hiring twenty people for research and restoration, ten of whom were graduate students or had already earned their PhDs. Observing Lee's progress, Chatelain recognized qualities that made him a "real Park Service man." In August 1934 Chatelain invited him to participate in a meeting to design a survey of Natchez Trace. One of Chatelain's assistants had become ill, and Chatelain asked Lee to stay in Washington, temporarily, to help with program and policy development. He never left.[25] Ronald Lee quickly became Chatelain's right-hand man and the face of the history program. Often it was Lee who traveled across the country to interview prospective history technicians and supervisors.

Documenting the Past

The New Deal gave the Park Service History Division a greater sense of purpose and a much stronger position of influence. The historians who came to work for the Park Service "had a very strong morale in those days. They felt they were engaging in new work—which indeed they were. They were evolving policies. They were setting standards and principles for a type of activity for which these did not exist." By and large, park superintendents and upper-level Park Service administrators were willing to accept historians' recommendations. Throughout the 1930s and into the 1940s, "the Director [and] . . . his principal advisers realized they had a vast expansion of responsibilities thrust upon them for which they weren't really competent by past experience to deal with effectively, and they were more inclined to listen to the recommendations of the new employees who'd been brought in to deal with this type of area."[26] From this position of influence, Chatelain, his staff, and his advisers began to press for a clear federal policy to guide site selection, acquisition, and protection. Carlton Qualey worked closely with Verne Chatelain, generating a report to explain the purpose of a federally mandated survey of historic sites.

The report described historians in the central and regional offices as facilitators who would help coordinate and rationalize preservation and programming servicewide by advising the staff at individual sites. In Qualey's estimation, areas of historic importance could be understood as "pegs on which American history can be conveniently hung." A survey of historic sites would help document the "specifically local, regional, state, national, and international importance" associated with each site and allow historical technicians to gather evidence to justify the acquisition of specific sites for the Park Service collection. Once acquired by the service, historic places became primary sources, raw material to be shaped by a program of historical research, interpretation, and education. The growing staff of the History Division would "coordinate them in such a manner that they may contribute a maximum of public service." Historical programming, not historic preservation alone, made the sites valuable for addressing a pressing public need. Qualey explained, "It is common knowledge that historic sites in the US have been inadequately utilized in the teaching of American history. This situation is largely due to two circumstances: (1) the failure of teachers of history in the schools and colleges to consider the value of historic sites in the teaching of American history; and (2) the inadequacy of the historical investigation and facilities for public education in the respective areas of historic importance." A national survey of historic sites, then, would allow the chief historian to "plan a national historical educational program into which each of the park units can be fitted with a maximum of educational efficiency."[27]

Although Qualey and Chatelain envisioned a symbiotic relationship between historic preservation and historical programming, the two evolved more as parallel programs during the New Deal. It was landscape architect Charles E. Peterson—not Verne Chatelain—who designed and implemented a New Deal historic preservation project for the National Park Service, the Historic American Buildings Survey (HABS). Peterson was brought into the Park Service by Horace Albright. Like Chatelain and Lee, he was connected to the University of Minnesota, but that connection did not convey much else on which the men might have formed a professional relationship. Peterson had put himself through school as a surveyor, working with road crews across the West. He met Horace Albright while he was doing survey work near Jackson Hole and expressed interest in a Park Service career.[28] Albright recommended Peterson for a position as a Park Service engineer in the western parks and then brought him east in 1930 to assist in designing Colonial National Parkway.

Peterson quickly gained a name for himself, and just as quickly, he differentiated his work from that of the historians. He designed entry structures and buildings for the eastern parks. He also participated in the restoration of Wakefield, dubiously protected as George Washington's birthplace. Design and construction projects in the military parks were overseen by the Eastern Division of the Park Service Branch of Planning, and by 1933 Peterson was its chief. In this capacity, he worked alongside Chatelain's historians, quickly developing a rather negative assessment of historical programming. Peterson dismissed the reports generated by historical technicians, arguing that "most of them were rubbish . . . they just didn't have any grasp of what they were doing . . . that was a product of the hurrying which was done." The reports typically contained recommendations for construction projects related to park interpretation. Peterson criticized Chatelain for wanting "a brick station with six historians at every entrance to every military park." From his perspective, the proposed work was frivolous, part of an ill-conceived effort to hire as many historians as possible. Chatelain, he thought, was nothing more than "a politician. . . . He never had any notions about quality or thoroughness."[29]

Such a brusque assessment has less to do with Chatelain's actual skills and professionalism and more to do with the fact that the two Park Service units—the Office of Planning and the History Division—were structured by distinct disciplines, sets of values, and personal ambitions. Their differences were evident in the proposals each office submitted through the Park Service director's office, to design and implement a survey of historic sites. Chatelain and Qualey's report, written in August 1933, recommended collecting information about historic structures as a means to a larger end, a springboard for expanding historical work in the Park Service. Peterson's report, submitted in November, argued that gathering quantifiable data about endangered American historic structures was itself a public service. In a thinly veiled swipe at Chatelain, Peterson criticized earlier efforts by the Park Service to catalog historic sites. The focus on places best suited for development as museums or tourist attractions had, he thought, obscured the significance of entire classes of buildings. Peterson argued the correct approach was scientific, not commercial. The "list of building types should be almost a complete resume of the builders' art. It should include public buildings, churches, residences, bridges, forts, barns, mills, shops, rural out-buildings and any other kind of structure of which there are good speci-mens extant." Because sites worthy of protection "comprise only a minor percentage of the interesting and important architectural specimens which remain from the old days," he wrote, "it is the responsibility of the American people that if the great number of our antique buildings must disappear through economic causes, they should not pass into unrecorded oblivion."[30] Peterson's proposal was successful; HABS received funding from the Civil Works Administration, and work began on December 1, 1933. Although certainly not the program Chatelain had envisioned—Peterson described it as a building survey "designed by architects for architects"—the project created a permanent administrative structure for historic preservation in the Park Service.[31]

Peterson's vision was in line with intellectual trends lending shape to the New Deal. Regionalism, so disdained by leading historians in the late nineteenth and early twentieth centuries, gained momentum during the 1920s and 1930s. Folklorists including B. A. Botkin and John Collier—a student of Native American life in the West who became the commis-sioner of Indian Affairs—sought an antidote to the consumerism, indus-trialism, and urbanization that had come to dominate, and ultimately endanger, American life. They found one in an idealized memory of the nation's agrarian past, a nostalgic longing for farming villages that fos-tered both strong communal bonds and self-reliant families. The decline of that lifestyle under the mad rush of modernization, they believed, also signaled the decline of cultural and social mores that defined the very heart of American life. That sensibility lent new urgency to an interdisciplinary effort to document unique cultures and lifestyles.[32] Adapting tools from the disciplines of history, anthropology, literature, and art, public intellectuals sought to rediscover America. In the words of the poet Allen Tate, "only a return to the provinces, to the small, self-contained centers of life, will put the all-destroying abstraction, America, safely to rest."[33]

This documentary impulse underlay a significant number of New Deal programs.[34] HABS architects were directed to document information about buildings erected prior to 1860. The date was chosen because, "after that time, the sectional characteristics of the country became less and less distinct. Steadily increasing movements of population and accelerated dis-tribution of information broadened architectural taste, and local differences in design and construction methods disappeared. There is little sectional difference in our architecture of today."[35] In the same vein, at the Farm Security Administration, Roy Stryker hired Dorothea Lange, Jack Delano, Gordon Parks, and other pioneering, documentary-style photographers to gather a complete visual record of unique and endangered ways of life.[36] Stryker certainly influenced what they saw, indeed, what they expected to see. He ordered each new hire to read J. Russell Smith's *North America,* a work of cultural geography. He saw the landscape, particularly the rural landscape, as the origin of the American character, and he drafted detailed shooting scripts in which he asked his photographers to document small towns and agricultural scenes.[37] Stryker instructed his staff to photograph family farms across the country because they were relics, landscapes on which American folkways persisted.

In the same vein, writers, anthropologists, and others employed by the Federal Writers' Project documented regional habits and perceptions. Project writers (including Zora Neale Hurston) gathered folktales in the south, recorded the impressions of farmers and workers about the impact of the Depression, and interviewed elderly African Americans, the last of the former slaves.[38] By the time New Deal funding dried up for these documentary programs—victims of a Congress increasingly uncomfortable with the idea of government-sponsored culture—they had accumulated massive numbers of images, sound recordings, performances, and published materials that have served as the raw materials for generations of artists, writers, architects, designers, and historians.

When the intellectual project of regionalism intersected with the federal government during the New Deal, however, some of the outcomes were more ironic than romantic. As the railroad had made the West more accessible to tourists and settlers, Native American potters and weavers had made significant changes to traditional crafts. They created new patterns and adopted new color schemes that reflected consumer demands for "real Indian" goods far more than they reflected indigenous preferences.[39] In much the same way, emergency work programs that sought to document authentic and indigenous ways of life in isolated corners of America did not protect regional forms of expression. Rather, they transformed local material culture, oral traditions, and architecture into icons of the "real America." The same HABS regional director who had marked 1860 as the year after which regional distinctions in building style and construction methods had declined also described the record of these differences as essential to crafting a common past for all Americans.[40] State guide-books, produced under the Federal Writers' Project, repackaged local places as tourist attractions, restructuring habits of life and work into arenas of performance. The National Park Service was not immune to the allure and popularity of folk art. Less than a decade after having evicted poverty-stricken communities from the Shenandoah and Great Smoky Mountains during the creation of the eastern parks, the agency now insisted "that only mountain peoples' handicraft work be sold" in shops on park grounds.[41]

The History Division staff viewed their work as both indebted to and distinct from the New Deal documentary impulse in general and from HABS in particular.[42] Chatelain recalled, "The Historic American Buildings Survey was . . . an architect's dream. . . . It was never too closely tied to our program and for that reason I think it failed to do some things that it could easily have done at the time it was carried on."[43] In fact, HABS was wildly productive. In its first six months, HABS employed 772 architects, pho-tographers, and drafters who assembled drawings and photographs of 860 historic buildings.[44] Peterson was insistent that these materials belonged to the public. As one regional architect from Richmond explained, acces-sibility was a cornerstone of the program: "This work of architectural con-servation by an agency of the federal government is a significant example of the functioning of democracy, [because] the interest and enthusiasm of the people have resulted in a study, recording and preservation of a natural heritage for the cultural benefit of all."[45] Peterson found that the organiz-ers of similar projects—at Williamsburg and the Royal Institute of British Architects, for example—had kept their drawings "nailed up in wooden boxes; they didn't know what to do with them." In contrast, he recalled, "We knew what we had to do with them. First of all, we had to take them away from the guys that drew them, because they're never through. There's always something they want to change in them no matter how long they have them. . . . Chatelain wanted to get his hands on them, too."[46] When Peterson learned that the chair of the National Preservation Committee, Leicester Holland, wanted to establish an archive of American architecture for the Library of Congress, he brokered a deal. The Park Service admin-istered HABS, the Library of Congress maintained its records, and the American Institute of Architects provided the labor. Throughout the 1930s HABS was kept afloat with money from various emergency relief pro-grams and voluntary student work.[47]

Uniqueness and Historical Value

Meanwhile, Chatelain and his staff began their own survey of historic sites, focusing less on physical details than on symbolic meaning. Roy Appleman, a Columbia University doctoral student recruited for the Park Service by Ronald Lee in the summer of 1935, explained, "I don't think HABS had any effect on the park development. HABS was a concept to put unemployed architects to work, recording historic structures, to develop a record of worthwhile buildings that might be useful in the future. It was a good idea, and it did have its effect eventually in historic preservation, but I don't think it had any great marked effect immediately."[48] Of course, this was not entirely true. Although personal biases, disciplinary preferences, and personalities worked against active cooperation between HABS and the History Division, in fact the Park Service historical program benefited greatly from the New Deal documentary impulse. The past became more popular and more ubiquitous as CCC workers identified and restored historic structures in state and regional parks, as HABS architects produced structural drawings of historic buildings, as state guidebook writers described unique tourist locations, and as photographers for the Farm Security Administration snapped—and published—evidence of distinctive local aesthetics. In this atmosphere, the impulse for preservation gained new momentum. Organizations began to press the Park Service to recognize and protect historic places across the country. A flood of proposals hit the Department of the Interior, as preservation organizations put houses, buildings, and other historic areas forward for consideration by the Park Service.

This was precisely what Chatelain had both hoped for and feared.[49] The steps he had taken to develop a systematic historical program were insufficient in light of the growing interest in his work. The sheer number of proposals was daunting, representative of a potentially endless historical landscape on which the Park Service could expand. Such demand required Chatelain to articulate a set of standards, a clear directive about how to mark the difference between distinctively local and appropriately national pasts. Popular interest lent him the push he needed. He recalled, "With Congress and the country in the mood of doing something, we felt that the time had come to strike."[50] Not everyone was supportive. President Roosevelt's secretary of the interior, Harold Ickes, brought an old-fashioned sensibility to his office, one that was in conflict with the goals of the National Park Service. He resisted the agency's expansion and held to a view of the

parks as primarily valuable for their natural surroundings. He argued that
the parks were best enjoyed by "people who appreciate and understand what
beautiful nature plots are. . . . I don't think the parks were intended to be
classrooms. Fortunately for Chatelain, Roosevelt thought otherwise. His
closest advisers urged Chatelain to draft a statement of standards to guide
the creation of national historic sites. His proposal "grew out of the programs we'd already developed."[51] Echoing the language of the Antiquities
Act and extrapolating key ideas from the proposal he had drafted with
Carlton Qualey, Chatelain's statement implicitly acknowledged that federal
policy already lent authority to the president and Congress to extend federal
protection to sites containing "unique qualities." Precedent had established
"uniqueness" as a quality inherent in scientific value (under the terms of the
Antiquities Act) or scenic beauty (in the establishment of national parks).
Chatelain's statement of standards extended the quality of uniqueness to
historic places.

In establishing HABS, Peterson had extended scientific value to historic properties, arguing that architectural styles could be categorized scientifically, and historic buildings could be documented in much the same
way that the Southwest monuments had been. Chatelain took a different
approach. Historical uniqueness, he argued, was created by context and narrative, not aesthetic evaluation or scientific typology. Reiterating Qualey's
argument, Chatelain wrote that nationally significant historic places were
"unique" if they were "points or bases from which the broad aspects of prehistoric and American life can best be presented." Furthermore, such sites
were useful for enabling the "student of history . . . [to] sketch the large
patterns of the American story," and they gained significance from their
"relationship to other areas, each contributing its part of the complete story
of American history." Bowing to pressure from preservation organizations,
Chatelain acknowledged that some sites achieved "uniqueness" from their
association with either "the life of some great American" or "some sudden or
dramatic incident in American history." In any case, historic sites may lack
the kind of physical indicators of uniqueness preferred by Peterson, but they
were nonetheless valuable because they were "symbolic of some great idea
or ideal."[52]

Park Service director Cammerer incorporated Chatelain's description of
standards into his formal recommendations for a new federal policy regarding historic sites. He added the suggestion that the Park Service should
conduct a regular survey of historic places, classifying them as "Potential

National" or "Non-Potential National." He also recommended the creation of a new national advisory board for the National Park Service, one focused more on historic sites than scenic properties, to replace the Educational Advisory Board. Under the proposal, history would become an independent division rather than a bureau of the Division of Research and Education. The reorganization would elevate Chatelain's status to associate director. Congress reviewed the proposal when Virginia senator Harry Byrd sponsored the Historic Sites Act in 1935. Testifying at the congressional hearing on the bill, Chatelain described the Park Service history program as a dialogue between local and national preservation entities, one that would result in a comprehensive program to preserve the nation's historic places. President Franklin Roosevelt signed the Historic Sites Act into law in August 1935, declaring that "it is a national policy to preserve for public use historic sites, buildings, and objects of national significance for the inspiration and benefit of the people of the United States." The law established the Advisory Board on National Parks, Historic Sites, Buildings, and Monuments to advise the secretary of the interior on matters of national significance, additions to the National Park System, and administrative policy. It also expanded the authority of the secretary of the interior, authorizing him to act through the National Park Service to conduct a new survey of historic places, acquire property, enter into cooperative management agreements, restore and preserve historic places, and, most important, "initiate a research program to determine the facts and develop an educational program to convey the information to the public."[53]

Chatelain began the program immediately. He pulled together a research group, calling four historical technicians to Washington from various CCC projects. Working in the Library of Congress and the U.S. National Museum, the young men—historians Alvin Stauffer, Charles Gates, and Vernon G. Setser, and archaeologist Summerfield Day—designed a thematic framework to guide site selection and aid interpretation. Recently minted graduate students with only limited experience on the ground, the researchers divided the project into periods—prehistoric, 1492 to 1775, 1775 to 1830 and 1830 to 1930—and each took responsibility for conducting thorough research for one phase. At first glance, the periodization is curious. One researcher was expected to cover the nearly three hundred years between Columbus's landing and the Revolution, while a second researcher had to cover only the fifty-five years between the Revolution and 1830. The scope of each research project was dictated not by the availability of archival or secondary source evidence but by the number of historic structures that remained standing from each period. Because only a small number of pre–Revolutionary War historic places had been identified by either HABS or private preservation groups, the researcher could cover a much broader period. But a large number of sites from the immediate post–Revolutionary Era had already been preserved by local societies, wealthy individuals, and community boosters, making a much smaller period a more promising arena for Park Service expansion.

Once they had selected a period focus, each man produced one piece of a larger narrative, called *Patterns of American History.* These reports addressed a common list of historical themes and a wish list of sites that might serve as "pegs" to ground the narrative. They also created a coherent account of American progress, covering the evolution of American civilization and moving through stages of development from "aboriginal occupation" to "exploration by the white man." Each contributed to that overarching sense of progress by addressing the same list of themes, including the "relationship between whites and Indians; sites associated with travel, transportation and communication; Industrial development; commerce, banking and exchange; development of political institutions; political events and struggles; humanitarian movements; military and naval events; maritime history; religious history; the frontier; [and] architecture."[54]

These categories functioned to establish historical standards that might guide site selection. Final decisions about whether or not to designate a national historic site remained with Congress, but the creation of *Patterns in American History* enabled Chatelain and his staff to make convincing arguments on behalf of a given site. "Frequently, we would excite the Congressman to make the request and he was glad to do it because it added to his own record of achievement."[55] By the fall of 1936, before he could effectively use the narrative for this purpose, Chatelain resigned: "I had accomplished in general what I had set out to do. I had gotten things set up. I had the Branch of Historic Sites and Buildings. I had the Historic Sites Act. I had generally the confidence of the people in the Park Service . . . [but] it was time for me to take care of my ulcers. . . . I was worn to a frazzle with the dizzy pace"[56]

With or without him, *Patterns in American History* had to pass through several layers of Park Service administration to achieve final approval. The Advisory Board on Historic Sites had the power to approve or reject any statement of policy issued by the Division of Historic Sites. That group consented to the overall narrative but rejected specific components and site recommendations that were too closely related to contemporary political or social conditions. During an October 1937 meeting the board rejected one thematic component in its entirety: Political and Military Affairs, 1865–1937. Board members reasoned that inclusion of the category would require the National Park Service to consider historic sites and events "pertinent to current or near current history, and therefore controversial."[57] Branch Spalding, Chatelain's temporary replacement as chief historian, also sought feedback from field historians and archaeologists in each of the Park Service's four regional offices. He asked them to make specific suggestions for the elimination or addition of proposed historic sites and assign priority to the development of an interpretive program at a given site.

The Landscape of Public History

The comments Branch Spalding gathered in 1936 and 1937 document a historical landscape still very much divided by regional preferences and perspectives. The Advisory Board on National Parks, Historic Sites, Buildings and Monuments reviewed the comments, submitted as formal memos by regional historians and archaeologists. A survey of these documents suggests that those experts located outside of the northeast region tended to reject the primacy that Gates, Day, Setser, and Stauffer had afforded to the British in their description of American cultural progress. William R. Hogan, a University of Texas–educated historian employed in the Oklahoma office, wrote, "It is doubtful whether English institutions are much more observable in the Southwest than those derivative from Spanish sources. A modern Englishman would be little more at home in Arizona today than a Mexican, and the typical Arizonan would very likely have more difficulty in conversing with his English cousin than with his American neighbor." In the margins of Hogan's memo, a handwritten "Oh no" scribbled perhaps by Spalding or by a member of the Advisory Committee captures a moment of visceral shock or defensiveness. Hogan strongly opposed the "tendency of this narrative ... to give the Spaniards and the French credit for explorations and the beginnings of a few local institutions but nothing that contributed to the mainstream of American culture." He cited specific, egregious examples, writing "Such statements as the following are questionable: 'Within the present United States neither France nor Spain had much influence in molding the type

of civilization.' And 'Spanish influence was most important in its modifica-
tion of Indian cultures.'" Such disdain for the cultural influence of Spain and
France was, Hogan thought, "New England historical poison."[58] He and his
colleagues also objected to the gentleness with which the British were treated
in the narrative. Thomas Pitkin particularly objected to a characterization
of the British as exhibiting a "tendency to grant the colonists more self-
government," arguing instead that there was a "tendency on the part of the
colonists to seek more self-government and to obtain it at the expense of the
royal authority, by one device or another."[59]

The comments from regional historians and archaeologists also indicate lingering differences of opinion regarding the appropriate location of
Native American people in the narrative of American history. Some archaeologists held to the belief that "prehistoric peoples" were culturally distinct
from historic and contemporary tribes, and they objected to any hint of historical continuity in the Park Service narratives. Erik K. Reed, for example,
pointed to the connection made between "Eastern Folsom" and "Southern
Mississippi Valley Cultures," worrying that the implication of continuity
might arouse criticism. The discovery of spear points in the remains of "prehistoric" mammals at Folsom had stirred considerable debate among scientists. They suggested that ancient Native Americans had, in fact, developed
a highly organized culture with advanced methods of tool making, which
called into question linear presumptions about human evolution. Some
scientists embraced these findings, altering their theories of civilization to
include older aboriginal peoples.[60]

This rather benign theory was highly controversial because it challenged
popular ideas about the civilizing influence of whites on Native Americans.
Opponents argued that the spear points were of a far more recent origin,
and they had simply become mixed up with the remains of ancient crea-
tures. Reed's comments indicate that he espoused the more conservative
perspective, arguing that "all the points of the Folsom type found east of
the high plains are, so far as I know, surface finds with no definite evidence
of great antiquity."[61] In sharp contrast, some of the historians commenting
on the narrative embraced this element, arguing that such evidence represented the "great antiquity" of human life. They objected to scientific dis-
continuities that relegated Native Americans to a prehistoric past. Edward
Hummel commented, "It is unfortunate that the writer of the section on
the Archaeological Periods in the United States made no attempt to trace
the (Indian) cultures through the historical period following European

contacts. This leaves a gap in the history of the Indian which should be eliminated when the outline is revised."[62]

Regional historians and archaeologists also raised questions about the uneven visibility of history on the nation's landscape. William Hogan wondered about the long-term effects of designating as historical those sites on which no physical remains were evident. He noticed a regional difference in how such designations were made. In the Northeast, there appeared to be a bias toward designating specific surviving buildings. In the South, it was more common for historic site status to be granted to places where no structures or markers existed—such as Nacogdoches, Texas, and Natchitoches, Louisiana. Hogan doubted the validity of such designations, arguing that they undermined standards and called Park Service professionalism into question. National historical sites, he argued, must be easy to distinguish from merely local or regional boosterism. He worried that "a too generous definition of a 'site' may result in . . . merely an embryo national historical marker system. The state of existing remains is no final criterion of historical importance, yet it is a factor which must be considered. The lack of physical remains . . . must inevitably limit the National Historic Sites program, just as the writers of histories are limited by available historical materials."[63] Thomas Pitkin, in contrast, argued that a bias toward historic houses in the Northeast might reduce the Park Service collection to a typological history of architecture and make it impossible actually to implement a thematic approach to the past.

Professionalism and History

The New Deal created at least two kinds of historical workers in the National Park Service. The architectural historians, engineers, and educators brought in to reconstruct historical landscapes were extremely good on the ground. Some were reluctant to see too much educational programming in the parks. They held to the belief that the value of the parks—all of the parks—was primarily inspirational. They found common cause with superintendents and administrators who held to older Park Service "scenic values." E. T. Scoyen, the superintendent of Zion National Park, preferred inspiration to instruction. In a telling anecdote, he explained the difference:

The other day, driving East, we stopped at Frankfort, KY, and we went up to Daniel Boone's grave. Now, I would have lost very much of the inspiration, if you choose to call it that, of my visit to Daniel Boone's grave if there had been anybody there to tell me about Daniel Boone or if there had been any museum of Daniel Boone's work or any instructor trying to point out his significance in the history of the United States. Those are some of the things that I just know. I do not know the details. I know something about Boone. In other words, just to go up there very quietly and stand in front of the grave of Daniel Boone was enough for me.[64]

Scoyen's comments point to the persistence of regional sensibilities among Park superintendents.

Nonetheless, the New Deal had brought a large wave of university-trained historians to the task of explaining sites like Daniel Boone's grave. Men such as Gates, Setser, Stauffer, and Day were extremely good in the books. They approached historical programming as they would any other kind of research project, viewing historic places not as sites of pilgrimage but as evidence useful for proving the thesis of American progress. Their work had a profound impact on public history. The narrative structure they devised in the middle of the 1930s guided interpretive development, site selection, designation, and interpretive programming through most of the twentieth century. Their narrative was replaced by a new thematic structure—one grounded in social and cultural history—in the 1990s. Nonetheless, the idea that a single, overarching historical framework should dictate programs on the ground remained intact. The American historical landscape was shaped by these two distinct groups of professionals, and the task of public history over the hundred years or more that followed would be to find their common professional ground.

John Wesley Powell, an adventure-seeking geologist best remembered for exploring the Grand Canyon, became the director of the Bureau of American Ethnology and a founder of the Cosmos Club. He played a crucial role in connecting the interests of science to those of government. (Smithsonian Institution Archives, John Wesley Powell and Native American, RU 95, box 18, folder 57, 2002-10682)

Stephen T. Mather (at left with hand in pocket), founding director of the National Park Service, at the dedication of Rocky Mountain National Park, 1915. With him (from his left) are Robert Sterling Yard, Mather's longtime friend whom he handpicked to serve as executive director of the National Parks Association; Park Superintendent Charles R. Trowbridge; Park Service photographer Herford T. Cowling; and Horace Albright, second director of the National Park Service and the man largely responsible for implementing the Park Service's educational mission. (Department of Interior, National Park Service Historic Photograph Collection, Harpers Ferry Center)

Frank Pinkley became custodian of Casa Grande Ruins National Monument in 1901, while the site was managed by the General Land Office. Though not an archaeologist, Pinkley conducted digs and became intimately familiar with the site's design and history. Pinkley built a small museum as a way to divert tourists from damaging the ruins. By the time this photograph was taken in 1934, Pinkley was a Park Service employee, serving as superintendent of the Southwest Monuments. (Department of Interior, National Park Service Historic Photograph Collection, Harpers Ferry Center, Photo by George A. Grant)

National Park Service superintendents posed with their wives and children on the Cliff Palace Ruins, during their conference at Mesa Verde National Park, October 1925. Stephen Mather is seated on the ladder in front. Jesse Nusbaum, the archaeologist responsible for the creation and professionalization of the museum at Mesa Verde, is seated next to the ladder on the brick structure. (Department of Interior, National Park Service Historic Photograph Collection, Harpers Ferry Center, Photo by James V. Lloyd)

In 1929 Horace Albright, second director of the National Park Service (seated at center) posed with the Mesa Verde Ranger force. Superintendent Jesse Nusbaum is seated to Albright's left. Both men were instrumental in designing an educational mission for the National Parks. Nusbaum fought with the Smithsonian Institution to establish park museums as legitimate federal institutions; Albright shepherded the Park Service into the realm of historical interpretation. (Department of Interior, National Park Service Historic Photograph Collection, Harpers Ferry Center, Photo by George A. Grant)

Successful Park Service historians recognized the value of material culture as well as documents. (Standing, left to right) Advisory Board member Herbert Bolton accompanies Thomas Pitkin, Ronald Lee, and (in hole) John Nagle to inspect evidence of vandalism at Tsankawi Ruin in Bandelier National Monument. Pitkin and Lee had joined the Park Service as historical technicians during the 1930s. (Department of Interior, National Park Service Historic Photograph Collection, Harpers Ferry Center)

Verne Chatelain, first chief historian of the National Park Service met regularly with the Educational Advisory Board, the body of experts responsible for justifying and guiding Horace Albright's vision of the Park Service as an educational agency. In this photograph of February 27, 1933, seated, left to right: Harold Bryant, Waldo Leland, Hermon Bumpus, Frank Oastler, Horace Albright, and W. W. Campbell; standing, left to right: Chatelain, Earl Trager, and Laurence Vail Coleman. (Department of Interior, National Park Service Historic Photograph Collection, Harpers Ferry Center, Photo by George A. Grant)

Smithsonian Curator of Archaeology handpicked J. C. Harrington to serve as the archae-ologist at Jamestown. Harrington's private correspondence with Setzler documents the emergence of historical archaeology as a research methodology and management strategy in the National Park Service. In this photograph, Harrington, at rear, conducts a dig with two CCC laborers. Although Harrington was sometimes skeptical that the "make work" labor force were adequate archaeologists, men like those pictured here were instrumental in linking archaeological research to historical interpretation. (National Park Service, Colonial National Historical Park, Jamestown Collection)

Historical archaeology was both a research method and a management tool at places like Colonial National Historical Park. Here, park staff members explain a dig site to visitors during the 1930s. (Department of Interior, National Park Service Historic Photograph Collection, Harpers Ferry Center, Colonial National Historical Park negative)

Throughout the 1920s, the National Parks became increasingly popular as more Americans had access to both leisure time and automobiles. Education programs helped Rangers manage the ways in which day trippers and auto-tourists used the parks. This 1929 photograph from Mesa Verde National Park shows Rangers preparing to lead a tourist party to the ruins. (Department of Interior, National Park Service Historic Photograph Collection, Harpers Ferry Center, Photo by George A. Grant)

During the New Deal, the National Park Service took advantage of the Civilian Conservation Corps program. Both Washington administrators and individual park rangers implemented projects they would otherwise have been unable to fund. In turn, the CCC "boys" took advantage of educational and recreational programs in the parks. They transformed the meaning of the park landscape. This group—Camp #4, Company 1240—was photographed at Glacier National Park on July 3, 1933. Most of the workers in this group were from New York City. (Department of Interior, National Park Service Historic Photograph Collection, Harpers Ferry Center, Photo by George A. Grant)

The Civilian Conservation Corps worked in segregated companies. This group of African American workers at Colonial National Historical Park contributed to historical interpretation at the site, building reconstructions of military fortifications. (Department of Interior, National Park Service Historic Photograph Collection, Harpers Ferry Center)

PART 3

Whom Do We Serve?
Public History and the Question of Authority

CHAPTER 6

Park Service Diggers

Public Historians and the Problem of Status

——— ❖ ———

The speed maniac, the low-brow, and the moron are as yet an item in the travel to national parks, and will always remain so. Lifting this limited class to a higher realization of park ideals and values is comparable to Joe Cannon's famous "boot strap aviation."

—JESSE NUSBAUM—

Park Service holdings, staff, and attendance had expanded exponentially by the end of the 1930s. In 1931 the average number of personnel employed by the Park Service each month was 2,044. In 1935 it was 17,047. During the same period, the number of park museums nearly doubled from twenty-seven in 1933 to fifty-three in 1936. Similarly, the number of historic sites held by the National Park Service increased dramatically. By 1941, in addition to the fifty-seven battlefields and monuments transferred from the War Department, the Park Service operated thirty-five historic house museums—eight west of the Mississippi and twenty-seven east of the Mississippi.[1] Attendance in the parks and monuments, which had grown steadily from the creation of the National Park Service, had declined during the start of the Great Depression. In 1930 total attendance was 3,246,656, but in 1933 the number was down to 1,872,000. The numbers rebounded during the New Deal, however, and 1936 saw 3,544,000 visitors enter the parks.[2]

The increase in visitation required better planning, and the Park Service implemented a number of visitor studies during the 1930s. Superintendents and rangers studied private campgrounds to evaluate automobile-friendly sites adjacent to national parks. They concluded that such operations were generally better run and less expensive than those inside park areas, and they used the results to set guidelines for better competition by park concession operators.[3] A much larger two-phase study took place in 1939, as part of a cooperative effort between the National Park Service and the state parks. During the first stage, park visitors filled out a questionnaire, answering demographic questions about their income and residence, as well as their modes and distance of travel. A full 12,081 questionnaires were returned from 126 state and municipal parks as well as 9 federal recreation areas in twenty-seven states. In phase two, park rangers counted the number of cars coming through park entryways and made note of the relative number of in-state and out-of-state tags. Rangers also counted the number of people making use of particular facilities and activities. No qualitative questions were asked in either phase of the study.[4] The survey goals were entirely pragmatic, and the Park Service used the information to determine the best location for parking lots, picnic tables, crowd-control barriers, exhibits, and interpretive signs.

Public interest in the national parks had dramatically expanded, at least in part because of circumstances well beyond the agency's control. In the years between the two world wars, economic and political conditions had made overseas travel less attractive. The U.S. Travel Bureau, established in 1937 with New Deal funding and staff, urged Americans to travel at home to help spark the economy.[5] The improvement of national transportation infrastructure, the broader availability of automobiles, and development of an integrated system of publishing and advertising helped foster the rise of a tourism industry in the United States. One particularly successful campaign—See America First—helped brand National Parks as icons of a uniquely American experience and compelled citizens to visit them as part of their patriotic duty. At the same time, tourism lent consumers some power to shape America's culture and heritage. New Deal documentary projects had enabled white-collar professionals—photographers, architects, historians, and writers—to transform local folkways into representations of quintessential Americana. Domestic tourism enabled average citizens to participate in that process. Their travel choices reflected their beliefs about which landscapes were the most meaningful representations of a shared American heritage. Tourists were consumers of America, and purchasing power gave them a measure of cultural authority.[6]

The expansion of tourism to the parks lent some urgency to the question of how park personnel understood and performed their professional authority. Although the dramatic increase in tourism was an indicator of the success of the National Park Service, the large number of visitors might damage any given park's physical resources. Furthermore, through their use—or neglect—tourists had an impact on the meaning and value of the Park Service landscape. The Park Service was always dependent on visitors, but the expansion of domestic tourism had broadened the class of tourists. During the nineteenth century, the parks had been the province of wealthy tourists and budding scientists. These individuals certainly presented challenges to administrators, superintendents, and rangers working to assert their authority. The women of the Association for the Preservation of Virginia Antiquities struggled with the Park Service over physical boundaries and the interpretation of the past. The Rockefeller family shaped the meaning of parks in both the West and the East in their disbursement of funds. Nonetheless, by and large, they shared with Park Service professionals an understanding of the parks as valuable and fragile resources. Between 1910 and 1930, however, members of both the working class and the growing middle class began to enjoy domestic travel as well.[7] Their interests and values were less predictable. Even Jesse Nusbaum considered the new tourists a "limited class," in need of uplift and enlightenment before they could fully comprehend the parks.[8] In the years leading up to World War II, Park Service professionals—from administrators in Washington to on-site staff—tried to articulate the terms of their authority. Policy initiatives, interactions with workers, and correspondence with colleagues all suggest that the "new technicians" were testing the boundaries of their own expertise and control.

Tourists as "The Limited Class"

Worry about tourists' values was directly related to concerns about the rise of consumer culture and the expansion of the middle class. Prior to the twentieth century, elites largely dictated the form and content of American culture. Over the course of the late nineteenth and into the early twentieth century, however, less wealthy, less well-educated, and more racially and ethnically diverse Americans gradually acquired more leisure time and some disposable income. They sought out cheap amusements, quickly and easily consumed during a single day or afternoon off from work.[9] As the

Park Service used CCC labor during the New Deal to construct comfort facilities, campgrounds, roads, and parking lots for the increasing number of visitors, some expressed worry that meeting the needs of tourists would irrevocably change the meaning of the parks.[10] Harold Ickes, secretary of the interior under Franklin D. Roosevelt and founding director of the U.S. Travel Bureau, expressed precisely this worry when he said, "I do not want any Coney Island. I want as much wilderness, as much nature preserved and maintained as possible. If I could have my way I would have much fewer roads than we now have in most parks."[11] The construction of roads in and around the parks had increased the number of middle-class and working-class visitors so dramatically that all accommodations were strained to their limit.[12] Park superintendents worked to improve camping facilities, restrooms, and parking areas for automobile travelers. After hearing about plans for such improvements in Yosemite National Park, Ickes further complained, "If you give them hot and cold running water for shower baths, the next thing they will want will be their breakfasts in bed. Frankly, we don't want that kind of people in the park."[13]

Ickes's own comment suggests, however, that the "kind of people" visiting the parks were not necessarily looking for "Coney Island." At least some expected to spend their tourist dollars on middle-class comforts. Also, according to the Park Service's own surveys, the vast majority of visitors sought out meaningful educational experiences. Each year, reports to the director of the National Park Service indicated the number of visitors who took advantage of park museums, guided tours, and campfire lectures. Although rangers' focus on auto tourism meant they could not account for day-trippers who hiked onto park property, they claimed most tourists—somewhere between 77 and 88 percent of all visitors—took advantage of formal educational opportunities.[14] This preference reflects the growing demand for the trappings of middle-class status, including education, during the 1930s.[15] For some white-collar professionals and intellectual elites, this trend was worrisome. The popularity of Coney Island was a foil against which elites could feel superior. The attraction of national parks for all classes was part of a broader series of trends, suggesting that elite taste was a commodity, not a symbol. As such, it could be bought.[16] Consumers familiarized themselves with works of classic literature, which they purchased in abridged form from *Readers Digest*.[17] They decorated their modest homes with inexpensive reproductions of great works of art. They listened to radio programs like *The World Is Yours*, produced by the

Department of the Interior's Office of Education in conjunction with the Smithsonian, absorbing information gathered by experts but communicated and packaged by scriptwriters. They became history buffs, reading biographies and accounts of historical events penned by journalists such as Claude G. Bowers, political figures like former senator Albert Beveridge, and artists such as the poet Carl Sandburg. These amateur historians portrayed themselves as populists, making history accessible as an antidote to the "smug" tomes produced by a professional "history writing tribe."[18]

Examining the rise of middle-class culture and the status anxiety it created for white-collar professionals pioneering new areas of expertise is crucial for understanding the origin of public history as a field. The historians and historical archaeologists in the Park Service were struggling to identify and claim a space somewhere between the "history writing tribe" and consumers. On multiple occasions Verne Chatelain sought to define the unique work practiced by his "new technicians" by contrasting it against that of academic historians. In 1936 he told the members of the advisory committee on historic sites that traditional scholarship was often incomplete. He said, "Very frequently, history is written by men who have never visited the physical conditions under which historical problems have arisen. Now, no amount of reading of books and the written record will bring an appreciation of that thing." Park Service historians' access to historic landscapes and artifacts provided them with a unique insight that could both enhance traditional scholarship and provide consumers with a more accurate picture of the past. Chatelain explained, "The Middle Westerner who has seen a great many of the pictures related to the story of Jamestown and has read a great many things, still does not have a clear appreciation of what Jamestown means, and he will not until he goes there."[19]

Chatelain's words gave shape to a Park Service program of education that included both nature study and history. His influence is clearly reflected in Harold Bryant and Wallace Atwood's 1936 study of research and education in the national parks. Bryant and Atwood emphasized the place of material culture in Park Service programs: "Contact with real things, with unusual things, awakens a desire for explanation, for an increase of knowledge. This awakened craving for knowledge needs to be satisfied when the desire is uppermost."[20] The study reflects Chatelain's optimism, both about the value of education in the parks and about park historians' unique skills and expertise. Arno Cammerer, who succeeded Horace Albright as director of the National Park Service in 1933, held a similar view. He described the preservation of parks as a "consistent part of our New World idealism," and he saw their growing popularity as evidence that "people have begun to look outward and to see with perspective." He viewed education as a vehicle by which the "native beauty of the land" and "homespun cultural fabrics"—nature and culture—would become part of a common national heritage.[21]

This optimism expressed by the top administrators in the History Division was more tempered among the staff in the parks, however. Chatelain, Lee, Albright and Cammerer conceptualized the history program as part of a top-down research and education initiative. Professionals in Washington and in the regional offices, typically removed from direct contact with tourists, established standards and developed the interpretive frameworks that they imagined would improve visitors' appreciation of both nature and history. They also enjoyed a measure of professional security that came from their proximity to Washington's political networks and their executive status. Frontline employees worked in entirely different circumstances. On the ground, it was difficult to consider tourists as passive, sleeping giants ready to be awakened by contact with "real things." Historians, rangers, archaeologists, and interpreters sought to balance the educational initiatives created in Washington against their mission to provide opportunities for enjoyment. Furthermore, more removed from professional and political networks, they had to work more actively to establish their authority and expertise, especially among visitors whose class identity was more similar to their own than their colleagues in Washington apparently expected. In each park, the calculations were somewhat different, and educational and historical initiatives were often as much about exerting control over recreational activities as they were about ensuring enlightenment. Frontline staff created distance between themselves and tourists, and they sought reinforcement from a diverse community of scholars to bolster their own authority. In so doing, they established a unique and often problematic cultural position for the public historians who would follow in their footsteps.

Creating Collective Memory

Top-down planning was designed to unify the Park Service landscape, making it a recognizable brand easily marketed to tourists. In this framework, historians such as Verne Chatelain and Ronald Lee viewed historic sites as the material remains of a common American experience and portrayed them as valuable educational tools, the "most important aids to social memory in existence."[22] They oversaw the design of an interpretive framework that clarified the specific place of each site in an overarching national story. The apparently mundane task of naming parks had enormous consequences in shaping tourists' understanding of the park landscape, but there had been no uniform policy to guide the designation of historic places. Historically significant places were identified by a number of different names, including national monuments, national historical parks, national historic sites, national military parks, national battlefield sites, and national cemeteries. Park designations provided visitors with important cues. They could convey something about the kinds of human experiences that had taken place on a given landscape in the past, and they established expectations regarding the kinds of tourist activities that were appropriate now.

The interpretive value of site designations in the middle of the 1930s was undermined by complicated legal precedent and past usage. The term "national monument" was particularly problematic. That designation had been established by the Antiquities Act, which defined it as any "historic landmark, historic or prehistoric structure, or other object of historic or scientific interest." In practice the term "national monument" had been assigned to landscapes deemed valuable by anthropologists, archaeologists, and ethnologists who were interested in conducting research on a given property and in discouraging amateur collectors from conducting digs of their own. Typically, Native American sites were designated as national monuments, but government scientists had been loath to link them to living populations of Native people. As a result, although most monuments provided graphic historical evidence of human activity on a given landscape, they were not clearly differentiated from natural parks. A government pamphlet printed in 1917 vaguely notes, "National monuments differ from national parks in several respects, particularly with regard to the method of creation, but it would be difficult to define one generally in terms that would exclude the other."[23] The absence of an active subject who might have influenced the "method of creation" represents the government's hesitation to formally recognize that some monuments were the result of historical actions taken by Native American people. Ultimately, then, both parks and monuments appeared primarily natural rather than historical in significance.

The Advisory Board on National Parks, Historic Sites, Buildings, and Monuments constantly discussed how they might simplify and clarify Park

Service terminology. Advisory board members specifically debated the logic of separating monuments from historic sites, and, in so doing, they struggled to clarify the location of Native people in a larger narrative of the American past. On the one hand, the members of the advisory board argued that both historical and archaeological sites might carry the designation "monument" if they contained the remains of some man made structure whose "age, beauty, or historical or archaeological significance makes them worthy of national recognition and preservation." At the same time, equating historical with archaeological remains in this manner might renew tensions between scientists and historians, reinvigorating debates over the proper disposition of Native artifacts excavated from park property. Such a designation strategy would situate Native American sites as the equals of historic sites, raising the possibility that Native people should be located inside the American past and included in American identity, rather than separated from it in the artificial category of "prehistory." Thus, the advisory board decided that the designation "National Historical Park" should apply only to a site that had been the scene of some event "of transcendent importance in *American* history [emphasis mine]." Such sites had value "because they afford the opportunity of using a park area to graphically illustrate some of the major themes of American history, of a military, political, social and economic nature." In contrast, the board understood that the objective of the Antiquities Act was, simply, to preserve beautiful and scientifically valuable "natural" artifacts.[24]

The sites that had been transferred to the Park Service from the War Department were also problematic. They had been designated as national military parks, national cemeteries, and national battlefield parks. Under the terms accepted by the advisory board, they were all obviously "historical" because major events in America's past had transpired on their soil. At the same time, the sites often also contained human remains—American soldiers and bystanders killed during military engagements. The presence of these bodies complicated the ability of the Park Service to implement educational programs there, because the bodies quite literally sanctified the landscape, infusing it with a complex mixture of grief and patriotism. The Educational Advisory Board attempted to make sense of these sites by situating them in a hierarchy. Thus, a national military park was the scene of a crucial action, and the educational objective was to "preserve the terrain on which the action took place, to mark the important sites and lines of battle, and to interpret to the visitor the story of the area, including not only the battle but its historic background and the history of the whole region." Interpretive objectives were the same at a battlefield site, but such sites were differentiated from military parks by the significance of the action. The narrative on a battlefield might include less historical context and more information about strategy and region. Finally, although a variety of sites were likely to include human remains, only national cemeteries were sanctified by formal burial practices, placing them outside the realm of interpretation.[25]

A service-wide historical education initiative grew out of these designation practices, establishing a set of expectations for potential visitors and providing a particular shape to "social memory." Some memories and emotions were integrated with American history, while others remained outside the borders of American identity. For example, most Native American monuments also contained human remains, sanctified by ceremony and personal emotion. Nonetheless, scientists and relic hunters alike had looted Native graves for years, often failing to distinguish between ancient and recent burials.[26] Instead, they designated all Native burials as "prehistoric," disconnected from both living communities of people and a larger American history. Under the emerging logic of historical education, the Park Service administered historic sites like battlefields and "prehistoric" Native sites as two interrelated but separate categories.

On a practical level, however, as the History Division collected and administered an increasing number of sites, it became impossible to effectively use so many site designations. In late 1938 the Educational Advisory Board streamlined the naming policy. Battlefields, cemeteries, and military parks were all redesignated as national historical parks and, eventually, as national historical sites. The decision was largely bureaucratic, enabling administrative consistency and simplifying the process of site designation. The change in designation terminology enabled individual historic sites to be interpreted as parts of a larger whole. The board agreed that the change meant that "our historical areas will become a series of great exhibits, which, taken in their entirety, will constitute a series of illustrations of the outstanding events and great basic themes of American history, re-creating something of the color, the pageantry and the dignity of our national past." The change also had ideological overtones, however. Most significantly, despite a board resolution that "battlefields, fortifications, buildings [and] pre-Columbian earthworks" were all historical in interpretive value, most Native sites retained the title "monument."[27]

Workers as Tourists

While park designation strategies certainly had an impact on marketing by the U.S. Travel Bureau, it is difficult to measure the actual extent to which the advisory board succeeded in shaping tourists' expectations and desires. Although the Park Service gathered information about visitor behavior, there was no systematic effort to collect visitor opinion. As a result, tourists' desires are difficult to measure directly in the pre–World War II era. Fortunately, another group has left a sparse but tantalizing record of their interests and activities—the laborers who made up the Civilian Conservation Corps.

Between 1933 and 1942 more than three million unemployed workers signed up with the CCC and were sent to live and work in national parks, national forests, state parks, and farms across the nation.[28] The vast majority of CCC enrollees were eighteen to twenty-five years old, male, in poor health, and lacking in any particular job skills. Quite literally, they entered the project as disenfranchised, sickly boys and left as vital, masculine citizens. Indeed, the second director of the corps titled his book *Now They Are Men*. In the CCC, enrollees were inoculated against disease and required to engage in forty hours a week of often demanding physical labor.[29] CCC workers at Mesa Verde National Park, for example, installed telephone lines, provided general sanitation work, built roads and guardrails, removed snow, and constructed foot trails, houses, office buildings, and a public campground. They also installed water stations, provided insect control, assisted in topographical surveys and landscaping, and provided maintenance and repair work in the park's museum exhibits.[30] In Arizona and New Mexico alone, a diverse corps of workers—"Indians, cowboys, homesteaders and trained archaeologists"—at fifteen national monuments built roads, improved visitor access and comfort facilities, and contributed to archaeological research by digging trenches and cataloging artifacts.[31] At historical parks in the eastern portion of the United States, CCC workers conducted historical research and improved the facilities at historic sites. Over the course of its tenure in the service, the CCC planted more than two billion trees, built retaining walls and installed vegetation to slow soil erosion on forty million acres of farmland, and participated in the development of eight hundred new state parks. It also built forty-six thousand automobile bridges, developed thirteen thousand miles of hiking trails, and installed nearly one million miles of fence to protect park property and wildlife from unchecked human traffic.[32]

The CCC enrollees experienced the parks like tourists, and park staff encouraged them to take advantage of the educational opportunities provided by professional guides and interpreters. Park Service rangers and concession operators provided recreational activities for the workers. They took them on guided tours—at reduced rates—on foot and by horseback and automobile. The enrollees sought out their own experiences as well. Many arrived in the camps with little direct experience of wildlife or wilderness. Writing for camp newspapers, they frequently commented on the impact that access to nature had on them. One enrollee reported, "The outdoors seems to make a fellow FEEL more."[33] Park staff encouraged them to think more as well, directing them to marked trails, museum exhibits, and other educational attractions. According to one annual report from Mesa Verde, the guided automobile trips were especially successful. "During the summer, trips were made to Hovenweep National Monument, to Battle Rock, to shiprock and Indian country, to the Aztec ruins and to other points of interest. To say that these trips were enjoyable is putting it mildly, as they were, for days and weeks, a prominent subject of conversation; so for many years it is believed they will bring memories of pleasant—and profitable—Recreational Activities."[34] Workers—like tourists—could explore the parks without an expert guide, but CCC leaders and park staff alike argued that the more "profitable" experiences required an expert to connect the material experience to intellectual growth. A variety of more directly educational classes rounded out the CCC experience. Workers were able to take elementary courses in English, math, spelling, penmanship, and typing. At some encampments, on-the-job training provided workers with marketable technical training as well.

The fact that workers in many CCC encampments conducted archaeological excavations and practiced collections management worried some professionals. Many remained doubtful that untrained and undereducated working-class boys were appropriate staff for research and interpretative projects. The archaeologist Carl Guthe conceded that the availability of a federal labor force might provide invaluable support to new and ongoing archaeological and historical research. But the quality of such a dig—done by untrained laborers overseen by unprofessional middle managers—would be more than suspect. Manual labor functioned best in routinized and tightly managed circumstances, but such an organization was contrary to meaningful scientific discovery. He argued that for the projects to function effectively, they required "the creation of a rather complex administrative machinery." He worried that too few archaeologists were available to oversee the projects, and, as a result, "inevitably more data will be destroyed than can possibly be recovered. And finally, when the work is done, we will have a great mass of improperly equipped individuals who think they are archaeologists because they have handled a shovel for a week or two in an archaeological project."[35] Guthe's criticism is telling. Just a decade earlier, Smithsonian scientists had expressed similar fears about the sense of entitlement Park Service men felt after seeing and handling Native artifacts. By describing workers requiring "administrative machinery" and equating the Works Progress Administration with an industrial mechanism, he expressed a distinctive class bias. Furthermore, he suggested that the predominant physicality of the working class was an inherent danger not only to the preservation of scientifically valuable landscapes but also to the clear boundary between experts and audiences. Guthe feared that simply because the workers "handled a shovel for a week or two" they would feel entitled to a measure of interpretive authority and expertise.

Museum-based education was available to workers at many of the Park Service CCC camps. While the vast majority of courses were elementary or technical in nature, some camp educators encouraged workers to design and direct their own educational projects. In more than one instance, participating in archaeological digs or museum conservation fired workers' imaginations. As the Park Service education staff had hoped, access to "real things" had inspired them. One camp education adviser—P. V. McCone— wrote a letter that was forwarded around the Smithsonian and the Park Service. According to McCone, the workers had been hiking in hills surrounding the camp and had discovered abandoned Native American structures and artifacts. McCone wanted permission to oversee a site dig. He argued that both he and his assistant had the expertise to conduct the dig with professionalism; McCone had an MA in sociology and his assistant had participated in digs while a student at Pacific University in Oregon. They intended to contribute to the site's historical records and to produce an exhibit. He assured, "THE UNDERTAKING WOULD BE PRIMARILY FOR THE PURPOSE OF GIVING EDUCATIONAL OPPORTUNITIES TO OUR BOYS WHO ARE INTERESTED."[36] Despite McCone's insistence on his own credentials and his appeal to the educational value of the project, the fact that laborers' interests were driving the request troubled federal historians and archaeologists. The request was quashed by a game of bureaucratic football, as various agents claimed they lacked the authority to grant McCone permission. The final rejection came from the Smithsonian's chief of ethnology.[37]

Ultimately, whether the relationship between CCC laborers and Park Service administrators was marked by camaraderie or frustration is almost immaterial. Just as laborers helped shape the Park Service landscape, the Park Service helped shape the laborers physically and intellectually. In this interdependent, dialogic relationship, a constituency of the working class exerted some influence in the evolving work culture of public history. Sometimes this mutual influence was quite literal; park rangers trained some CCC workers to serve as site guides and official greeters. Furthermore, the emergency work projects in the Park Service led to the employment of both laborers and specialists. Thrown together by unemployment, they worked in sync on a variety of interpretive projects. On occasion, the line between professionals and laborers was quite vague. At Mesa Verde, Wally Hagan lived in the CCC labor camp and worked on a variety of construction projects. He was also a geology graduate from the University of Illinois. He identified himself to camp operators and began to develop new education programs for his fellow enrollees. He "was successful in inspiring his class with much of his own enthusiasm."[38] Hagan represents the complexity of the "tourist class," at least as it was embodied in the CCC workforce. His dual role as worker and interpreter represents the success of Arno Cammerer's "New World idealism" for creating a more informed working class. More broadly, the relationship between Park Service educators and CCC workers suggests there was room for dialogue regarding the use and meaning of the parks.

Authority and Expertise

The extent to which tourists could shape their own experiences in the parks raised questions about the legitimacy of the authority exerted by park staff. Frontline interpreters experienced some anxiety about their status and professionalism. Questions of status were particularly potent for men practicing younger sciences such as historical archaeology or engaged in interpretive work. Working on-site in historical parks and archaeological monuments required park staff to conduct research to ensure they understood the meaning of the landscape. Verne Chatelain insisted that their proximity to the material remains of the past gave them a unique expertise. Yet, their primary responsibility was to interpret the landscape for non-experts, tourists who understood education as recreational. Their private correspondence with colleagues suggests that on-site staff experienced a sense of uncertainty about their professional stature. They struggled to create a coherent interpretation that addressed the needs of visitors while also advancing their disciplinary expertise. Ultimately, their effort documents the formation of a rather complex cultural foundation for public history professionalism.

Scientists from other federal agencies—particularly the Smithsonian Institution—were invested in the creation of a strong program of research in the national parks. In the nineteenth century, geologists and other naturalists had been pivotal in justifying the creation of national parks. At the turn of the twentieth century, ethnologists and archaeologists had fought to extend federal protections to landscapes containing evidence of the human past and to establish an agency for their efficient management. After the creation of the National Park Service, Smithsonian curators had worried that park museums would usurp their status as the keepers of national collections. Nonetheless, they had also lent their expertise to excavations at Jamestown, Mesa Verde, and various other park sites. In the latter half of the 1930s, personal relationships between Park Service research staff and Smithsonian curators had an important impact on the ways in which Park Service professionals defined and defended their expertise.

Park Service researchers depended on their relationships with Smithsonian curators to bolster their own authority. When the National Park Service found itself engaged in a dispute with the Association for the Preservation of Virginia Antiquities over the creation of Colonial National Historical Park, Frank Setzler had stepped in. He pushed the Park Service to hire a scientist for site evaluation. Leveraging his broad professional network, the Smithsonian curator of archaeology sought recommendations from colleagues across the country and identified J. C. Harrington as the best candidate for the position of site archaeologist.

Like Nusbaum, Chatelain, and other "Park Service men" who had arrived before him, Harrington had taken a rather circuitous route to his eventual profession. He had completed undergraduate studies in architecture at the

University of Michigan. For his senior thesis, rather than working in an architect's office, he went to work as one of two architecture students at the School of American Research in Santa Fe, recording structural reports of Spanish missions. He became acquainted with Edgar Hewett and Alfred Kidder, entering into a network of scientists who encouraged him to switch fields. His interdisciplinary interests did not make him an easy fit for formal schooling, but he applied to the graduate program in anthropology at the University of Chicago, where he was accepted, by his account, "somewhat reluctantly" by faculty. After struggling through courses in linguistic and social anthropology, he returned to his real interest: archaeology. Still Harrington was reluctant to accept the archaeology position at Jamestown. He recalled, "I had no interest in working for the Federal government, preferring an academic association, nor did I see any future in digging a site only 300 years old."[39] After some procrastination, however, Harrington found that the job perfectly suited his diverse interests and background. Once at work for the Park Service, Harrington combined archaeological excavation with archival research to investigate competing claims regarding the historical significance of Jamestown Island. Still something of a novice, he relied on advice from his mentors and repeatedly turned to Setzler for advice.

Harrington's correspondence with Setzler documents his personal maturation as a historical archaeologist; his initial research provided the Park Service with the evidence necessary to expand their control of the site. More broadly, examining the experiences of multidisciplinary prospective scholars at work in the Park Service demonstrates that their personal uncertainty about the path of professional advancement is significant in the larger history of the agency and its historical projects. In November 1937 Harrington wrote a lengthy letter describing the techniques of historical archaeology that he and his staff had put to use on-site. He assured Setzler that he had implemented the most cutting-edge methods of excavation, storage, and interpretation of artifacts. He planned to put together a field manual to guide future site research and establish himself as a key figure for the advancement of his profession. He was wary, however, about who else might make use of his technique, writing, "I am not sure that I want to make it available to Park Service 'diggers' as a whole."[40] Harrington likely meant he did not want the manual to be used by the CCC workers conducting the most strenuous labor on-site. But his comment also reflects his understanding that a gap remained in the perceived professionalism of

Park Service staff and the more established scientific network. After his first year at Jamestown, Harrington lent his expertise not only to the work of excavation but also to the effort to reconstruct the historic village. He recalled, "It had become clear that the American archaeological fraternity was not going to accept this new use of archaeology without a struggle."[41]

Setzler played his own role in that struggle. When an opportunity arose for the Smithsonian to gain more control over professional standards in Park Service research, Setzler advised his superiors to act. In 1934, anticipating the passage of the Historic Sites Act, National Park Service historians and educators turned to the Smithsonian Institution for advice. The act, passed in 1935, authorized a massive study of the nation's untapped archaeological and historical resources. Chatelain and Lee believed the project would be temporary, especially because similar surveys had already begun under HABS and under the auspices of the History Division. The Historic Sites Act, they believed, would provide the final push to create a complete list of nationally significant sites. Under this assumption, the Smithsonian shared with the Park Service the results of its own survey of archaeological sites and provided the service with recommendations about which might be most worthy of national status.

By 1938, however, it had become obvious that the work generated by the Historic Sites Act was neither temporary nor manageable by the small Washington staff. Park Service administrators began to inquire about establishing a more formal partnership with the Smithsonian. There was more than enough precedent to support such an arrangement. In addition to Frank Setzler, other curators had conducted or advised scientific projects on Park Service properties. Mathew Stirling, chair of the Bureau of American Ethnology, had detailed researchers to examine various Native American sites. Jesse Nusbaum and Frank Pinkley had worked alongside Smithsonian researchers at various southwestern monuments and western parks. Nonetheless, cooperation and support between the two agencies often had taken place not so much as a gesture of professional courtesy, but rather to minimize competition and assert control. Even as he made the case for formalizing a relationship between the two agencies, Frank Setzler expressed old professional jealousies. He wrote to Smithsonian Secretary Alexander Wetmore, "If we neglect to cooperate we will not only be criticized but will give the National Park Service a legitimate reason for creating a duplicate archaeological staff."[42]

Clearly, Setzler believed the Historic Sites Act had created an opportunity to expand the professional reach of federal archaeologists. At Jamestown, solving the Park Service boundary dispute with the Association for the Preservation of Virginia Antiquities had depended on Smithsonian authority. Setzler sought to take advantage of that dependence. He advised Wetmore that a more formal arrangement would mean that "all archaeological work sponsored by the National Park Service would come under the jurisdiction of the Smithsonian Institution." Furthermore, expanding the Smithsonian's jurisdiction would not necessarily expand its workload. Setzler argued, "Such an agreement should not require more than the selection of a competent archaeologist to be placed temporarily on our staff or even on the staff of the Park Service.... If demands from the National Park Service become too involved, we could convincingly request an increase in our regular staff, both departments sharing in the expense of an increased budget." Rather than diluting Smithsonian authority, he argued, "These suggestions would seem to increase our own independence as a research organization."[43] Wetmore agreed. When the Park Service identified a potentially significant site, the Smithsonian Institution would send its scientists to conduct field studies. The research would take place at the request—and the expense—of the Park Service. Mathew Stirling and Frank Setzler resolved to serve as the official points of contact between the two agencies. In practice, the agreement gave the Smithsonian a sense of entitlement and control in designing and managing archaeological and ethnological research in the parks. Both Stirling and Setzler were named to Park Service advisory boards, and both influenced the creation of policies on research and education.[44] By taking on a role in Park Service planning, Setzler and Stirling were able to monitor its projects, offering assistance even when none was requested.

Over time, Setzler, Stirling, and other Smithsonian scientists exerted a strong influence not only on scientific work but also on the conduct of historical research in the parks. In 1938 word began to spread that the Park Service intended to hire a historian who would assist its associate archaeologist, A. R. Kelly, in his Macon, Georgia, offices. After a kind of apprenticeship under Kelly, that historian would be installed as the site administrator of Ocmulgee National Monument. Ocmulgee, designated in June 1934, is the site of "prehistoric" earthworks and burial mounds dating back about twelve thousand years. The Smithsonian was not pleased that the service planned to select a historian to oversee research and the development of site interpretation. Frank Setzler sprang to action again. He convinced the Park Service that hiring a historian would be a serious mistake. Monument sites had been designated as archaeologically significant, and Setzler doubted a historian would understand the value and meaning of cultural resources, particularly the remains of a culture with no written record. Instead, he recommended the archaeologist Jess Jennings as a more appropriate choice. Jennings had been working in Arizona as an assistant to Frank Pinkley, then superintendent of the Southwestern Monument. Setzler believed that Jennings's professional training was being wasted in the National Park Service. Setzler approached assistant director Arthur Demaray, who oversaw the Branch of Research and Education as well as the History Division. He complained that Jennings was doing primarily "custodial" duty under Pinkley, and he reported that Demaray and assistant director for operations Hillory Tolson were both "dismayed" to learn about the plans to hire a historian. He told Jennings, "They realized immediately that such a move would not be in keeping with a strictly archaeological site."[45]

Setzler's belief that Jennings's talents were "wasted" in the Southwest is particularly telling. Far from simply engaging in custodial work, Jennings was actively engaged in interpretation. He served as a site guide, conducting tours. He also assisted researchers working on archaeological digs on park properties. Both Setzler and Jennings agreed, however, that this work was not sufficiently professional. Jennings's task was not necessarily to advance science among experts but rather to interpret scientific information and techniques for tourists. When Pinkley was reluctant to transfer him to Georgia, Jennings made a point of emphasizing the potentially greater value his work would have at Ocmulgee. He echoed the words of J. C. Harrington when he wrote to Setzler, "I emphasized to Pinkley that research was my interest; not digging." In Georgia, Jennings argued, he would analyze data alongside the better established Kelly, thereby contributing to new scholarship. Jennings found his role as an educator in the Southwest tiresome and unsatisfying. He wanted to "do something more than contact work, which I definitely do not care to continue." He believed that producing specialized scholarship from Ocmulgee would advance both "the Park Service and archaeology, as well as benefit me personally."[46] When Jennings was ultimately offered the position and Pinkley relented on his efforts to block the transfer, Setzler expressed his pleasure that Jennings would be "in a much more academic and research atmosphere" at Ocmulgee.[47] Much as he had with Harrington at Jamestown, Setzler encouraged Jennings to "write me very frankly" regarding the politics and work at Ocmulgee.

Jennings, much like Harrington, preferred to think of himself as a scientist rather than an interpreter. He expressed frustration with the Park Service effort to quantify visitor behavior. In an exasperated note to Setzler he explained, "If my visitors' average time on the Monument is forty-five minutes and that time slowly increases to sixty minutes, I and the Service assume that the guide personnel is giving more information to the average person, and there is a further assumption that he is doing his job better when he interests his parties for this increased time." At the same time, he also began to resent the Smithsonian's efforts to control the production of scholarship. In 1938 he made an attempt to assert his own expertise to block the transfer of a rather large collection from Ocmulgee to the Smithsonian. The artifacts had been excavated on-site between 1936 and 1937, with a combination of private and federal funds. According to the original project plans, they belonged to the Smithsonian Institution. Jennings wrote to Setzler, presumably to ask for instructions about how to transport the materials, but he clearly believed that the artifacts should remain on-site. He explained that "digging" funded by the New Deal had nearly come to a halt and that the reduction of labor activity gave him some time to properly study the material. He continued, "I intend to emphasize the cataloging and correlation of the raw data which has been amassed during the past four years, with a consequent temporary lull in digging activity. Your knowledge of the situation is probably such that you agree with me in this change of policy."[48] By describing the material as "data" and sharing his plans to catalog and correlate the information they contained, Jennings placed himself as Setzler's equal rather than his student and, in so doing, claimed a role for the Park Service in the advancement of scientific knowledge.

Jennings's monthly reports and correspondence with Setzler indicate that he was increasingly caught in an intellectual middle ground, sensitive to the Park Service emphasis on visitor education but still invested in the belief that his professional identity depended on scientific scholarship. In his first report as superintendent in April 1938, Jennings noted, "Our problem at Ocmulgee lies in achieving the proper balance between the two imperative programs—research and educational presentation—in such a way that the excavation program will not outstrip the physical development of Monument facilities. Neither can the excavation be allowed to advance too far ahead of laboratory analysis of data."[49] Despite his own distaste for frontline interpretation, he recognized it as a safety valve—a way to help visitors understand and respect the boundaries between professional research and personal curiosity. He hired guides to lead visitors around active dig sites and to conduct cautious tours of the mounds. He continued to observe and report on visitor behavior, and he used this information in his reports as a way to demonstrate his educational success.

By far the most significant gesture Jennings made to balance the competing interests of scientific professionalism and park popularity was his effort to rebuild the on-site museum. Although he understood the museum would be a tourist destination, his goal was to emphasize the site's value as a research facility. His reports indicate that he got the most satisfaction from scholarly visits to the museum and collections. In August 1938, for example, Jennings expressed enthusiasm that the site museum had begun to attract legitimate researchers. He reported that a recent graduate of the University of Arizona had spent a week conducting research in the museum collections. He described the visit as "the item of main importance this month [that] will interest supporters of the Museum program more than anything which has been reported in the last several months." He explained, "The significant thing is not that he spent a few days with us but that he represents the type of individual to whom we wish our museum to be attractive."[50]

For Jennings, the most important "supporters of the Museum" were not necessarily private funders or increasing numbers of visitors but professional archaeologists and advanced students. In his estimation, the Park Service could harness the archaeological value of Ocmulgee to advance its professional standing. In his July 1938 report he wrote, "Ocmulgee is an ideal situation so far as the Park Service is concerned, because we have here a vast quantity of raw data in which the professional archaeologist has a great interest. The Service can set a research precedent, and gain for itself new laurels if it makes the point of having detailed scientific reports prepared at the earliest possible time." Perhaps it was because of this emphasis on scientific advancement and professional standards that Jennings found that "all the professional archaeologists are much in sympathy with the proposed Southeastern Museum now being built in Ocmulgee. All promised cooperation and any assistance which they can render."[51]

Scientists acting as site supervisors sought to achieve balance between the demands of professional expertise and the demands of visitors. It is significant that one of the first tasks J. C. Harrington undertook at Jamestown was also the construction of a museum. Although he had been markedly uncomfortable allowing archaeological authority to rest with CCC work-ers, he had far less trepidation about assigning them a variety of museum tasks such as cleaning, repairing, and cataloging artifacts for museum dis-play: "The final story of the development of Jamestown, and its place in American history, is too distant and hinges on too many factors for us to attempt to set up a far-reaching program at this time. But it is important . . . to formulate a tentative program . . . for planning and carrying out more immediate work."[52] Among the "immediate work" he felt was most impor-tant was the creation of a museum that would help control the impact that tourists could have on the site by providing them with a safe space in which to satisfy their curiosity about the process of archaeological work. Museums, guides, and other controlled educational experiences created a buffer between experts and audiences, limiting the kinds of dialogue that could shape the meaning and value of the park landscape.

Historical Expertise and Professionalism

Over the course of the 1930s, history became more integrated into top-down administrative planning and on-the-ground management and education in the National Park Service. In Washington, D.C., and in the Park Service regional offices, historians were research technicians, administrators, and members of advisory boards. There, they applied what Verne Chatelain had called "historical mindedness" to the task of site selection and site des-ignation. Park names and structures identified as historically significant reflected both a belief in the logical advancement of American history over time and a set of cultural values regarding the kinds of sites worthy of fed-eral protection. On the ground in historic parks and national monuments, historians accepted jobs as professional supervisors for CCC site develop-ment and museum work. Historians were also increasingly considered for superintendent and ranger positions at national monuments.

Despite this success, the work of site management and interpretation exposed the professional landscape on which Park Service historians stood as inherently unstable. Museums and educational programs were designed to control the behavior of tourists, elevating the popularity of sites but minimizing the ability of middle- or working-class tourists to alter their meaning. The potential of the "limited class" to affect perceptions and pop-ularity of various historical resources was a problem because Park Service historians had only a small cohort of colleagues. Scientists, on the other hand, continued to enjoy a broad network of professional support. Their common reliance on research collections meant that academics and museum professionals were bound by professional interests. Historians remained divided, and the proximity of Park Service historians to landscapes and artifacts infused with patriotism and other emotional attachments meant that academics were reluctant to help bolster their legitimacy. Scientists filled that gap, recommending archaeologists for key positions at sites such as Colonial National Historical Park, Ocmulgee, and other monuments to the human past.

Archaeologists such as Jess Jennings and J. C. Harrington brought the interdisciplinary methodology of historical archaeology to bear on their work. They came to understand the necessity of documenting site popularity and even to enjoy curating exhibitions that attracted the attention of tourists. Nonetheless, the preference for scientific modes of research and interpretation had an impact on the evolution of public history for the remainder of the twentieth century. As the New Deal ended and funds evaporated, the Park Service history program retreated to a less narrative and more archival kind of historical practice.

Toward a New Genealogy of Public History

— ❊ —

Historians function at the intersection of the natural rhythm of life and the cultural context of human enterprise. They bring the historical perspective of our natural and cultural worlds to the National Park Service's management table. That table, we now understand, is large enough to accommodate a wide range of perspectives and professions. And we are better managers because of it.

—DWIGHT PITCAITHLEY—

By the 1930s the National Park Service had become a standard bearer for historical planning and interpretation. Under the leadership of Harold Albright, a small but significant group of men crafted new strategies for the expansion of park holdings and the education of tourists, introducing history into the National Park Service management structure. Together, forward-looking and ambitious administrators such as Albright, archaeologists such as Jesse Nusbaum, and historians such as Verne Chatelain and Ronald Lee crafted a new profession. Between 1916 and 1936 their actions helped to establish history as a function of government service, as they struggled to find an appropriate balance between the desires of tourists and the demands of their discipline's gatekeepers. They developed a research strategy to guide site selection, designation, and interpretation and they defined artifacts as viable historical documents, not simply scientific specimens. For thirty years after the end of the New Deal, the decisions they made shaped the values applied by federal historians, local preservationists, historical archaeologists, and history consumers.

Yet, just as federal historians such as Jack Holl, David Trask, and others felt marginalized by the public history movement of the 1970s, the historians who carved out a new profession in the Park Service during the 1930s have been relegated to a supporting role in histories of the field. Recent efforts to define and historicize public history often gloss over their work or minimize its significance. For example, in his valuable analysis of interpretive planning at Colonial Williamsburg, Cary Carson credits its founders and managers with conceptualizing historical interpretation as part of a broader management strategy. He acknowledges the earlier work by Chatelain and the Park Service History Division but argues that it "produced little that resembles an interpretive plan."[1] Ian Tyrell credits Chatelain and his men with influencing the practice of history in local and regional historical societies, and he describes Verne Chatelain's vision as "strikingly contemporary." Nonetheless, because his work traces the extent to which the discipline of history always has involved public practice—rather than tracing a separate evolution for public history—he devotes only a few pages to Chatelain and Lee specifically.[2] Scholars within the Park Service have most certainly recognized the important role played by Chatelain, Lee, and other early historians in the service, but their work has inadvertently compartmentalized them, measuring their significance within the agency, rather than their larger contributions to the field of public history.[3]

Reframing the ongoing effort to define public history illuminates the importance of Park Service historians more clearly, shedding light on the distinct path from which their professional practice emerged. At the end of the twentieth century, the then Park Service chief historian Dwight T. Pitcaithley defined history in his agency not simply as a discipline but more broadly as an educational enterprise, a management strategy, and an interpretive middle ground on which tourists and educators met to make sense of the relationship between nature and culture. His comments opened up an opportunity to reconsider the long process by which history became a government job.[4] As Pitcaithley suggested, public history is an interdisciplinary practice that adapts research methodologies and interpretive perspectives from a variety of fields to raise important questions about the meaning of the past and impose order on a diverse and otherwise incoherent landscape.[5] While most observers and practitioners acknowledge interdisciplinary work as part of the practice of public history today, few have adequately recognized it as having been central in the field's development over time. Reconsidering the events that created space for historians as government workers broadens the field's family tree, making clear the professional debt public historians have to generations of naturalists and adventurers as well as to other historians. This perspective is important not simply because it helps to establishes men such as Chatelain and Lee as central figures in the public history movement. It also intervenes in stubborn debates regarding the term "public history." Tracing the gradual emergence of public history as a government job rather than as a specialty within the larger discipline of history sheds new light on the complicated role public historians play in the institutions in which they work and among the audiences they serve.

Public History as a Tool of Expansion, Authority, and Management

The history of public history is, at its most basic level, a story about expansion—of federal authority, disciplinary expertise, and public space. Historians entered into public service in the twentieth century because the federal government's reach had stretched over the course of the nineteenth century. Prior to the Civil War, individuals seeking legitimacy for the natural sciences cast their lot with politicians and diplomats similarly interested in raising the stature of the nation. Over time, they nurtured a mutually dependent relationship between science and government. This was a slow process, complicated by Americans' general resistance to the expansion of federal authority and protectiveness regarding private property and individual rights. In this cultural atmosphere, budding naturalists connected their intellectual pursuits to pragmatic concerns. They abandoned the European model of research as an elite pursuit and demonstrated instead that gathering scientific specimens and analyzing their meaning had direct, practical ramifications for entrepreneurs and for the nation. Their work enabled governments—local, state, and federal—to influence economic development and to define the landscape as a public resource, one that housed the nation's wealth, reinforced its military defenses, and reflected its uniqueness.

After the Civil War the cultural and political influence of researchers and collectors expanded even more dramatically. The postwar period was defined by rapid change. The end of slavery, the rise of industry, the growth of cities, and the emergence of new social norms created both anxiety and optimism. In this atmosphere, science moved to the center of American public life, promising objectivity and efficiency as an antidote to economic, social, and cultural upheaval. With the maturation of a national publishing industry—made possible by technological advancements in the realm of printing—scientific expeditions were popularized as adventure stories. As life east of the Mississippi became increasingly routinized, crowded, and urban, the exploration of the Grand Canyon and the Yellowstone River fired interest in the wild western landscapes and fueled the expansion of the railroad and the development of a tourist industry. At the same time, scientific research and development became essential to the economic well-being of the nation. Work became more mechanical in factories and on farms, and the potential labor force required better access to specialized instruction. In response, Congress pressed federal influence even further— into the realm of higher education—by passing the Morrill Act, which encouraged the establishment of state colleges and universities that provided practical, vocational training in states in the Midwest and the West. It also enabled older universities in the East and the South to develop applied research programs and institutes to complement classical education offerings.

The popularization of science and the rise of research-based education accelerated the professionalization of various disciplines and established a broad well-connected network of scientists, educators, and policymakers. Entrepreneurial scientists such as Ferdinand Hayden and John Wesley Powell, who had begun their research careers prior to the Civil War, became linchpins connecting government and science through both their personal relationships and their research ventures. They accepted professorial positions in land grant universities established under the Morrill Act, curated collections in university museums, shared data and specimens with colleagues at the Smithsonian, and courted support from federal and local governments, regional boosters, and new media outlets, as they sought to explore ever more remote landscapes. Their adventures spawned a diverse movement to protect natural resources and produced new collections for the Smithsonian, new fodder for the popular press, and new legitimacy for their own professional goals. Powell moved to Washington, D.C., to head the Bureau of American Ethnology, a division of the Smithsonian Institution. He organized the Cosmos Club—a social organization where men of science mingled with policymakers and other elites.

Scientists like Powell leveraged their popularity, their ties to wealthy industrialists, their broad professional connections, and their relationships with policymakers. They created powerful coalitions and lobbied successfully to formalize a role for the federal government in the protection of natural and cultural resources. Congress acted on reports by geologists, eth-nologists, and archaeologists. Beginning with the creation of Yellowstone National Park in 1872, and bolstered by the passage of the Antiquities Act in 1906, the federal government defined large swaths of land as "useless" to investors and redefined them as primarily valuable for science. By the turn of the twentieth century, then, researchers enjoyed broad influence in the realm of policymaking, and policymakers enjoyed broad influence in determining the use and value of public lands.

The establishment of federally protected landscape also broadened Americans' acceptance of government influence in the realm of economic development. Local boosters and business investors recognized parks and monuments as potential tourist attractions. Representatives heard propos-als from entrepreneurial constituents as well as geologists, ethnologists, anthropologists, and other scientists, and the pace at which properties were set aside for preservation accelerated rapidly. Between 1872 and 1906 Congress approved the creation of seven national parks in the American West. At least ten other sites—battlefields, military cemeteries, and monu-ment structures—also gained federal recognition. In the ten years after the passage of the Antiquities Act, the president and Congress designated more than forty additional sites. The growing number of parks and monu-ments led to calls for more federal control, not less. Concern spread about the ability of existing federal agencies to enforce the protection of natural and cultural resources. Neither individual park bills nor the Antiquities Act contained clear or uniform instructions regarding enforcement. Sites fell under the responsibility of various federal entities, including the Depart-ment of War, the Bureau of Public Lands, the Department of the Interior, and the Department of Agriculture. In practice, many were guarded in a rather haphazard fashion by local ranchers or business owners. The large national parks were policed by the U.S. Cavalry, making them more like battlefields than recreation or research areas. In the meantime, western set-tlers, tourists, and other curiosity seekers continued to inflict irreparable damage on fragile scientific resources, carting off artifacts as souvenirs and defacing natural formations and ancient structures.

In this cultural environment, the history of public history also became a story about management. A variety of professional associations and pro-gressive reform organizations began to demand a rational approach to the management of public lands. Some emphasized the need for standards to guide park and monument selection to protect only the most spectacular and unique landscapes from development. Others sought to impose sharp limits on public access to protected spaces, ensuring that wilderness remained unsullied by the human touch. Still others believed that public spaces should provide opportunities for outdoor recreation, particularly for those who lived and worked in urban America. Despite significant differences in tone and emphasis, most of these organizations agreed that a single agency must be established to manage park landscapes and park visitors more efficiently. All of this pressure led Congress to establish the National Park Service in 1916. The agency's mission transformed the federal government's responsibility for public lands, moving beyond custody to management—broadly defined.

As with earlier laws, however, the Park Service mandate to both protect fragile landscapes and make them available and accessible to tourists came without instructions. Stephen Mather and Horace Albright, the first two directors of the National Park Service, identified education as a management tool, one that could bridge the agency's two core responsibilities. On the ground in individual parks, interpretive programs, including guided tours, campfire talks, and museum exhibitions, protected fragile resources by controlling the movements and training the perceptions of tourists. The development of educational programs for park visitors became the focus not only of Park Service administrators in Washington but also of individual superintendents and rangers, who—by the middle of the 1920s—were often well-trained scientists in their own right.

This seemingly innocuous decision to harness education as a strategy for park management, however, meant that professionals in the National Park Service were often in conflict with their colleagues in other agencies and institutions. Scientists had long gathered specimens in the parks and monuments, shipping valuable artifacts to curatorial units at the Smithsonian Institution in Washington. Some early site custodians, lacking scientific training, had tended to support this practice, recognizing the attention of legitimate collectors as an appropriate antidote to the damage inflicted by treasure hunters. Others challenged the removal of Park Service property. Historical archaeologists such as Jesse Nusbaum argued that artifacts made more sense when displayed in context, helping visitors to recognize the landscape as historical as well as scientific, cultural as well as natural.

The establishment of the National Park Service also created competition among various government bureaus and agencies tasked with land management. This competition was pivotal, drawing attention to history as an area ripe for federal expansion and management. Within a decade of its founding, the agency remained—for the most part—a regional entity, managing a large number of parks and monuments in the West and Southwest. In the meantime, the Forest Service, the War Department, and the Bureau of Public Lands retained responsibility for a number of monuments, battlefields, and natural resource areas across the country. Mather and Albright recognized the need to expand Park Service holdings east of the Mississippi to justify its national stature. Following the advice of an advisory board focused on education in the national parks, Albright created a Park Service history program as a first step toward acquiring managerial control of various historic properties from other agencies. Park Service history became a tool of expansion and development, enabling states in the South and Northeast to attract tourists. It provided a canvas on which local boosters could portray regional culture. As museum exhibits, guided tours, campfire talks, and archaeological demonstrations presented artifacts to tourists for inspection, history began to serve a public good, providing a window through which average Americans might catch a glimpse of the past and recognize their own place in the nation's story.

Public Historians and the Discipline of History

The historians hired by Verne Chatelain and Ronald Lee were somewhat isolated as federal workers. During the nineteenth century, a well-connected and well-respected network of scientists had helped to expand the reach of the federal government, define the value of the public landscape, and shape education as a strategy for management. Most historians remained on the margins of these larger processes. Although their efforts to attain status and legitimacy followed many of the same patterns established by the scientific disciplines, historians were unable—or, perhaps, unwilling—to integrate voluntary preservationists, artifact collectors, commemorative organizations, or history-buff writers into their professional network. As a result, the practice of history remained splintered, and the most popular efforts to explore the past were marginalized by the discipline's gatekeepers.

At first, history-making failed to influence government expansion because the past was perceived as a source of shame, not strength. In the latter half of the nineteenth century, Americans celebrated novelty and looked to the future. African American and white homesteaders alike moved west to escape the weight of history and tradition. Construction of cities and towns was more likely to involve the demolition of old buildings than their preservation. History lacked the popular appeal of science. This early lack of popularity compounded internal divisions evident in the discipline's formative years. The first American-educated historians valued written documents and sought to craft objective narratives about the nation's past. In much the same way that naturalists sought out government sponsors, individual historians sought legitimacy by attaching themselves to the effort to collect political papers or craft political histories. Their work—requiring much less adventure and resulting in much less colorful report-ing—achieved congressional recognition, but not much funding or popular enthusiasm.

During the same period, however, historic preservation did begin to gain popularity as an expression of vernacular forms of patriotism and as an outgrowth of women's domestic politics and reform. Seeking to protect and elevate to national significance the icons of a predominantly white, Anglo-Saxon American past, amateur preservationists identified the pri-vate homes of presidents, governors, and other political figures as artifacts worth saving. They protected landscapes and artifacts made meaningful by blood, sentiment, and pedigree. Their efforts attracted popular atten-tion, and engaged white Americans in a process of commemorating and honoring past sacrifices. Civil War battlefields lost their connection to the war and instead became stages for the reunification of white people in the North and South. House museums became evidence of the superior-ity of middle-class values. Displays of clothing, presidential relics, and other artifacts were designed to influence tourists to approximate main-stream culture. Academic historians discounted preservation, commemo-ration, and museum display as all part and parcel of the same illegitimate impulse. They were too emotional, too feminine, too soft to be equated with scholarship.

The division between objective scholarship and subjective preservation became less clear during the late nineteenth century, splintering the dis-cipline of history in unpredictable and often illogical ways. By the late nineteenth century, the efforts of preservationists had become more for-mal. A growing number of states and cities had organized historical asso-ciations and had worked to preserve locally significant documents and to craft regional histories. These organizations were increasingly led by PhD historians, and local history topics began to appear in the work of budding scholars. Yet the leading members of the discipline's professional association—the American Historical Association—tended to discount this work as well. Its origins in preservation made it appear less objective and less important than work that addressed large national trends. By 1907 regional historians had established a separate professional association, the Mississippi Valley Historical Association, and had begun to lash out against disrespect from their peers. This infighting cut against the ability of history to achieve the kind of broad public influence scientists enjoyed.

The rise of local and regional historical societies and the ongoing process of voluntary commemoration grew increasingly popular after the turn of the twentieth century. Massive immigration from southern and eastern Europe had changed the complexion of America in the same way that decades of industrialization and urbanization had changed its landscape. Wealthy capitalists and average Americans alike turned to the past as an antidote to modernism, seeking evidence of simpler times in an idealized agricultural folk culture or an adventurous and virtuous colonial experience. Ironically, it was often those who had driven the engine of modernism who now crafted nostalgic pageants of a mythic American history. John D. Rockefeller established Colonial Williamsburg. Henry Ford constructed Greenfield Village. Tourists flocked to these places, and history buffs consumed historical accounts crafted by poets and politicians.

When the National Park Service created a History Division, it created an opportunity for historians to establish a broad professional network, one that might unify amateur preservationists, academic scholars, and museum curators around a common goal. Unfortunately, leading members of the American Historical Association did not embrace this popularity. The expanding number of historic properties in the Park Service collection enabled the agency to capitalize on the popularity of history. Efforts by Verne Chatelain, Ronald Lee, and others to adapt history as a strategy for management and education had the potential to expand the discipline's influence on federal policymaking. But the reluctance of key leaders in the field to join forces with amateurs, to work with researchers from other disciplines, to recognize the resonance of regionalism, and to court the interests of lowbrow and middlebrow audiences stymied the rise of a truly public history. As a result, Park Service historians were largely disconnected from academics and could not become the linchpin in a broad and unified network of influential researchers and policymakers. Instead, history emerged in the federal government as a somewhat disjointed program, disconnected from the discipline by its proximity to regionalism, its reliance on voluntary preservation organizations, and its dependence on popular appeal.

A second factor further complicated the ability of public history to earn legitimacy and influence. On the ground in parks, historical archaeology became the centerpiece of historical planning and management. But, like preservationists and local historians, historical archaeologists were not fully integrated into their parent discipline of archaeology. Through the 1930s historical archaeologists such as Jess Jennings and J. C. Harrington walked a fine line. They relied on their connections with archaeologists at the Smithsonian, maintaining correspondence that helped bolster their sense of disciplinary competency. At the same time, their work forced them to acknowledge the validity of arguments made by their predecessor, Jesse Nusbaum, at Mesa Verde National Park during the 1920s, that artifacts were not simply the material of scholarly inquiry. They were also valuable for educating—and managing—site tourists. This realization set men such as Jennings and Harrington apart, perhaps foreshadowing divisions between academic and federally employed scientists that would become sharper as the twentieth century wore on.[6]

In any case, in this atmosphere, at least two kinds of historical workers emerged in the upper-level administration of the National Park Service. On the one hand, historians hired by Chatelain and Lee conducted more or less traditional research, searching for documents in the National Archives and other formal repositories, scouring the literature to design a thematic outline they believed would guide site selection and site interpretation. Although several of these young men succeeded as federal historians by displaying sensitivity to material culture and an interest in the needs of tourists, they nonetheless imported academic history into government service. The theme study format they devised tended to minimize the importance of emotional resonance and material culture as elements of site selection. A second group of administration-level historical workers were less interested in interpretation than in assembling objective evidence. Architectural historians and engineers recorded evidence of historical structures, mapping trends of design in the American-built environment. Despite a common approach to research, the members of these two groups were often in conflict, disagreeing over the standards by which historic sites should be selected for the national collection.

On the ground in parks, a third group of historical workers had the most direct interaction with tourists and laborers. Historical archaeologists conducted research, opened museums, and led tours in parks such as Colonial National Historic Site or Ocmulgee National Monument. Their efforts introduced a final theme into the history of public history. Caught somewhere between the effort to educate and direct park visitors and the impulse to advance and protect the stature of their discipline, frontline workers in historical parks and monuments hesitated to fully engage tourists in a process of interpretation. They invited visitors to see the landscape historically, but they stopped short of valuing visitors' own perceptions of meaning and significance. At Colonial National Historical Park, historical archaeologists took tourists on guided tours of their digs and conducted artifact research in full view of museum visitors. Nonetheless, at most parks and monuments in the years leading up to World War II, tourists were considered as a mass to be managed, not an audience of stakeholders to engage. The collaborative and reflexive processes so valued by contemporary public historians would not emerge for at least three more decades.

Throughout the 1930s the expansion of tourism in the parks lent some urgency and anxiety to the relationship between visitors and interpreters. The national parks were always dependent on visitors, but the expansion of domestic tourism broadened the class of tourists and made visitor interests and values more difficult to predict. In the years leading up to World War II, Park Service professionals—from administrators in Washington to on-site staff—tried to articulate the terms of their authority. Policy initiatives, interactions with workers, and correspondence with colleagues all suggest that the "new technicians" were constantly testing the boundaries of their own expertise and control.

The Long Reach of the New Deal

Given that so many recent histories of the field emphasize the establishment of public history as a profession in the 1970s, it may seem strange that this study ends in the late 1930s. But the decisions made by the Park Service History Division and the intellectual conditions in which they worked during the years leading up to World War II were profoundly influential. They shaped the nation's historical landscape for the rest of the twentieth century. Additional development of historical programming and interpretive practices was interrupted by America's entry into World War II. Shortly after Pearl Harbor, the Civilian Conservation Corps program ended. Military mobilization and the expansion of defense industries put a quick end to any lingering unemployment issues. The New Deal documentary impulse that had fostered numerous efforts to collect and preserve evidence of authentic American folkways and histories shifted in focus and purpose. Film and photography projects were repurposed for war propaganda. Photographers documented services available to military personnel, defense industries, and homefront mobilization efforts to build morale and foster unity. Filmmakers worked for the Department of War to demonize the enemy and foster a fighting spirit among troops of draftees.[7] As the nation mobilized, the Park Service director was under constant pressure to sacrifice natural resource protection for the sake of national defense, and several parks were commandeered for soldiers' training as well as for their rest and relaxation. Federal appropriations for the National Park Service dropped precipitously from $21 million in 1940 to $5 million in 1943, and the number of tourists entering the parks fell as well.[8]

After the war, the priorities of the National Park Service changed along with the basic conditions of American life. The attention of Congress was redirected to demobilization and development. The GI Bill enabled veterans to transition back to domestic life by pursuing higher education or technical training.[9] In turn, better-educated veterans achieved better-paying jobs, and they expanded the middle class as white-collar professionals. In addition, the availability of mortgages through the Veterans Administration fueled an explosion of suburban development. Suburban living was less consolidated than urban life had been, and Americans became increasingly dependent on their automobiles. All of these demographic shifts required massive infrastructure development in the form, most notably, of a more efficient federal transportation policy and an interstate highway system.[10]

The National Park Service was both a beneficiary and a victim of these cultural transformations. Along with the middle class and automobile ownership, domestic tourism expanded. More and more tourists flocked to the parks each decade—six million in 1942, thirty-three million in 1950, seventy-two million in 1960. Rapid suburban development reenergized the park movement.[11] The number of state parks grew, and fifty new national parks were added to the federal system between 1956 and 1966. Such popularity also stressed park facilities, overwhelming roads, campgrounds, and sanitary systems. In response, the National Park Service implemented Mission 66, a ten-year program designed to improve the visitor experience by upgrading existing facilities and employing a new staff of resource managers. Fifty-six new visitor centers were built as part of the Mission 66 initiative, and the Park Service dramatically expanded its environmental education programs.[12]

In the meantime, middle-class white families, many of which had anchored ethnic neighborhoods for generations, abandoned cities. Entire neighborhoods were demolished to make way for highways and public transportation systems. Such destruction created a sense of crisis and galvanized new preservation efforts. In response, Congress authorized the National Historic Preservation Act of 1966, establishing the National Register of Historic Places. Just as Verne Chatelain had believed a survey of historic places would help identify sites appropriate for management in the federal system, so did proponents of the 1966 law imagine it would facilitate the growth of the Park Service history collection. It quickly became evident—again—that the number of potentially significant sites was far too large for the Park Service to handle.[13] Instead, the National Register quickly took shape as a dialogue between local and regional preservationists on the one hand and federal historians on the other.

In some significant ways, the creation of the National Register of Historic Places broadened the influence of the National Park Service in general and of New Deal–era historical workers in particular. The thematic approach to history adopted by the National Park Service advisory board in 1936 served as a guide for those proposing sites for the register from its 1966 creation until 1994.[14] The notion—essential to the original framework—that American history can be understood as a narrative of progress through recognizable stages remained intact through most of the twentieth century. Groups and individuals wishing to list a property in the National Register had to craft a proposal, reporting on both the physical integrity and historical significance of the site. To ensure that their proposals were accepted by Park Service historians (who have final authority to approve or reject sites) they relied on the 1936 framework. Houses, buildings, and landscapes across the country, approved for inclusion in the National Register, thus illustrate and reinforce a now-dated narrative of progress.[15] This remained true even as Park Service historians and new advisory boards reviewed the themes from time to time. The framework was revised in 1970 and 1987, only to provide more detail and to expand the number of themes and subthemes.[16]

The original theme structure was finally abandoned in 1994 and replaced with a more inclusive set of guidelines. Rather than a set of themes that reinforce the notion of American progress, the new guidelines are represented in a graphic of overlapping circles, emphasizing the role of people—rather than processes or trends—in shaping the natural and cultural world over time.[17] American history, in this assessment, is neither necessarily progressive nor degenerative. The new framework will undoubtedly have an important impact on the selection and interpretation of historic sites in the twenty-first century. Indeed, it has already raised questions about how best to preserve sites that are somewhat more humble than the homes of presidents. After all, people influenced their social, cultural, and physical environment from slave cabins, apartment buildings, basements, and other, even more ephemeral, sites. In the meantime, it has proven challenging to implement interpretive changes in the existing historical landscape. The logic used to designate and explain (not to mention denigrate and destroy) historic structures and landscapes between 1930 and the end of the twentieth century has shaped an official public memory of the common American past in ways that sometimes seem impossible to change. It has also trained park enthusiasts to see material traces of the past in a particular way, one that has unintentionally integrated the sentiment of voluntary preservationist and commemorative organizations with seemingly objective evidence. These conditions are the inheritance of contemporary public historians.

Toward a New Definition of Public History

Public history has profoundly interdisciplinary roots. History became a managerial strategy and educational enterprise in the federal government only after two generations of scientists had demonstrated that conducting research, assembling collections, and advancing interpretations about the value and meaning of the landscape had practical value for the federal government. By forging a powerful network with business owners and politicians and courting popular appeal with stories of adventure and discovery scientists were responsible for crafting policy and husbanding reform movements that established a diverse and rich public landscape. Historians built on the success of naturalists, advancing history as a strategy for the expansion of the public landscape, management of protected places, and a source of meaning and value.

Many of the challenges faced by public historians today were established in the past. Historians inside and outside the federal government were unable to forge broad, lasting connections with scholars and amateurs. In the eyes of many of the discipline's leaders, the fact that Park Service historians necessarily sought to integrate sites infused with local and regional meaning into the national collection reflected poorly on their professionalism. Despite the fact that the historians in both the Park Service History Division and in the New Deal Historic American Buildings Survey program conducted rather traditional forms of research, emphasizing the construction of a progressive narrative, their proximity to preservation associations marginalized them. Furthermore, their emphasis on different kinds of historical evidence and their unequal interactions with visitors distanced them from one another. As a result, Park Service historians—whether on the ground in parks or in the Washington office—tended to seek approval and sanction from other experts. Until very late in the twentieth century, most historians held fast to a belief that only scholarship grounded in documents and disconnected from popular emotion was legitimate. Park Service historical workers found stronger kinship with historical archaeologists and preservationists and, as a result, became increasingly involved in efforts to excavate sites and protect buildings rather than engage fully in an interpretive discourse with audiences.

Such complexity and contradiction are not necessarily causes to despair, however. Thinking about public history as a government enterprise opens up new opportunities to think more broadly about its public value. In recent years the National Park Service has implemented new interpretive programs designed to broaden Americans' perception of the common past. Many rangers and educators complain that audiences resist stories about slavery, labor, and protest, but the problem lies not simply in audience hostility but rather in the long trajectory by which public landscapes became infused with historical meaning. In the federal government, history has developed not simply as an intellectual exercise but as a tool for the expansion of governmental authority and the management of both landscapes and people during the twentieth century. This is a contradictory inheritance for contemporary public historians. No doubt, the emergence of history as a function of government has provided the field with a firm foundation on a well-defined cultural landscape, but it has also distanced practitioners from their stakeholders.

The good news is that public historians come from a long line of public servants who have addressed questions of immediate concern to various groups of citizens and stakeholders. Public historians can produce original interpretations that connect scholarship and everyday life by respecting the ways in which their partners and audiences use history and by balancing professional authority against community needs. To do so more effectively, they must cast a clear eye on their professional inheritance. This book begins to polish the looking glass. Public historians are not to blame for persistent disciplinary divisions. They may, however, be able to build important bridges in the larger historical landscape. In the same way that nineteenth-century scientists worked to temper the anxiety generated by social change, so too can twenty-first-century public historians ease fears regarding the future of the nation.

A Note on Sources

This book rests on research I conducted in the following collections and archives. Abbreviations used in the notes are given in parentheses.

NATIONAL ARCHIVES AND RECORDS ADMINISTRATION, COLLEGE PARK, MARYLAND (NARA)

NATIONAL PARK SERVICE, PARK HISTORY PROGRAM, U.S. DEPARTMENT OF THE INTERIOR, WASHINGTON, D.C. (PHP)

This informal collection, located in the offices of the chief historian and the Park Service historian, was organized by Barry Mackintosh. The files contain the most directly relevant material related to the creation of historical policies in the National Park Service.

NATIONAL PARK SERVICE HISTORIC PHOTOGRAPH COLLECTION AND NATIONAL PARK SERVICE HISTORY COLLECTION, DEPARTMENT OF THE INTERIOR, HARPERS FERRY CENTER, WEST VIRGINIA (NPSHC)

These two collections of primary and secondary sources include minutes and correspondence related to superintendent's conferences, advisory board meetings, and policy development. In addition, they contain oral histories conducted with key figures in National Park Service history, as well as photographs taken of personnel on-site in various parks and offices.

SMITHSONIAN INSTITUTION ARCHIVES, WASHINGTON, D.C. (SIA)

TRANSPORTATION COLLECTIONS, DIVISION OF WORK AND INDUSTRY, NATIONAL MUSEUM OF AMERICAN HISTORY, SMITHSONIAN INSTITUTION, WASHINGTON, D.C.

This collection contains primary and secondary source material assembled by curator Roger White and related to various aspects of the automobile industry and automobile tourism.

NATIONAL ANTHROPOLOGICAL ARCHIVES AND HUMAN STUDIES FILM ARCHIVES, DEPARTMENT OF ANTHROPOLOGY, NATIONAL MUSEUM OF NATURAL HISTORY, SMITHSONIAN INSTITUTION, WASHINGTON, D.C. (NAA)

ARCHIVES OF AMERICAN ART, SMITHSONIAN INSTITUTION, WASHINGTON, D.C. (AAA)
This archive contains, among others, all of the oral histories conducted by
Charles Hosmer for his landmark study of American preservation in the
Papers of Charles B. Hosmer (Hosmer Papers).

THE NATIONAL PARK SERVICE HISTORY E-LIBRARY.
The site contains electronic versions of individual park administrative histories as well as broader histories of the National Park Service. Some of these
sources were originally published in article or monograph form, but many
were issued as government pamphlets and internal reports, of which only
a handful of hard copies exist. Wherever possible, I have cited hard copy
versions of these documents. If the citations direct readers to an Internet
resource, I have made an effort to ensure that links include the quotation or
idea I have cited.

Notes

Prologue

1. Charles B. Hosmer Jr., "Pioneers of Public History: Verne E. Chatelain and the Development of the Branch of History of the National Park Service," *Public Historian* 16, no. 1 (Winter 1994): 25–38, 32–33.
2. Harlan Unrau and G. Frank Williss, "The National Park Service, 1933–1939," in *Expansion of the National Park Service in the 1930s: Administrative History*, National Park Service, last modified March 14, 2000, www.nps.gov/history/history/online_books/unrau-williss/adhi6a.htm.
3. There is a vast literature on these subjects. See, e.g., Rebecca Conard, *Benjamin Shambaugh and the Intellectual Foundations of Public History* (Iowa City: University of Iowa Press, 2002); Julie Des Jardins, *Women and the Historical Enterprise in America: Gender, Race and the Politics of Memory* (Chapel Hill: University of North Carolina Press, 2003); Michael Holleran, *Boston's Changeful Times: Origins of Preservation and Planning in America* (Baltimore: Johns Hopkins University Press, 2001); Barbara J. Howe, "Women in Historic Preservation: The Legacy of Ann Pamela Cunningham," *Public Historian* 12, no. 1 (Winter 1990): 31–61; Michael Kammen, *Mystic Chords of Memory: The Transformation of Tradition in American Culture* (New York: Vintage Books, 1993); James M. Lindgren, *Preserving the Old Dominion: Historic Preservation and Virginia Traditionalism* (Charlottesville: University Press of Virginia, 1993); Charlene Mires, *Independence Hall in American Memory* (Philadelphia: University of Pennsylvania Press, 2002); and Patricia West, *Domesticating History: The Political Origins of America's House Museums* (Washington, D.C.: Smithsonian Institution Press, 1999).
4. In addition to several of the studies cited in note 3, other works frequently assigned in introductory public history courses recount the history of the field in this manner. See, e.g., David Glassberg, *Sense of History: The Place of the Past in American Life* (Amherst: University of Massachusetts Press, 2001); Barbara J. Howe and Emory L. Kemp, *Public History: An Introduction* (Malabar, Fla.: R. E. Krieger, 1986); Phyllis K. Leffler and Joseph Brent, *Public History Readings* (Malabar, Fla.: R. E. Krieger, 1992).

5. Kristin Ahlberg and others, "Report of the Working Group on Evaluating Public History Scholarship" (unpublished draft, November 2008), 2.

6. Pete Daniels, a curator in the Smithsonian Institution's National Museum of American History, Division of Work and Industry, served as president of the Organization of American Historians from 2008 to 2009.

7. Roy Rosenzweig and David Thelen, *The Presence of the Past: Popular Uses of History in American Life* (New York: Columbia University Press, 2000), 105.

8. Recent works have been well received, including the winner of the 2007 NCPH Book Award, Cathy Stanton, *The Lowell Experiment: Public History in a Postindustrial City* (Amherst: University of Massachusetts Press, 2006). See also Amy M. Tyson, "Crafting Emotional Comfort: Interpreting the Painful Past at Living History Museums in the New Economy," *Museum and Society* 6, no. 3 (November 2008): 246–62. In contrast, research conducted by Richard Handler and Eric Gable created an ongoing and rather public debate between the authors and Cary Carson, then vice president for research at Colonial Williamsburg. To trace their debate, see Gable and Handler, "On the Uses of Relativism: Fact, Conjecture, and Black and White Histories at Colonial Williamsburg," *American Ethnologist* 19, no. 4 (November 1992): 791–805; Gable and Handler, "The Authority of Documents at Some American History Museums," *Journal of American History* 81, no. 1 (June 1994): 119–36; Cary Carson, "Lost in the Fun House: A Commentary on Anthropologists' First Contact with History Museums," *Journal of American History* 81, no. 1 (June, 1994): 137–50; and Handler and Gable, *The New History in an Old Museum: Creating the Past at Colonial Williamsburg* (Durham, N.C.: Duke University Press, 1997).

9. Peter Novick, *That Noble Dream: The "Objectivity Question" and the American Historical Profession* (New York: Cambridge University Press, 1988), 574.

10. G. Wesley Johnson, "The Origins of *The Public Historian* and the National Council on Public History," *Public Historian* 21, no. 3 (Summer 1999): 167–79.

11. Robert Kelley, "Public History: Its Origins, Nature and Prospects," *Public Historian* 1, no. 1 (Autumn 1978): 16; Johnson, "Origins," 168; Kelley, "Public History," 18.

12. Johnson, "Origins," 168–69.

13. Ibid., 169.

14. Jack M. Holl, "Cultures in Conflict: An Argument against 'Common Ground' between Practicing Professional Historians and Academics," *Public Historian* 30, no. 2 (Spring 2008): 29–50, quote on 32.

15. Jack M. Holl, "Getting on Track: Coupling the Society for History in the Federal Government to the Public History Train," *Public Historian* 21, no. 3 (Summer 1999): 43–55, quote on 50.

16. Ibid., 44, 49.

17. Kristen L. Ahlberg, "Making a Living, Making a Life: The Fellowship of Federal Historians," *OAH Newsletter* 35, no. 3 (August 2007): 9.

18. Otis Graham, "The Uses and Misuses of History: Roles in Policymaking," *Public Historian* 5, no. 2 (Spring 1983): 5–19, quote on 15.

19. James B. Gardner and David F. Trask, "Serving Time in the Trenches: David F. Trask, Public Historian and Federal Historian," *Public Historian* 22, no. 2 (Spring 2000): 9–27, 15; Holl, "Cultures in Conflict," 32.

20. Philip Scarpino, "Common Ground: Reflections on the Past, Present and Future of Public History and the NCPH," *Public Historian* 16, no. 3 (Summer 1994): 11–22, quotes on 13–14.

21. Kelley, "Public History," 16.

22. Theodore Karamanski, "Making History Whole: Public Service, Public History and the Profession," *Public Historian* 12, no. 3 (Summer 1990): 91–101, quote on 96. ·

23. Scarpino, "Common Ground," 15.

24. See, e.g., James B. Gardener, "The Redefinition of Historical Scholarship: Calling a Tail a Leg," *Public Historian* 20, no. 4 (Fall 1998): 43–59.

25. See, e.g., Michael J. Devine, "The Education of a Public Historian: A Case Study with Reflections on Professional Wrestling," *Public Historian* 22, no. 4 (Fall 2000): 10–18.

26. See, e.g., Arnita A. Jones, "Public History Then and Now," *Public Historian* 21, no. 3 (Summer 1999): 21–29.

27. J. Ronald Grele, *Envelopes of Sound: The Art of Oral History* (Chicago: Precedent, 1975).

28. J. Ronald Grele, "Whose Public, Whose History? What Is the Goal of the Public Historian?," *Public Historian* 3, no. 1 (Winter 1981): 40–48, quote on 41.

29. Ibid., 47–48.

30. Michael H. Frisch, *A Shared Authority: Essays on the Craft and Meaning of Oral and Public History* (Albany: State University of New York Press, 1990), xxi–xxii.

31. Rebecca Conard, "Public History as Reflective Practice: An Introduction," *Public Historian* 28, no. 1 (Winter 2006): 9–13, quote on 11.

32. Howard S. (Dick) Miller and Katharine T. Corbett, "A Shared Inquiry into Shared Inquiry," *Public Historian* 28, no. 1 (Winter 2006): 15–38, 18.

33. Cathy Stanton, "What Is Public History?—Redux," *Public History News* 27, no. 4 (September 2007): 1.

34. Margo Shea, comments at the closing plenary, NCPH annual meeting, Louisville, Ky., April 10–13, 2008.

35. Stanton, "What Is Public History?," 14.

36. Ibid.

37. See, e.g., the multidisciplinary essays that compose Steven Lubar and W. David Kingery, eds., *History from Things: Essays on Material Culture* (Washington, D.C.: Smithsonian Institution Press, 1995).

38. Robert Weible, comments at the closing plenary, NCPH annual meeting, Louisville, Ky., April 10–13, 2008.

39. See, e.g., Edward T. Linenthal, "Healing Wounds, Opening Wounds: The Burdens of Remembrance," and Max Page, moderator, "Common Ground: Moving Audiences Outside Their Own Experiences," papers presented at NCPH annual meeting, Louisville, Ky., April 10–13, 2008.

40. Conard, "Public History as Reflective Practice."
41. Calinda Lee, comments at the closing plenary, NCPH annual meeting, Louisville, Ky., April 10–13, 2008.
42. See, e.g., John R. Gillis, ed., *Commemorations: The Politics of National Identity* (Princeton, N.J.: Princeton University Press, 1996); Glassberg, *Sense of History;* Paul Shackel, *Myth, Memory, and the Making of the American Landscape* (Gainesville: University Press of Florida, 2001); Stanton, *Lowell Experiment.*
43. Park Service administrative histories demonstrate that documents such as these provide crucial insight into the establishment of the agency's philosophical and administrative stance and help explain its larger significance and underlying schools of thought. The National Park Service maintains an online resource of full-text "Administrative Histories" on its website: see History E-Library, www.cr.nps.gov/history/hisnps/NPSHistory/adminhistory.htm. In addition, a number of administrative histories have been published as scholarly monographs and articles. See, e.g., Seth C. Bruggeman, *George Washington Birthplace National Monument: Administrative History, 1930–2000* (Washington, D.C.: National Park Service, 2006); Joan Zenzen, *Fort Stanwix National Monument: Reconstructing the Past and Partnering for the Future* (Albany: State University of New York Press, 2008).
44. Horace Albright, oral history interview by Charles B. Hosmer, December 2, 1969, transcript, 1, Hosmer Papers, AAA; Chatelain, quoted in Hosmer, "Pioneers of Public History," 32–33; Jesse L. Nusbaum, oral history interview by Sylvia Loomis, December 12, 1963, microfilm reel 3419, frames 661–83, AAA, 11.

1. A Matter of National Dignity

1. Joel Roberts Poinsett, *Discourse on the Objects and Importance of the National Institution for the Promotion of Science* (Washington, D.C.: Force, 1841), 22.
2. John Winthrop, "A Model of Christian Charity," Religious Freedom Page, University of Virginia Library, last modified September 10, 2001, http://religiousfreedom.lib.virginia.edu/sacred/charity.html.
3. Gerald N. Grob and George Athan Billias, eds., *Interpretations of American History: Patterns and Perspectives,* 6th ed. (New York: Free Press, 1992), 1–6.
4. For more on this subject, see Charles A. Miller, *Jefferson and Nature: An Interpretation* (Baltimore: Johns Hopkins University Press, 1988), and Keith Thompson, *A Passion for Nature: Thomas Jefferson and Natural History* (Chapel Hill: University of North Carolina Press, 2009).
5. See Patricia West, *Domesticating History: The Political Origins of America's House Museums* (Washington, D.C.: Smithsonian Institution Press, 1999).
6. John C. Calhoun, quoted in Nina Burleigh, *The Stranger and the Statesman: James Smithson, John Quincy Adams and the Making of America's Greatest Museum: The Smithsonian* (New York: Harper Perennial, 2004), 234.
7. See Kevin J. Hayes, *The Road to Monticello: The Life and Mind of Thomas Jefferson* (New York: Oxford University Press, 2008), and Susan Stein, *Worlds of Thomas Jefferson at Monticello* (New York: Abrams, 1993).

8. See Charles Coleman Sellars, *Mr. Peale's Museum* (New York: Norton, 1980), and David Brigham, *Public Culture in the Early Republic: Peale's Museum and Its Audience* (Washington, D.C.: Smithsonian Institution Press, 1995).

9. Charles Card Smith, *A Short Account of the Massachusetts Historical Society* (Boston: Massachusetts Historical Society, 1918), 7–8.

10. *Proceedings of the New-York Historical Society* (New York: Historical Society Press, 1843), 175.

11. Smithson had died in 1829 and left his estate to his nephew, but his will transferred the estate to the United States if his nephew should die without any heirs. The estate became the property of the U.S. government in 1835, after the death of Smithson's nephew in 1833 and two years of negotiations between U.S. and British courts.

12. Heather Ewing, *The Lost World of James Smithson: Science, Revolution, and the Birth of the Smithsonian* (New York: Bloomsbury, 2007), 317.

13. Calhoun, quoted in Burleigh, *Stranger and the Statesman*, 232–33.

14. Ibid., 240–43.

15. For John Quincy Adams, ibid.; for Richard Rush, ibid., 245; for Joel Poinsett, ibid., 240.

16. Pamela M. Henson, "Planning a National Museum," *Spencer F. Baird's Vision for a National Museum*, Institutional History Division, Office of Smithsonian Institution Archives, http://siarchives.si.edu/history/exhibits/baird/bairdb.htm.

17. Poinsett, *Discourse on the Objects*, 15.

18. "Joel Roberts Poinsett," *Biographical Directory of the United States Congress*, U.S. House of Representatives, http://bioguide.congress.gov/scripts/biodisplay.pl?index=p000404.

19. Burleigh, *Stranger and the Statesman*, 239.

20. Joel Roberts Poinsett, *Notes on Mexico, Made in the Autumn of 1822, Accompanied by a Historical Sketch of the Revolution* (Philadelphia: Carey and Lea, 1824), 96.

21. Natural Science was then a broad category of inquiry that included a number of still-to-be-distinguished disciplines from geology and botany to anthropology and paleontology.

22. John P. Herron, *Science and the Social Good: Nature, Culture, and Community* (New York: Oxford University Press, 2009), 22–23.

23. "Ann Pamela Cunningham, Phoebe Apperson Hearst, and Frances Payne Bolton," George Washington's Mount Vernon Estate and Gardens, http://www.mountvernon.org/content/ann-pamela-cunningham-phoebe-apperson-hearst-and-frances-payne-bolton.

24. Barbara J. Howe, "Women in Historic Preservation: The Legacy of Ann Pamela Cunningham," *Public Historian* 12, no.1 (Winter 1990): 31–61, 33.

25. Cited in "To the Daughters of Washington," *Southern Literary Messenger* (Richmond, Va.) 21, no. 5 (May 1855): 318.

26. "The Formation of the Mount Vernon Ladies' Association and the Dramatic Rescue of George Washington's Estate," George Washington's Mount Vernon

Estate and Gardens, http://www.mountvernon.org/content/formation-mount
-vernon-ladies-association.

27. Anne Pamela Cunningham, quoted in James M. Lindgren, *Preserving the Old Dominion: Historic Preservation and Virginia Traditionalism* (Charlottesville: University Press of Virginia, 1993), 43.

28. Mount Vernon Ladies' Association, *Historical Sketch of Ann Pamela Cunningham: The Southern Matron* (Jamaica, N.Y.: Marion, 1911), 19–20.

29. See Julie Des Jardins, *Women and the Historical Enterprise in America: Gender, Race and the Politics of Memory* (Chapel Hill: University of North Carolina Press, 2003); Charlene Mires, *Independence Hall in American Memory* (Philadelphia: University of Pennsylvania Press, 2002); and West, *Domesticating History.*

30. Henry P. Beers, "A History of the U.S. Topographical Engineers, 1813–1863," *Military Engineer* 34 (June 1942): 287–91 and (July 1942): 348–52, as excerpted on U.S. Corps of Topographical Engineers, http://topogs.org/History.htm.

31. Ibid.

32. John James Abert, quoted in Mary C. Rabbit, "Geological Surveys before the Civil War," *The United States Geological Survey: 1879–1989,* U.S. Geological Survey Circular 1050, Department of the Interior, last modified April 10, 2000, http://pubs.usgs.gov/circular/c1050/before.htm.

33. Ibid.

34. William Ragan Stanton, *The Great United States Exploring Expedition of 1838–1842* (Berkeley: University of California Press, 1975), 291.

35. Ibid., 63.

36. W. John Kress, "Botanical Exploration: Yesterday, Today, and Tomorrow," *The United States Exploring Expedition,* Smithsonian Institution Libraries Digital Collection, www.sil.si.edu/digitalcollections/usexex/learn/Kress.htm.

37. Nathaniel Philbrick, *Sea of Glory: America's Voyage of Discovery, the U.S. Exploring Expedition* (New York: Penguin, 2003), 331–47.

38. The problem that such collections pose for museums today is a frequent topic in the literature: see Claire L. Lyons and John K. Papadopoulos, *The Archaeology of Colonialism* (Los Angeles: Getty, 2002); Barbara Kirshenblatt-Gimblett, *Destination Culture: Tourism, Museums, and Heritage* (Berkeley: University of California Press, 1998); and Ivan Karp et al., eds., *Museum Frictions: Public Cultures/Global Transformations* (Durham, N.C.: Duke University Press, 2007).

39. Philbrick, *Sea of Glory.*

40. Henson, "Planning a National Museum."

41. Burleigh, *Stranger and the Statesman,* 240, 249.

42. "Board of Regents, Meeting Minutes, September 7, 1846," SIA, RU 1, vol. 1.

43. Burleigh, *Stranger and the Statesman,* 254.

44. Joseph Henry to Joseph Bradley Varnum Jr., June 22, 1847, *The Papers of Joseph Henry,* vol. 7 (Washington, D.C.: Smithsonian Institution Press, 1996), 121–22.

45. Herron, *Science and the Social Good,* 41, 46.

46. The Topographical Bureau was reorganized a second time in 1838, reconstituting it as the United States Corps of Topographical Engineers, a move that

enabled the military corps to conduct the work that had been hired out to civilians.

47. Philbrick, *Sea of Glory,* 344.

48. Arthur A. Socolow, ed., preface to *The State Geological Surveys: A History* (Tallahassee, Fla.: Association of American State Geologists, 1988).

49. William H. Emory, *Notes of a Military Reconnaissance from Fort Leavenworth in Missouri to San Diego in California* (Washington, D.C.: Wendell and Van Benthuysen, 1848), 64.

50. Laura E. Mathew and Michel R. Oudijk, *Indian Conquistadors: Indigenous Allies in the Conquest of Mesoamerica* (Norman: University of Oklahoma Press, 2007), 167.

51. Hubert Howe Bancroft and Alfred Bates, *History of Utah: 1540–1886* (San Francisco: History Company, 1890), 1–5.

52. John L. Kessell, *Spain in the Southwest: A Narrative History of Colonial New Mexico, Arizona, Texas, and California* (Norman: University of Oklahoma Press, 2002), 46.

53. Stuart Nixon, *Redwood Empire* (New York: Dutton, 1966), 175.

54. Special Agent Alexander L. Morrison, "Report on the Condition of Casa Grande," *Magazine of Western History* 11, no. 1 (November 1889): 107–8.

55. Emory, *Notes of a Military Reconnaissance,* 68.

56. Antoine Leroux, quoted in Lieutenant A. W. Whipple, Thomas Ewbank, Esq., and Professor Wm. W. Turner, *Report upon the Indian Tribes* (Washington, D.C.: G.P.O., 1856), 14–15.

57. Bruce G. Trigger, *A History of Archaeological Thought* (New York: Cambridge University Press, 2006), 211–314.

58. David Hurst Thomas, *Skull Wars: Kennewick Man, Archaeology, and the Battle for Native American Identity* (New York: Basic, 2000), 137.

59. Alfred Hunter, quoted in Curtis Hinsley, *The Smithsonian and the American Indian: Making a Moral Anthropology in Victorian America* (Washington, D.C.: Smithsonian Institution Press, 1981), 66–67.

60. Philbrick, *Sea of Glory,* 344.

61. Frank Millikan, "Joseph Henry's Grand Meteorological Crusade," *Weatherwise* 50 (October/November 1997): 14–18, as excerpted in "Joseph Henry: Father of Weather Service," Joseph Henry Papers Project, Smithsonian Institution, http://siarchives.si.edu/history/jhp/joseph03.htm.

62. Marc Rothenberg, "Henry and the National Museum: Making a Deal," *Smithsonian Material Culture Forum Grapevine* (Washington, D.C.: Smithsonian Institution, May 2000), as excerpted in Joseph Henry Papers Project, http://siarchives.si.edu/history/jhp/joseph24.htm.

63. Henson, "Baird as Assistant Secretary and the Growth of a Dream," *Spencer F. Baird's Vision,* www.siarchives.si.edu/history/exhibits/baird/bairdc.htm.

64. Alfred Goldsborough Meyer, "Biographical Memoir of William Stimpson, 1832–1872," in *National Academy Biographical Memoirs,* vol. 8 (Washington, D.C.: National Academy of Sciences, 1919), 419–33.

65. David G. Smith and Inci A. Bowman, "Naturalist Collectors: Robert Kennicott, 1835–1866," *Spencer Baird and Ichthyology at the Smithsonian, 1850–1900,* Division of Fishes, National Museum of Natural History, Smithsonian Institution, http://vertebrates.si.edu/fishes/ichthyology_history/ichs_colls/kennicott_robert .html.

66. Henson, "Baird as Assistant Secretary." For more information on the U.S. National Museum, see the website of the SIA, "Smithsonian History, Arts and Industries Building," http://siarchives.si.edu/history/arts-and-industries -building. The Smithsonian's Arts and Industries Building opened to the public in 1881 as the U.S. National Museum. In 1910, the museum moved to the build- ing that is now the National Museum of Natural History. It retained the name U.S. National Museum until the 1960s. The original collections are now located in several of the Smithsonian museums.

67. Socolow, *State Geological Surveys,* 323–26.

68. Mike Foster, "Ferdinand Vandeveer Hayden as Naturalist," *American Zoologist* 26, no. 2 (1986): 343–49.

69. James G. Cassidy, *Ferdinand V. Hayden: Entrepreneur of Science* (Lincoln: University of Nebraska Press, 2000), 34, 36–37.

70. Ibid., 36–41.

71. U.S. Geological Survey Information 74-24, *John Wesley Powell: Soldier, Explorer, Scientist* (Washington, D.C.: U.S. Geological Survey, 1976).

72. Donald Worster, *A River Running West: The Life of John Wesley Powell* (New York: Oxford University Press, 2000), 82.

73. "A Brief History of the Illinois Natural History Society," Illinois Natural History Survey, Prairie Research Institute, www.inhs.illinois.edu/organization/ history.html.

74. Charles Dana Wilber, *Transactions of the Illinois Natural History Society* (Springfield, Ill.: Bailhache and Baker, 1861), 15.

2. Managing the Landscape

1. In his essay "The New Negro" (1925) Alain Locke, considered by many the father of the Harlem Renaissance, coined the term to describe transformations in African American culture.

2. Joel Chandler Harris, *Life of Henry W. Grady* (1890), in *Major Problems in the History of the American South: Documents and Essays,* vol. 2, *The New South,* ed. Paul D. Escott and David R. Goldfield (Lexington, Mass.: D. C. Heath, 1990), 71–73.

3. This optimistic interpretation of the period is expressed by Rebecca Edwards, *New Spirits: Americans in the Gilded Age, 1865–1905* (New York: Oxford University Press, 2005).

4. Michael Holleran, *Boston's Changeful Times: Origins of Preservation and Planning in America* (Baltimore: Johns Hopkins University Press, 2001), 3.

5. Margaret Deland, "The Change in the Feminine Ideal," *Atlantic Monthly* 105, no. 3 (March 1910): 289–302, quote on 289.

6. Edwards, "New Spirits."

7. William Howard Taft, "Special Message to Congress, February 3, 1911," quoted in *National Park Service: Hearing before the Committee on the Public Lands, H.R. 104*, 63rd Cong., 58 (April 29, 1914).

8. Craig L. LaMay, "Justin Smith Morrill and the Politics and Legacy of the Land-Grand College Acts," in *A Digital Gift to the Nation: Fulfilling the Promise of the Digital and Information Age*, ed. Lawrence K. Grossman and Newton N. Minnow (Washington, D.C.: Century Foundation, 2001), 73–95, quote on 75.

9. John P. Herron, *Science and the Social Good: Nature, Culture, and Community* (New York: Oxford University Press, 2009), 24.

10. LaMay, "Justin Smith Morrill," 79–80.

11. Ibid., 78.

12. Herron, *Science and the Social Good*, 24.

13. Charles H. Warren, "The Sheffield Scientific School from 1847 to 1947," in *The Centennial of the Sheffield Scientific School*, ed. George Alfred Baitsell (New Haven: Yale University Press, 1950), 156–68.

14. Programs, such as the Office of Economic Ornithology, designed to study specific species of American wildlife were reorganized as the Bureau of Biological Surveys in 1905. U.S Fish and Wildlife Service, "Who We Are," www.fws.gov/who/.

15. See W. Fitzhugh Brundage, ed., *Where These Memories Grow: History, Memory, and Southern Identity* (Chapel Hill: University of North Carolina Press, 2000), esp. 79–218.

16. James M. Lindgren, "'For the Sake of Our Future': The Association for the Preservation of Virginia Antiquities and the Regeneration of Traditionalism," *Virginia Magazine of History and Biography* 97, no. 1 (1989): 47–74, 53.

17. Patricia West, *Domesticating History: The Political Origins of America's House Museums* (Washington, D.C.: Smithsonian Institution Press, 1999), 43.

18. Lindgren, "For the Sake," 58–60.

19. Kathleen Ann Clark, *Defining Moments: African American Commemoration and Political Culture in the South, 1863–1913* (Chapel Hill: University of North Carolina Press, 2005), 37.

20. Mary Jeffrey Galt, quoted in West, *Domesticating History*, 43.

21. Ibid., 44.

22. Annual Report of the Illinois Chapter of the Society of the Colonial Dames, Reported by Anne Hollingsworth Wharton, "Address of the Historian, Executive Meeting of the National Society of the Colonial Dames of America, April 24, 1900," included in the Minutes of the Council of the National Society of the Colonial Dames of America, Washington, D.C., The Arlington, April 25–28, 1900, 40.

23. Michael Kammen, *Mystic Chords of Memory: The Transformation of Tradition in American Culture* (New York: Vintage Books, 1993), 159.

24. Peter Novick, *That Noble Dream: The "Objectivity Question" and the American Historical Profession* (New York: Cambridge University Press, 1988), 182–83.

25. Mark R. Nemec, *Ivory Towers and Nationalist Minds: Universities, Leadership, and the Development of the American State* (Ann Arbor: University of Michigan Press, 2006), 57.

26. Robert Wiebe, *The Search for Order: 1877–1920* (New York: Hill and Wang, 1967). Wiebe's landmark work argues that while Progressive Era reforms established important avenues for improving industrial safety, children's health, urban living conditions, and other side effects of change, they are also equally notable for reasserting the right of white, well-educated, native-born, elite citizens to dictate the form and function of American social conventions. Although perhaps too dismissive of the noble intentions of reformers, Wiebe's emphasis on the ways in which social change created a desire for order is a useful window for viewing the emergence of government-sanctioned historic and natural preservation. For more on the continuing significance of his work, see "Robert Wiebe's *The Search for Order: A Thirty Year Retrospective*," H-Net, Humanities and Social Sciences Online, www.h-net.org/~shgape/wiebe/wiebeindex.html.

27. James G. Cassidy, *Ferdinand V. Hayden: Entrepreneur of Science* (Lincoln: University of Nebraska Press, 2000), 26.

28. Larry Anderson, *Benton MacKaye: Conservationist, Planner and Creator of the Appalachian Trail* (Baltimore: Johns Hopkins University Press, 2002), 35.

29. Cassidy, *Ferdinand V. Hayden*, 28.

30. Mary C. Rabbitt, "The Four Great Surveys of the West," *U.S. Geological Survey Circular 1050: The United States Geological Survey: 1879–1989*, U.S. Geological Survey, Department of the Interior, last modified April 10, 2000, http://pubs.usgs.gov/circ/c1050/surveys.htm.

31. William Goetzmann, "Desolation Thy Name Is the Great Basin: Clarence King's Fortieth Parallel Survey," in *Perpetual Mirage: Photographic Narratives of the Desert West*, ed. May Castleberry, John Chávez, and Martha A. Sandweiss (New York: Whitney Museum of Art, 1996), 57–63.

32. Martha A. Sandweiss, *Passing Strange: A Gilded Age Tale of Love and Deception across the Color Line* (New York: Penguin, 2010), 60.

33. L. F. Schmeckebier, *Catalogue and Index of the Publications of the Hayden, King, Powell and Wheeler Surveys. Department of the Interior, United States Geological Survey* (Washington, D.C.: G.P.O., 1904), 38–40.

34. "A Guide to the 'Wheeler Survey' Field Notebooks of the U.S. Geographical Survey West of the 100th Meridian Collection, No. NC319," *Special Collections*, Mathewson-IGT Knowledge Center, University of Nevada, Reno, last modified August 12, 2008, http://knowledgecenter.unr.edu/specoll/mss/nc319.html.

35. Cassidy, *Ferdinand V. Hayden*, 84, 87, 86, 87–102.

36. Donald Worster, *A River Running West: The Life of John Wesley Powell* (New York: Oxford University Press, 2001), 132–34.

37. Ibid., 157–68.

38. William deBuys, *Seeing Things Whole: The Essential John Wesley Powell* (New York: Island, 2004), 14; J. W. Powell, *Lands of the Arid Region of the United States*

with a More Detailed Account of the Lands of Utah with Maps (Washington, D.C.: G.P.O., 1879).

39. Herron, *Science and the Social Good,* 26.

40. Kris Fresonke, "Inventing the Grand Canyon: E. O. Beaman's National Landscape," *Journal of the Southwest* 39, no. 2 (Summer 1997): 153–64.

41. In addition to Goetzmann, "Desolation," on O'Sullivan, see also Toby Jurovics, Carol M. Johnson, Glenn Willumson, and William F. Stapp, *Framing the West: The Survey Photographs of Timothy H. O'Sullivan* (New Haven: Yale University Press, 2010).

42. M. John Lubetkin, *Jay Cooke's Gamble: The Northern Pacific Railroad, the Sioux, and the Panic of 1873* (Norman: University of Oklahoma Press, 2006), 20, 48–49.

43. Ibid., 75.

44. Nathaniel Langford, "The Wonders of Yellowstone," pt. 1, *Scribner's Monthly* 2, no. 1 (May 1871): 10.

45. Langford, "Wonders of Yellowstone," pt. 2, *Scribner's Monthly* 2, no. 2 (June 1871): 128.

46. Rocky Barker, *Scorched Earth: How the Fires of Yellowstone Changed America* (Washington, D.C.: Island, 2005), 33.

47. David Sievert Lavender and Duane A. Smith, *The Rockies* (1968; repr., Lincoln: University of Nebraska Press, 2003), 240.

48. Spencer Baird, quoted in Aubrey L. Haines, "The Hayden and Barlow Parties," *Yellowstone National Park: Its Exploration and Establishment* (Washington, D.C.: National Park Service, Department of the Interior, 1974), www.nps.gov/history/history/online_books/haines1/iee2e.htm.

49. Nancy K. Anderson, *Thomas Moran* (Washington, D.C.: National Gallery of Art, 1997), 46–48.

50. Ferdinand V. Hayden, "The Wonders of the West: More about the Yellowstone," *Scribner's Monthly* 3, no. 4 (February 1872): 338.

51. See Angela Miller, *The Empire of the Eye: Landscape Representation and American Cultural Politics, 1825–1875* (Ithaca, N.Y.: Cornell University Press, 1993).

52. Lubetkin, *Jay Cooke's Gamble,* 72–73.

53. John Warfield Simpson, *Visions of Paradise: Glimpses of Our Landscapes Legacy* (Berkeley: University of California Press, 1999), 170.

54. Ibid., 174.

55. See Karl Jacoby, *Crimes against Nature: Squatters, Poachers, Thieves, and the Hidden History of American Conservation* (Berkeley: University of California Press, 2001).

56. Ronald F. Lee, "Origins of the Antiquities Act," in *The Antiquities Act: A Century of American Archaeology, Historic Preservation and Nature Conservation,* ed. David Harmon, Francis P. McManamon, and Dwight T. Pitcaithley (Tucson: University of Arizona, 2006), 17–41.

57. Alfred M. Tozzer, "Biographical Memoir of Frederic Ward Putnam, 1839–1915," *National Academy of Sciences Biographical Memoirs,* vol. 16, 4th memoir (Washington, D.C.: National Academy of Sciences, 1933), 136–37, 145.

58. Don D. Fowler and David R. Wilcox, "From Thomas Jefferson to the Pecos Conference: Changing Anthropological Agendas in the North American Southwest," in *Surveying the Record: North American Scientific Exploration to 1930,* ed. Edward Carlos Carter (Philadelphia: American Philosophical Society, 1999), 197–223, quote on 211–12.

59. Lee, "Origins of the Antiquities Act."

60. Women pioneers in science formed separate associations. Their inability to join the Cosmos Club contributed to the marginalization of women's contributions to various disciplines. Women anthropologists, for example, found the American Anthropological Association so hostile to their efforts to conduct meaningful research that they formed a separate association. Work conducted by women pioneering anthropologists such as Matilda Stevenson and Ruth Benedict was typically viewed as supporting—or sometimes threatening—the work conducted by their husbands and male mentors.

61. Wilcomb E. Washburne, *The Cosmos Club of Washington: A Centennial History, 1878–1978* (Washington, D.C.: Cosmos Club, 1978), 345.

62. See James Kirkpatrick Flack, *Desideratum in Washington: The Intellectual Community in the Capital City, 1870–1900* (Cambridge, Mass.: Schenkman, 1975).

63. William Wroth, "Bandelier, Adolph F.," *New Mexico Office of the State Historian, Courtesy of the State Records Center and Archives,* New Mexico State Record Center and Archives, www.newmexicohistory.org/filedetails.php?fileID=517.

64. Fowler and Wilcox, "From Thomas Jefferson to the Pecos Conference," 214–15.

65. Alex F. Chamberlain, "In Memoriam: Frank Hamilton Cushing," *Journal of American Folklore* 13, no. 48 (January–March 1910): 129–34.

66. Philip Joseph Deloria, *Playing Indian* (New Haven: Yale University Press, 1991), 141.

67. Jesse Green, ed., *Zuni: Selected Writings of Frank Hamilton Cushing* (Lincoln: University of Nebraska Press, 1979), 136.

68. Adolph Bandelier, "Historical Introduction to Studies among the Sedentary Indians of New Mexico," *Papers of the Archaeological Institute of America,* American Series (Boston: Williams, 1881), 42.

69. Lee, "Origins of the Antiquities Act," 17–18.

70. Susan H. Haskell, "Mary Hemenway and the Hemenway Southwestern Archaeological Expedition" (unpublished manuscript, 1993), cited in Sarah R. Demb, "Creator Sketch," in *Hemenway Expedition Records, 1886–1919,* Peabody Museum Archives, Harvard University, http://oasis.lib.harvard.edu/oasis/deliver/~pea00009.

71. Joan T. Mark, *A Stranger in Her Native Land: Alice Fletcher and the American Indians* (Lincoln: University of Nebraska Press, 1989), 223.

72. Lee, "Origins of the Antiquities Act," 19.

73. After Yellowstone was established in 1872, Congress created Mackinac National Park in 1875, which was then transferred to the state of Michigan in 1895.

74. For more on Hewett and his influence on the passage of the Antiquities Act, and in addition to Ronald F. Lee's frequently cited history, "Origins of the Antiquities Act," see Hal Rothman, *Preserving Different Pasts: The American*

National Monuments (Champaign: University of Illinois Press, 1989), 22–23, 37–51; and Hal Rothman, *America's National Monuments: The Politics of Preservation* (Lawrence: University Press of Kansas, 1994), 42–48, 143–46.

75. David Harmon, Francis P. McManamon, and Dwight T. Pitcaithley, eds., "Introduction: The Importance of the Antiquities Act," in Harmon, McManamon, and Pitcaithley, *Antiquities Act.*

76. Kris Hirst, "Nuts and Bolts: Designate National Monuments," *A Visionary Act,* March 20, 2006, Archaeological Institute of America, www.archaeology.org/online/features/act1906/.

77. Ibid.

78. Ronald F. Lee, "Beginnings: National Monument Line I, 1906–1916, Department of the Interior," *Family Tree of the National Park System* (Philadelphia: Eastern National Park and Monument Association, 1972), www.nps.gov/history/history/online_books/lee2/lee1a.htm.

79. Richard West Sellars, *Preserving Nature in the National Parks: A History* (New Haven: Yale University Press, 1997), 30.

80. Ibid., 42–60.

81. See Robert Righter, *The Battle over Hetch Hetchy: America's Most Controversial Dam and the Birth of Modern Environmentalism* (New York: Oxford University Press, 2005).

82. Ibid., 15–16.

83. Rodrick Nash, *The Rights of Nature* (Madison: University of Wisconsin Press, 1989), 39.

84. John Muir, *Muir: Complete Writings* (New York: Penguin, 1997), 849.

85. Righter, *Battle over Hetch Hetchy,* 121.

86. See Char Miller, *Gifford Pinchot and the Making of Modern Environmentalism* (Washington, D.C.: Island Press, 2001).

87. Anne Wintermute Lane and Louise Herrick Wall, eds., *The Letters of Franklin K. Lane: Personal and Political* (Cambridge: Riverside, 1922), 272–73.

88. Righter, *Battle over Hetch Hetchy,* 117–32.

89. Horace M. Albright, Marian Albright Schenck, and Robert Utley, *Creating the National Park Service: The Missing Years* (Norman: University of Oklahoma Press, 1999), 20.

90. Righter, *Battle over Hetch Hetchy,* 195.

91. Henry G. Law, Laura E. Soulliere, and William C. Tweed, "The Landscape Influence, 1916–1918," *Rustic Architecture: 1916–1942* (National Park Service, Western Regional Office, Division of Cultural Resource Management, 1977), www.nps.gov/history/history/online_books/rusticarch/part2.htm.

92. The National Park Service Organic Act, 16 U.S.C. § 1 2 3, 4 (August 25, 1916).

93. See Albright, Schenck, and Utley, *Creating the National Park Service,* 94. Horace M. Albright, oral history interview by Erskine, January 28, 1959, transcript, 16, NPSHC.

95. Albright, Schenck, and Utley, *Creating the National Park Service,* 316, 271–72, 213–15.

96. Albright interview, 25.

97. See Mark David Spence, *Dispossessing the Wilderness: Indian Removal and the Making of the National Parks* (New York: Oxford University Press, 2000).

98. See Jacoby, *Crimes against Nature.*

99. Harmon, McManamon, and Pitcaithley, "Introduction," 6.

100. See David Hurst Thomas, *Skull Wars: Kennewick Man, Archaeology and the Battle for Native American Identity* (New York: Basic, 2001).

101. Horace Albright, quoted by Barry Mackintosh, "The Park Service Assumes Responsibility: *Interpretation in the National Park Service: A Historical Perspective* (Washington, D.C.: History Division, National Park Service, Department of the Interior, 1986), www.nps.gov/history/history/online_books/mackintosh 2/origins_nps_assumes_responsibility.htm.

102. Albright, Schenck, and Utley, *Creating the National Park Service,* 275–76. Although different versions of the creed appear in various publications, Albright recounted this version as the most important.

3. Losing Their Identity

1. Jesse Logan Nusbaum, oral history interview by Herbert Evison, December 9, 1962, transcript, 3, 51, 48, NPSHC.

2. Raymond Harris Thompson, "Edgar Lee Hewett and the Politics of Archaeology," in *The Antiquities Act: A Century of American Archaeology, Historic Preservation and Nature Conservation,* ed. David Harmon, Francis P. McManamon, and Dwight Pitcaithley (Tucson: University of Arizona Press, 2006), 35–47.

3. Thomas Carl Patterson, *A Social History of Anthropology in the United States* (New York: Berg, 2001), 51.

4. Thompson, "Edgar Lee Hewett," 44.

5. Regna Darnell, "Neil M. Judd 1945," in *Celebrating a Century of the American Anthropological Association,* ed. Regna Darnell and Frederic Wright Gleach (Washington, D.C.: American Anthropological Association, 2002), 109–12.

6. Florence Cline Lister, *Troweling through Time: The First Century of Mesa Verdean Archaeology* (Albuquerque: University of New Mexico Press, 2004), 50–52.

7. Nusbaum interview (Evison), 2, 48–49.

8. Ricardo Torres-Reyes, "Launching of Park Operations," *Mesa Verde National Park: An Administrative History, 1906–1970,* National Park Service, History E-Library, last modified August 21, 2004, www.nps.gov/history/history/online_books/meve/adhi/adhi2.htm.

9. Torres-Reyes, "Development of Services and Facilities," ibid., /adhi3b.htm.

10. Torres-Reyes, "Nusbaum's Crash Program," ibid., /adhi5.htm.

11. Nusbaum interview (Evison), 10.

12. Torres-Reyes, "Nusbaum's Crash Program."

13. Stephen Mather, *Report of the Director of the National Park Service to the Secretary of the Interior for the Fiscal Year Ended June 30, 1921, and the Travel Season 1921* (Washington, D.C.: G.P.O., 1921), 85.

14. Horace Albright, quoted in Torres-Reyes, "Nusbaum's Crash Program."

15. Nusbaum interview (Evison), 13, 11.

16. Ibid., 47, 14, 13.

17. Ibid., 16, 17.

18. Stephen Mather, *Report of the Director of the National Park Service to the Secretary of the Interior for the Fiscal Year Ended June 30, 1924, and the Travel Season 1924* (Washington, D.C.: G.P.O., 1924), 7.

19. See Steven Conn, *Museums and American Intellectual Life, 1876–1926* (Chicago: University of Chicago, 1998), esp. 75–114.

20. George Brown Goode, quoted in Conn, *Museums and American Intellectual Life*, 75–76.

21. Conn, *Museums and American Intellectual Life*, 26, 106–8, 110–12.

22. Ralph Lewis, *Museum Curatorship in the National Park Service, 1904–1982* (Washington, D.C.: National Park Service, 1993), 2–3.

23. Mather, *Report of the Director* (1924), 8.

24. Rose Houk, *Casa Grande Ruins National Monument* (Tucson: Western National Parks Association, 1996), 8.

25. Frank Pinkley, quoted in Horace Albright, Marian Albright Schenck, and Robert Utley, *Creating the National Park Service: The Missing Years* (Norman: University of Oklahoma Press, 1999), 283.

26. J. Walter Fewkes, "Casa Grande, Arizona," in *Twenty-Eighth Annual Report of the Bureau of American Ethnology to the Secretary of the Smithsonian, 1906–1907* (Washington, D.C.: G.P.O., 1912), 120.

27. Stephen Mather, "Annual Report of the Director of the National Park Service," in *Reports of the Department of the Interior for the Fiscal Year Ended June 30, 1919*, vol. 1 (Washington, D.C.: G.P.O., 1919), 945.

28. Mather, "Annual Report of the Director" (1919), 31.

29. Stephen Mather, *Report of the Director of the National Park Service to the Secretary of the Interior for the Fiscal Year Ended June 30, 1922, and the Travel Season 1922* (Washington, D.C.: G.P.O., 1922), 69.

30. Now known as the Chapin Mesa Archeological Museum, it was referred to as the Mesa Verde museum throughout the period.

31. Torres-Reyes, "Nusbaum's Crash Program."

32. Edwin Booth to Arno Cammerer, letter regarding disposition of artifacts, January 17, 1923, NAA, American Antiquities Act Permits Prior to 1960, box 9, folder Interior Secretary, 1932–1944, National Park Service, hereafter cited as NAA, AAAP.

33. "Charles Doolittle Walcott (1850–1927)," Smithsonian History, Secretaries of the Smithsonian, http://siarchives.si.edu/history/charles-doolittle-walcott.

34. T. T. Belote, "Division of History, Annual Report, 1932–3," SIA, RU 158, series 1, box 64, folder 18.

35. Annual Report, 1927, SIA, RU 240, series 5, box 10, folder 14.

36. Ibid.

37. Ibid.

38. John Bodnar, *Remaking America: Public Memory, Commemoration, and Patriotism in the Twentieth Century* (Princeton, N.J.: Princeton University Press, 1992), 249. For more on American patriotism during and after World War I, see Christopher Capozzola, *Uncle Sam Wants You: World War I and the Making of the Modern American Citizen* (New York: Oxford University Press, 2009).

39. Belote, "Division of History, Annual Report, 1931–2," SIA, RU 158, series 1, box 63, folder 12.

40. Belote, "Division of History, Annual Report, 1930–1," SIA, RU 158, series 1, box 62, folder 12.

41. Herbert Krieger, "Division of Ethnology, Annual Report, 1931–2," SIA, RU 158, box 63, folder 1.

42. Briann Greenfield, *Out of the Attic: Inventing Antiques in Twentieth Century New England* (Amherst: University of Massachusetts Press, 2009). Greenfield argues, in part, that the collection of everyday artifacts at the Smithsonian was a side effect of the rise of an antiques market, which made it impossible for the institution to purchase highly priced items.

43. Mathew Stirling, "Report of the Division of Ethnology, 1932–3," SIA, RU 158, box 64, folder 6.

44. Krieger, "Division of Ethnology, Annual Report."

45. For more on the expansion of museums and museum education, see Edward P. Alexander and Mary Alexander, *Museums in Motion: An Introduction to the History and Functions of Museums,* 2nd ed. (Lanham, Md.: Alta Mira, 2008); Conn, *Museums and American Intellectual Life;* Jane R. Glaser, *Museums: A Place to Work; Planning Museum Careers,* with Artemis A. Zenetou (New York: Routledge, 1996); and Warren Leon and Roy Rosenzweig, eds., *History Museums in the United States: A Critical Assessment* (Champaign: University of Illinois Press, 1989).

46. Lewis, *Museum Curatorship,* 2–3.

47. Watson Smith, "Ansel Franklin Hall, 1894–1962," *American Antiquity* 29, no. 2 (October 1962): 228–29.

48. Lewis, *Museum Curatorship,* 4.

49. Ibid.

50. Smith, "Ansel Franklin Hall."

51. For more on the role of the Park Service in the development of historical archaeology, see Staley South, ed., *Pioneers in Historical Archaeology: Breaking New Ground* (New York: Plenum, 1994), esp. J. C. Harrington, "From Architraves to Artifacts: A Metamorphosis," 1–14.

52. Bruce G. Trigger, review of *Archaeology and History: A Plea for Reconciliation* by David P. Dymond, *American Antiquary* 40, no. 4 (October 1975): 510–11.

53. Anders Andren, *Between Artifacts and Texts: Historical Archaeology in Global Perspective* (New York: Springer, 1998), 97–98.

54. Charles E. Orser Jr., "The Anthropology in American Historical Archaeology," *American Anthropologist* 103, no. 3 (September 2001): 621–32.

55. Bernard L. Fontana, "Bottles, Buckets, and Horseshoes: The Unrespectable in American Archaeology," *Keystone Folklore Quarterly* (Fall 1968): 171–84.

56. Booth to Cammerer, January 17, 1923, American Antiquities Act Permits.

57. The Bureau of Ethnology, established in 1879, changed its name to the Bureau of American Ethnology in 1897.

58. Neil Judd to Alexander. Wetmore, memorandum, February 21, 1928, NAA, AAAP.

59. Ibid.

60. This incident is documented in a series of letters dated September 7 through 15, 1927, between Acting Secretary of the Smithsonian Alexander Wetmore and Jesse L. Nusbaum. Nusbuam sent a copy of his September 7 letter to Dr. R. S. Lipscomb, disputing the doctor's ownership of the piece, to Wetmore. This exchange was integrated into a larger set of correspondence among archaeologists in the field, Jesse Nusbaum, Director of the National Park Service Arthur Demaray, Alexander Wetmore, and a number of Smithsonian curators, July 31, 1927–February 21, 1928. NAA, American Antiquities Act Permits Prior to 1960, box 9, folder Interior, National Park Service.

61. Frank H. H. Roberts Jr. to Mr. Dorsey, July 31, 1927, NAA, AAAP.

62. Alexander Wetmore to John Edwards, Assistant Secretary of the Interior, October 19, 1927, NAA, AAAP.

63. Ibid.

64. Jesse Nusbaum to Arthur Demaray, Director, National Park Service, January 10, 1928, NAA, AAAP.

65. Ibid.

66. Paragraph 16 of the Antiquities Act, quoted in R. W. Pugh to Mr. Patterson, memorandum, February 2, 1928.

67. Neil Judd to Alexander Wetmore, February 21, 1928.

68. Walter Hough to Alexander Wetmore, February 21, 1928, NAA, AAAP.

69. Neil Judd to Mathew Stirling, memorandum, February 15, 1933. NAA, AAAP.

4. Ignorant and Local-Minded Influences

1. James Reed, quoted in Daniel S. Pierce, *The Great Smokies: From Natural Habitat to National Park* (Knoxville: University of Tennessee Press, 2000), 50.

2. Pamela J. Belanger, *Inventing Acadia: Artists and Tourists at Mount Desert* (New York: Farnsworth, 1999).

3. Subcommittee of House Committee on Appropriations, Interior Department Appropriations Bill of 1924, 67th Cong., 4th Sess. (1922), 699.

4. Ibid., 697.

5. Stephen Mather, *Report of the Director of the National Park Service to the Secretary of the Interior for the Fiscal Year Ended June 30, 1923, and the Travel Season 1923* (Washington, D.C.: G.P.O., 1923), 14.

6. Pierce, *Great Smokies*, 50.

7. Mather, *Report of the Director* (1923), 13.

8. Pierce, *Great Smokies*, 54.

9. See John C. Miles, *Guardians of the Parks: A History of the National Parks and Conservation Association* (Bristol, U.K.: Taylor and Francis, 1995).

10. Verne Chatelain, "Comments," Conference of Park Superintendents, 1932, unpublished bound volume, General Library Collection, NPSHC.

11. John Albright, "Robert Sterling Yard," in *National Park Service: The First 75 Years; Biographical Vignettes*, ed. William H. Sontag (Eastern National Park and Monument Association, 1990), www.nps.gov/history/history/online_ books/sontag/yard.htm.

12. Verne Chatelain, interview by Charles B. Hosmer, September 9, 1961, transcript, 1, NPSHC.

13. Robert Sterling Yard, *The Book of the National Parks* (1919; repr., New York: Charles Scribner and Sons, 1921), 3.

14. Robert Sterling Yard, "Educational Day," January 3, 1917, *Proceedings of the National Parks Conference Held in the Auditorium of the New National Museum, Washington, D.C., January 2, 3, 4, 5, and 6, 1917* (Washington, D.C.: G.P.O., 1917), 80.

15. Stephen R. Mack, *Preserving the Living Past: John C. Merriam's Legacy in the State and National Parks* (Berkeley: University of California Press, 2005), 106.

16. Dwight Pitcaithley, *National Parks and Education: The First Twenty Years* (Washington, D.C.: National Park Service, 2002), www.nps.gov/history/history/resedu/education.htm.

17. Robert Sterling Yard, quoted in Pierce, *Great Smokies*, 51.

18. Mather, *Annual Report of the Director* (1923), 14.

19. Robert Sterling Yard, "Gift-Parks the Coming National Park Danger," *National Parks Association Bulletin*, no. 4 (October 1923): 4.

20. Miles, *Guardians of the Parks*, 78.

21. See Edward T. Linenthal, *Sacred Ground: Americans and Their Battlefields* (Urbana: University of Illinois Press, 1993).

22. Horace Albright, quoted in Harlan Unrau and G. Frank Williss, "Early Efforts to Transfer War Department Parks," in *Administrative History: Expansion of the National Park Service in the 1930s* (Denver: National Park Service, Denver Service Center, September 1983), www.nps.gov/history/history/online_books/ unrau-williss/adhi2b.htm.

23. John C. Miles, *Wilderness in National Parks: Playground or Preserve* (Seattle: University of Washington Press, 2009), 71.

24. Albright, quoted in Unrau and Williss, "Early Efforts."

25. Robert Sterling Yard, "To Double Our National *Military* Parks System—But Let Us Not Mix Systems," *National Parks Bulletin*, no. 5 (January 1924): 8.

26. Ralph H. Lewis, *Museum Curatorship in the National Park Service, 1904–1982* (Washington, D.C.: Department of the Interior, National Park Service, 1993), 29–31.

27. Stephen Mather, *Report of the Director of the National Park Service to the Director of the National Park Service to the Secretary of the Interior for the Fiscal Year Ended*

June 30, 1924, and the Travel Season 1924 (Washington, D.C.: G.P.O., 1924), 8.

28. Burton E. Livingston, "Scientific Events: National Park Museums" *Science* 60, no. 1563 (December 12, 1924): 543.

29. Harold C. Bryant, Hermon Bumpus, Vernon Kellogg, John C. Merriam, and Frank R. Oastler, *Reports with Recommendations from the Committee on Study of Educational Problems in National Parks,* January 9, 1929, NPSHC.

30. Ibid., 6.

31. Ibid., 22, 24.

32. Robert Sterling Yard, *National Parks Association Information Circular,* 71st Cong. (1929), SIA, RU 46, box 69, folder 3.

33. Ibid., 23.

34. Stephen Mather, *Report of the Director of the National Park Service to the Secretary of the Interior for the Fiscal Year Ended June 30, 1920, and the Travel Season 1920* (Washington, D.C.: G.P.O., 1920), 17–19.

35. Yard, "Gift-Parks," 4.

36. See John Bodnar, *Remaking America: Public Memory, Commemoration and Patriotism in the Twentieth Century* (Princeton, N.J.: Princeton University Press, 1993), and Max Page and Randall Mason, eds., *Giving Preservation a History: Histories of Historic Preservation in the United States* (New York: Routledge, 2003).

37. Committee on Graduate Education, Dexter Perkins, Chair, "The Growth of Doctoral Training in History," in *The Education of Historians in the United States* (New York: McGraw Hill, 1962), 33.

38. William B. Hesseltine and Louis Kaplan, "Doctors of Philosophy of History: A Statistical Study," *American Historical Review* 47, no. 4 (July 1942): 765–800.

39. Morey Rothberg, ed., *The Carnegie Institution of Washington and the Library of Congress, 1905–1937,* vol. 3 of *John Franklin Jameson and the Development of Humanistic Scholarship in America* (Athens: University of Georgia Press, 2001), 278, 279.

40. Ibid., 137, 136.

41. Clark Wissler, quoted in Bryant et al., *Reports with Recommendations,* 24.

42. Horace M. Albright, *Origins of National Park Service Administration of Historic Sites* (Philadelphia: Eastern National Parks and Monument Association, 1971), www.nps.gov/history/history/online_books/albright/origins.htm.

43. John Davison Rockefeller, Horace Marden Albright, and Joseph W. Ernst, *Worthwhile Places: Correspondence of John D. Rockefeller, Jr., and Horace M. Albright* (New York: Rockefeller Archive Center, 1991), 4–5, 338.

44. See Seth Bruggeman, *Here George Washington Was Born: Memory, Material Culture, and the Public History of a National Monument* (Athens: University of Georgia Press, 2008).

45. Congress voted to convert the Colonial National Monument to a National Historical Park in 1936.

46. Edwin Bearss, "The History Division and the Chief Historians—An Overview," *CRM Bulletin* 11, no. 1 (February 1988): 4.

47. Rockefeller, Albright, and Ernst, *Worthwhile Places,* 156.

48. Barry Mackintosh, "The National Park Service Moves into Historical Interpretation," *Public Historian* 9, no. 2 (Spring 1987): 51–63.
49. Albright, *Origins.*
50. Verne Chatelain, interview by Herb Evison, July 18, 1973, transcript, 4, 5–6, NPSHC.
51. Chatelain interview (Hosmer), 3.
52. Chatelain interview (Evison), 9.
53. Chatelain interview (Hosmer), 2, 1.
54. Chatelain interview (Evison), 17.
55. Chatelain interview (Hosmer), 5.
56. Chatelain interview (Evison), 23, 24.
57. Ibid., 12, 11, 12.
58. Peter Novick, *That Noble Dream: The "Objectivity Question" and the American Historical Profession* (New York: Cambridge University Press, 1988), 193–94.
59. Carl L. Becker, "Everyman His Own Historian: Annual Address of the President of the American Historical Association, Delivered at Minneapolis, December 29, 1931," *American Historical Review* 37, no. 2 (January 1932): 22.
60. Novick, *That Noble Dream,* 182–83.
61. Rothberg, *Carnegie Institution of Washington,* 15.
62. Rebecca Conard, *Benjamin Shambaugh and the Intellectual Foundations of Public History* (Iowa City: University of Iowa Press, 2002), 148.
63. Rothberg, *Carnegie Institution of Washington,* 16.
64. For more on the rift between traditionalists and pragmatists, see Novick, *That Noble Dream,* and Ian Tyrell, *Historians in Public: The Practice of American History, 1890–1970* (Chicago: University of Chicago Press, 2005), 173.
65. Chatelain interview (Hosmer), 6.
66. Chatelain interview (Evison), 6.
67. "About MHS: Collecting and Telling Minnesota History for 150 Years," Minnesota Historical Society, 2011, www.mnhs.org/about/mnhistory.html.
68. "Our History," Minnesota State Archives, Minnesota Historical Society, www.mnhs.org/preserve/records/about.html.
69. Julie Des Jardins, *Women and the Historical Enterprise* (Chapel Hill: University of North Carolina Press, 2003), 97.
70. "The Development of the U.S. Archival Profession and Timeline for the National Archives: 1899," "About the National Archives," www.archives.gov/about/history/milestones.html.
71. Clarence Alvord, quoted in Rothberg, *Carnegie Institution of Washington,* 356.
72. Minnesota Historical Society, "Notes and Documents: The Local History Conference, 1922," *Minnesota History Bulletin* 4 (1921–22): 250.
73. Solon J. Buck, ed., "The 1921 Annual Meeting of the Minnesota Historical Society," *Minnesota History Bulletin* 4 (1921–22), 20, 24.
74. Ibid., 25.
75. Minnesota Historical Society, "Historical Society Notes," *Minnesota History Bulletin* 4 (1921–22): 176.
76. Chatelain interview (Evison), 6.

77. Verne Chatelain, "The 1929 Annual Meeting of the Minnesota Historical Society," *Minnesota History Bulletin* 10, no. 1 (March 1929): 54.

78. Chatelain interview (Evison), 6.

79. Chatelain interview (Hosmer), 3.

80. James Lindgren, *Preserving the Old Dominion: Historic Preservation and Virginia Traditionalism* (Charlottesville: University of Virginia Press 1993), 92.

81. Fiske Kimball, letter to Ronald F. Lee regarding efforts to create a cooperative agreement with the APVA, n.d. This and following citations, PHP, Archival Records, folder Colonial National Historical Park—Jamestown, 1934–1939.

82. J. C. Harrington, "Significance of the Site and General Scope of the Interpretive Program," May 18, 1939, ibid.

83. J. C. Harrington, "Report: Statement of Problems of Research, Development, and Use at Jamestown," May 2, 1939, ibid.

84. Ronald F. Lee to Fiske Kimball, July 19, 1939, ibid.

85. Verne E Chatelain, Memorandum for Mr. Demaray, April 21, 1933.

86. Ibid.

87. Verne Chatelain quoted in Barry Mackintosh, "Inaugurating the Program," *Interpretation in the National Park Service: A Historical Perspective* (Washington, D.C.: History Division, National Park Service, Department of the Interior, 1986), www.cr.nps.gov/history/online_books/mackintosh2/branching_inagurating.htm.

88. Chatelain interview (Hosmer), 13, 14.

89. "Glenn Frank: President, 1925–1937," "Chancellors and Presidents of the University of Wisconsin–Madison," last modified February 21, 2011, http://archives .library.wisc.edu/chancellors/chancellors.htm.

90. Glenn Frank, "Salesman of Knowledge," 1933, uncredited clipping, box code K1810, History of Interpretation to 1935, Early 1930s Education file, General Collection, NPSHC.

91. Charles B. Hosmer, "Pioneers of Public History: Verne E. Chatelain and the Development of the Branch of History of the National Park Service," *Public Historian* 16, no. 1 (Winter 1994): 32–33.

5. Real Park Service Men

1. Horace Albright, interview by Erskine, January 28, 1959, transcript, 29, NPSHC.

2. Statement by Verne Chatelain recalled by Charles B. Hosmer during his interview of Horace M. Albright, December 2, 1969, transcript, 18, NPSHC.

3. Ibid.

4. David M. Kennedy, *Freedom from Fear: The American People in Depression and War, 1929–1945* (New York: Oxford University Press, 2001).

5. Verne Chatelain, interview by Charles B. Hosmer, September 17, 1971, transcript, 26, NPSHC.

6. Richard West Sellars, "The National Park System and the Historic American Past: A Brief Overview and Reflection," *George Wright Forum* 24, no. 1 (2007): 8–22.

7. Albright interview (Hosmer), 26, 27.

8. See Edward T. Linenthal, *Sacred Ground: Americans and Their Battlefields* (Urbana: University of Illinois Press, 1993).

9. Sellars, "National Park System," 10.

10. Lary Dilsaver, ed., "The New Deal Years: Organization of Executive Agencies, 1933," in *America's National Park System: The Critical Documents* (New York: Rowman and Littlefield, 1994), www.nps.gov/history/history/online_books /anps /anps_3b.htm.

11. Albright interview (Hosmer), 41.

12. Harlan Unrau and G. Frank Williss, "Federal Emergency Relief Administration," in *Administrative History: Expansion of the National Park Service in the 1930s* (Denver: National Park Service, Denver Service Center, 1983), www.nps.gov/ history/history/online_books/unrau-williss/adhi3b.htm.

13. Unrau and Williss, "Civil Works Administration," in ibid., /adhi3c.

14. Unrau and Williss, "Public Works Administration," in ibid., /adhi3d.

15. Unrau and Williss, "Works Progress Administration," in ibid., /adhi3e.

16. Ronald F. Lee, *Family Tree of the National Park System: A Chart with Accompanying Text Designed to Illustrate the Growth of the National Park System, 1872–1972* (Philadelphia: Eastern National Park and Monument Association, 1972), 37.

17. Harold C. Bryant, interview by Herbert Evison, October 25, 1962, transcript, 16, 17, reel 75, AAA.

18. Chatelain interview (Hosmer), September 17, 1971, 12–13.

19. Verne Chatelain, interview by Charles B. Hosmer, September 9, 1961, transcript, 5, NPSHC.

20. Chatelain interview (Hosmer), September 17, 1971, 12–13.

21. Thomas Pitkin to Charles B. Hosmer, n.d., Hosmer Papers, AAA.

22. Robert D. Cross, "A Tribute to Carlton C. Qualey," *Journal of American Ethnic History* 8, no. 1 (Fall 1988): 7–9, 7.

23. "Biographical Note," "Guide to the Charles M. Gates Papers," 2005, Northwest Digital Archives, Special Collections, University of Washington Libraries, http://nwda-db.wsulibs.wsu.edu.

24. Pitkin to Hosmer, n.d., 1–2.

25. Ronald F. Lee, interview by Charles B. Hosmer, August 17, 1962, transcript, 4, Hosmer Papers, AAA.

26. Roy Appleman, interview by Charles B. Hosmer, April 15, 1970, transcript, 33, 4, Hosmer Papers, AAA.

27. Carlton C. Qualey, "A National Parks Historical-Educational Program," August 21, 1933, 2, PHP.

28. Albright interview (Hosmer), 1.

29. Charles Peterson, interview by Charles B. Hosmer, February 9, 1970, transcript, 25–26, NPSHC.

30. Charles E. Peterson, "Thirty Years of HABS," *Journal of the American Institute of Architects* 40 (November 1963): 83–84.

31. Charles E. Peterson, "The Historic American Buildings Survey: Its Beginnings,"

in *Historic America: Buildings, Structures, and Sites,* ed. C. Ford Peatross and Alicia Stamm (Washington, D.C.: Library of Congress, 1983), 9.

32. See Robert L. Dorman, *Revolt of the Provinces: The Regionalist Movement in America, 1920–1945* (Chapel Hill: University of North Carolina Press, 1993), esp. 81–104 and 145–218.

33. Allen Tate, quoted in Robert L. Dorman, "Revolt of the Provinces: The Regionalist Movement in America, 1920–1945," in *The New Regionalism,* ed. Charles Reagan Wilson (Jackson: University Press of Mississippi, 1998), 1–17, 5.

34. See William Stott, *Documentary Expression and Thirties America* (Chicago: University of Chicago Press, 1986).

35. Orin M. Bullock Jr., "Preserving Our Architectural Heritage," in *Regional Review* 3, no. 3 (September 1939): 20.

36. For a broader perspective on innovations and artistry of 1930s-era photography, see John Raeburn, *A Staggering Revolution: A Cultural History of Thirties Photography* (Champaign: University of Illinois Press, 2006).

37. Stu Cohen, *The Likes of Us: America in the Eyes of the Farm Security Administration,* ed. with foreword by Peter Bacon Hales (Boston: Godine, 2008), xv; see also examples of shooting scripts, 153–82.

38. See Jerrold Hirsch, *Portrait of America: A Cultural History of the Federal Writers' Project* (Chapel Hill: University of North Carolina Press, 2003).

39. See Erika Marie Bsumek, *Indian Made: Navajo Culture in the Marketplace, 1868–1940* (Lawrence: University Press of Kansas, 2008).

40. Bullock, "Preserving Our Architectural Heritage," 22.

41. "Conference of Superintendents and Field Offices," November 19–23, 1934, vol. 1, Sessions of November 19th and 20th, p. 34, box code A 40, Conferences and Meetings, 1934, General Collection, NPSHC.

42. It is difficult to track with certainty the number of employees in specific Park Service divisions at any given time. For a discussion of the impact of the New Deal on employment, see Unrau and Williss, "Growth of the National Park Service," in *Administrative History,* www.nps.gov/history/history/online_books /unrau-williss/adhi6a.htm.

43. Chatelain interview (Hosmer), September 9, 1961, 7.

44. Unrau and Williss, "Historic American Buildings Survey," in *Administrative History,* www.nps.gov/history/history/online_books/unrau-williss/adhi5f.htm.

45. "Conference of Superintendents," 22.

46. Peterson interview (Hosmer), 27–28.

47. Unrau and Williss, "Historic American Buildings Survey."

48. Appleman interview (Hosmer), 38–39.

49. Chatelain interview (Hosmer), September 17, 1971, 23.

50. Chatelain interview (Hosmer), September 9, 1961, 7.

51. "Conference of Superintendents," 102.

52. Verne Chatelain, quoted in Unrau and Williss, "Movement toward Passage of Legislation for National Program of Historic Preservation," in *Administrative History,* www.nps.gov/history/history/online_books/unrau-williss/adhi5g.htm.

53. Unrau and Williss, "Significance of the Historic Sites Act and the National Park Trust Fund Board Act," in ibid., /adhi5i.

54. Alvin P. Stauffer, "Memorandum for Mr. Chatelain: The Report to the Advisory Board on the Types of Historic Sites Worthy of Preservation," n.d., pp. 1–2, PHP, Files of the Branch of History, National Park Service History Division, folder Policy Relating to Early History Programs in the National Park Service, General Section, Policy, 1933–1937.

55. Chatelain interview (Hosmer), September 17, 1971, 25.

56. Chatelain interview (Hosmer), September 9, 1961, 28–29.

57. "Minutes, Second Session of the Committee," p. 7, Advisory Board on National Parks, Historic Sites, Buildings and Monuments, Fifth Advisory Board Meeting, 1937, PHP, Educational Advisory Board Files.

58. William R. Hogan, "Comments on Historical Section of 'Preliminary Outline of the Main Period of American History' with Special Reference to Region III," pp. 3, 1, Third Advisory Board Meeting, 1936, PHP, Educational Advisory Board Files.

59. Thomas Pitkin, "Memorandum to Mr. Hagen regarding the Preliminary Outline of Main Periods in American History," p. 2, ibid.

60. See David Hurst Thomas, *Skull Wars: Kennewick Man, Archaeology, and the Battle for Native American Identity* (New York: Basic, 2000).

61. Erik K. Reed, "Suggestions with Respect to the Archaeological Section of the 'Preliminary Outline of American History,'" p. 1, Third Advisory Board Meeting, 1936, PHP.

62. Edward Hummel, "Memorandum to Olaf T. Hagen Regarding Historic Sites," p. 1, ibid.

63. Hogan, "Comments on Historical Section," p. 4.

64. E. T. Scoyen, quoted in Verne E. Chatelain, "Committee on Archaeologic and Historic Sites," p. 15, Educational Advisory Board Files, 1936, PHP.

6. Park Service Diggers

1. "Growth of the National Park Service under Director Cammerer," 1936, NARA, RG 79, entry 18, Records of Arno B. Cammerer, 1922–40, box 2.

2. Horace Albright, foreword to *National Parks Portfolio* by Robert Sterling Yard and Isabelle Story, 6th ed. (Washington, D.C.: G.P.O., 1931).

3. "Proceedings of Joint Council of National Park Operators and Superintendents Held at Grand Canyon National Park," AZ, May 1–5, 1934, box code A 40, Conferences and Meetings, General Collection, NPSHC.

4. *Part I. A Report Covering the Attendance, Activity, Participation and Preference Studies Conducted in Cooperation with the Several State Park Agencies in 248 State Parks and Related Recreational Areas in 1938* and *Part II. A Report Covering the Organization, Conduct, and Results of Park Use Program Demonstrations in 1939,* in *Park Use Studies and Demonstrations* (Washington, D.C.: G.P.O., 1941).

5. Shelley Baranowski, *Being Elsewhere: Tourism, Consumer Culture, and Identity* (Ann Arbor: University of Michigan Press, 2001), 203.

6. Marguerite Shaffer, *See America First: Tourism and National Identity, 1880–1940* (Washington, D.C.: Smithsonian Institution Press, 2001), 309.

7. See Cindy S. Aron, *Working at Play: A History of Vacations in the United States* (New York: Oxford University Press, 1999).

8. Jesse Nusbaum, "Response to National Park Standards Drafted by the Camp Fire Club of America," 1930, NARA, RG 79, entry 7, Central Classified Files, 1907-49; 1907-32, General Files, box 82, item no. 201-15: National Park Service Administration, National Park Standards, 1929–1932.

9. See Lawrence W. Levine, *Highbrow/Lowbrow: The Emergence of Cultural Hierarchy in America* (Cambridge: Harvard University Press, 1990).

10. Tourism and its pitfalls were a constant topic of discussion, and evidence of this can be found in the proceedings of superintendents' conferences, including "Group Conference of Historical and Archaeological Superintendents Held in Conjunction with National Park Service Superintendents' Conference," 1934, Conferences and Meetings, General Collection, NPSHC; "Proceedings of Joint Council," NPSHC.

11. "Conference of Superintendents and Field Offices," November 19–23, 1934, vol. 1, Sessions of November 19th and 20th, p. 96, box code A 40, Conferences and Meetings, 1934, General Collection, NPSHC.

12. See Aron, *Working at Play*.

13. "Conference of Superintendents," p. 96.

14. "Growth of the National Park Service under Director Cammerer."

15. See Joan Shelley Rubin, *The Making of Middle Brow Culture* (Chapel Hill: University of North Carolina Press, 1992).

16. See Theodor W. Adorno, *The Culture Industry: Selected Essays on Mass Culture* (New York: Routledge, 2001).

17. See Janice Radway, *A Feeling for Books: The Book-of-the-Month Club, Literary Taste, and Middle-Class Desire* (Chapel Hill: University of North Carolina Press, 1999).

18. Carl Sandburg quoted in Peter Novick, *That Noble Dream: The "Objectivity Question" and the American Historical Profession* (New York: Cambridge University Press, 1988), 252.

19. Verne E. Chatelain, "Committee on Archaeologic and Historic Sites," pp. 7–9, Educational Advisory Board Files, 1936, PHP.

20. Harold C. Bryant and Wallace W. Atwood Jr., *Research and Education in the National Parks* (Washington, D.C.: G.P.O., 1936), 3–4.

21. Arno Cammerer, "National Parks and New World Idealism," *Regional Review* 4, no. 6 (June 1940): 3–12, 6.

22. Advisory Board on National Parks, Historic Sites, Buildings and Monuments, "Definitions and Objectives of National Historical and Archaeological Monuments, National Military Parks, etc.," p. 3, Fourth Meeting of the Advisory Board on Historic Sites, 1957, Educational Advisory Board Files (hereafter EABF), PHP.

23. *General Information Regarding the National Monuments, Set Aside under the Act of Congress, Approved June 8, 1906* (Washington, D.C.: G.P.O., 1917), booklet,

National Monuments, A-Ce, box 17, American Antiquities Act Permits Prior to 1960, NAA.

24. Advisory Board on National Parks, "Definitions and Objectives," p. 1.

25. Ibid., pp. 1–2.

26. See David Hurst Thomas, *Skull Wars: Kennewick Man, Archaeology, and the Battle for Native American Identity* (New York: Basic, 2000).

27. Dr. Clark Wissler, "Resolution Regarding Organization of Historic Sites," p. 1, Minutes of the Ninth Advisory Board Meeting, EABF, PHP.

28. See Neil Maher, *Nature's New Deal: The Civilian Conservation Corps and the Roots of America's Environmental Movement* (New York: Oxford University Press, 2008).

29. Neil M. Maher, "A New Deal Body Politic: Landscape, Labor and the Civilian Conservation Corps," *Environmental History* 7, no. 3 (July 2002): 435–61, 436.

30. CCC Encampment, Mesa Verde National Park, Colorado, Narrative Report, 4th Enrollment Period, October 1, 1934–March 31, 1935, NARA, RG 79, entry 42, Narrative Reports Concerning CCC Projects in National Park Service Areas, box 9, Colorado, 1935.

31. Director Arno Cammerer, "Final Report of Civil Works Activities under the Jurisdiction of the National Park Service, May 31, 1934," NARA, RG 79, entry 18, Records of Park Service Director Arno B. Cammerer, 1922–40, box 3, file C, Civil Works Administration.

32. Maher, "New Deal Body Politic," 437.

33. Alfred E. Cornebise, *The CCC Chronicles: Camp Newspapers of the Civilian Conservation Corps, 1933–1942* (Jefferson, N.C.: MacFarland, 2004), 219.

34. Narrative Reports Concerning CCC Projects in National Park Service Areas, 1933–1935, box 10, Colorado.

35. Carl Guthe to H. J. Boekelman, Department of Middle American Research, Tulane, 1936, folder 2, box 3, Frank Maryl Setzler Papers, NAA (hereafter Setzler Papers).

36. P. V. McCone, Letter requesting permission for CCC workers to conduct an independent excavation, SIA, RU 46, folder 1, box 156, CCC 1933–1935.

37. Letter denying request by P. V. McCone, Department of Ethnology, ibid.

38. Narrative Reports Concerning CCC Projects in National Park Service Areas, 1933–1935, box 10, Colorado.

39. J. C. Harrington, "From Architraves to Artifacts: A Metamorphosis," in *Pioneers in Historical Archaeology: Breaking New Ground,* ed. Staley South (New York: Plenum, 1994), 2–3.

40. J. C. Harrington to Frank Setzler, November 19, 1937, Setzler Papers, series 1, subseries 1, box 3, General Correspondence.

41. Harrington "From Architraves to Artifacts," 6.

42. Frank Setzler, letter to Secretary Wetmore regarding a request from the Park Service for professional assistance, 1938, SIA, RU 192, box 498.

43. Ibid.

44. Charles Abbot, letter to Harold Ickes regarding formal cooperation between the Smithsonian and the Park Service, 1938, SIA, RU 192, box 498.

45. Frank M. Setzler, Head Curator, Department of Anthropology, to Jesse D. Jennings, January 7, 1938, pp. 1–2, Setzler Papers, series 1, subseries 1, box 3, General Correspondence—Jennings, 1938.
46. Jesse D. Jennings to Frank M. Setzler, January 24, 1938, p. 2, ibid.
47. Frank M. Setzler to Jesse D. Jennings, February 8, 1938, p. 1, ibid.
48. Jesse D. Jennings to Frank M. Setzler, June 18, 1938, p. 1, ibid.
49. Jesse D. Jennings, "Monthly Report, Ocmulgee National Monument, Prepared for the National Park Service," Setzler Papers, box 29, folder Ocmulgee National Monument, file 1 of 2, 1938.
50. Jesse D. Jennings, "Monthly Narrative Report, Ocmulgee National Monument, Prepared for the National Park Service," p. 3, Setzler Papers, series 1, subseries 1, box 3, General Correspondence—Jennings, 1938. Page 3.
51. Jennings, "Monthly Report, Ocmulgee National Monument" (box 29).
52. J. C. Harrington, "Report for Jamestown Archaeological Project for October, 1936," Setzler Papers, series 1, subseries 1, box 3, General Correspondence, 1936.

Conclusion

1. Cary Carson, "Colonial Williamsburg and the Practice of Interpretive Planning in American History Museums," *Public Historian* 20, no. 3 (Summer 1998): 11–51, 21.
2. Ian Tyrell, *Historians in Public: The Practice of American History, 1890–1970* (Chicago: University of Chicago Press, 2005), 172–76.
3. In this vein, e.g., see Barry Mackintosh, "The National Park Service Moves into Historical Interpretation," *Public Historian* 9, no. 2 (Spring 1987): 51–63; and Dwight Pitcaithley, "National Parks and Education: The First Twenty Years," 2002, National Park Service, *History E-Library*, www.nps.gov/history/history/resedu/education.htm.
4. Dwight T. Pitcaithley, "The Role of History in Managing NPS Areas," *The Guadalupe Mountains Symposium: Proceedings of the 25th Anniversary Conference on Research and Resource Management in Guadalupe Mountains National Park,* ed. Fred Armstrong and Keller Lynn (Salt Flat, Tex.: National Park Service, Guadalupe National Park, 1998), 347–52, 351–52.
5. See also Dwight T. Pitcaithley, "Taking the Long Way from Euterpe to Clio," in *Becoming Historians,* ed. James M. Banner Jr. and John R. Gillis (Chicago: University of Chicago Press, 2009), 54–75.
6. It is certainly true that the necessarily pragmatic approach of scientists employed by the federal government has created fissures in the broad network of scientific professionalism. Federal scientists are currently engaged in a discussion about their own sense of marginalization. But examining the history of public history through the lens of science makes the case that internal divisions among scientists, at least during the nineteenth and early twentieth century, were less totalizing, because leading scientists have always relied on artifact collections and their curators in ways that historians simply did not until much later in the twentieth century.

7. For more on World War II propaganda, see John Whiteclay Chambers and David Culbert, eds., *World War II, Film, and History* (New York: Oxford University Press, 1996); George Roeder Jr., *The Censored War: American Visual Experience During World War Two* (New Haven: Yale University Press, 1995); and Allan M. Winkler, *The Politics of Propaganda: The Office of War Information, 1942–1945* (New Haven: Yale University Press, 1978).

8. Barry Mackintosh, "Parks and People: Preserving Our Past for the Future," in *National Park Service: The First 75 Years; Revising the Mission,* ed. William Sontag (Philadelphia: Eastern National Park and Monument Association, 1990), www.cr.nps.gov/history/online_books/sontag/sontag5.htm.

9. On the impact of the GI Bill, see Glenn C. Altschuler and Stuart Blumin, eds., *The GI Bill: A New Deal for Veterans* (New York: Oxford University Press, 2009).

10. For more on the interstate highway system, see Mark H. Rose, *Interstate: Express Highway Politics, 1939–1989,* rev. ed. (Knoxville: University of Tennessee Press, 1990), 15–28, 55–68.

11. Ney C. Landrum, *The State Park Movement in America: A Critical Review* (Columbia: University of Missouri Press, 2004), 155–68.

12. Mackintosh, "Parks and People."

13. Sara K. Blumenthal, *Federal Historic Preservation Laws* (Washington, D.C.: U.S. Department of the Interior, National Park Service, Cultural Resource Programs, 1994), 6, 42.

14. Edwin Bearss, introduction to *History and Prehistory in the National Park System and the National Historic Landmarks Program,* 1987, www.cr.nps.gov/history/online_books/thematic87/themeo.htm.

15. Nominations are submitted by groups or individuals through local and state preservation offices. They are made available for public comment. After passing through these stages, they are submitted for consideration to the National Register of Historic Places, and the Park Service conducts a final review before making a listing decision.

16. National Park Service, Organization of American Historians, and National Coordinating Committee for the Promotion of History, *History in the National Park Service: Themes and Concepts,* 1994, History E-Library, www.nps.gov/history/history/hisnps/NPSThinking/themes_concepts.htm, "Preamble."

17. Ibid., "Overview of the Revised Thematic Framework."

Index

Abert, John James, 13, 15
academic historical profession, 94,
  113–14, 160–61; and "alternative
  careers," xviii–xix; narrow focus of,
  xviii–xix, xx, 32, 75, 94–95, 152, 160,
  161; Park Service historians and,
  xiii–xiv, xxviii, 101, 107, 113–14, 115,
  135, 159, 161–62, 167; public history
  movement within, xiv–xxiii, xxvi,
  153. *See also* American Historical
  Association
Acadia National Park, 84
Adams, John Quincy, 3, 6, 8, 9, 16
Advisory Board on National Parks,
  Historic Sites, Buildings, and
  Monuments, 123, 124–25, 137–38
African Americans, 31, 119
Agassiz, Louis, 21
Albright, Horace, xxviii–xxix, xxxi,
  52–55, 92, 109; background of, xxviii,
  51, 66; and Charles Peterson, 116–17;
  and educational function of parks,
  55, 87, 92, 98, 158; and Hetch Hetchy
  dam controversy, 50, 51; and Park
  Service expansion, 86, 89–90, 92–93,
  95, 96–98, 105, 111–12, 159; and Park
  Service history program, 86, 92,
  98, 99, 136, 153; park visits by (1917),
  53–55, 62, 63; and Stephen Mather,
  52–53, 92, 109, 158; and Verne
  Chatelain, xxviii, 98, 99, 104; at
  Yellowstone National Park, xxviii,
  66, 93, 109
Allen, George, 23

Alvord, Clarence, 102
American Anthropological Association,
  46, 47, 182n60
American Association of Museums, 74,
  90–91
American Civic Association, 49–50
American Historical Association
  (AHA), 31–32, 94–95; narrow focus
  of, 95, 100, 101, 102, 161; and 1970s
  history jobs crisis, xvi, xviii
American Historical Review, 100
American Institute of Architects, 120
American Museum of Natural History,
  65, 91, 92
anthropologists, xv, 19–20, 46, 65–66; and
  the Smithsonian, 19, 66, 67, 70–72,
  73, 76, 82 (*see also* Fewkes, J. Walter;
  Judd, Neil); women as, 19, 182n60
Antiquities Act (1906), 48, 63, 96,
  122, 157; and definition of national
  monuments, 137, 138; Edgar Lee
  Hewett and, 47–48, 60; and Native
  Americans, 54; origins of, 44–48;
  and park museums, 67, 69–70, 76,
  78, 81–82; permits issued under, 48,
  54, 78; and the Smithsonian, 66, 67,
  69–70, 81–82
Appleman, Roy, 121
Archaeological Institute of America, 43,
  44, 46, 47, 60, 70
archaeology, 74–75. *See also*
  Archaeological Institute of America;
  historical archaeology
artifacts, 46, 54, 63–64, 65–66, 75; conflict

DENISE D. MERINGOLO began her career in the political history division of the National Museum of American History. Between 1989 and 1995, she provided research, writing, and collections management support for two major exhibitions. In 1995, Meringolo became curator of the Jewish Historical Society of Greater Washington, where she curated three exhibitions and worked closely with a variety of community organizations, volunteers, and collections donors. She left that position in 1997 to pursue a doctoral degree. She received her PhD in American studies from George Washington University in 2005. Throughout her graduate studies, she continued her work in public history, serving as an independent contractor for a variety of historical institutions. During 2005–2006 she was scholar-in-residence at the Accokeek Foundation at Piscataway Park. She is associate professor of history and director of Public History at the University of Maryland, Baltimore County. Meringolo lives in Alexandria, Virginia, with her husband, Kevin Tucker, their son, Shane, and a beagle named Lolly.